BETTER HUMANS?

UNDERSTANDING THE ENHANCEMENT PROJECT

Michael Hauskeller

ACUMEN

First published in 2013 by Acumen

Acumen Publishing Limited
4 Saddler Street
Durham
DH1 3NP, UK

ISD, 70 Enterprise Drive
Bristol, CT 06010, USA

www.acumenpublishing.com

ISBN: 978-1-84465-556-4   (hardcover)
ISBN: 978-1-84465-557-1   (paperback)

British Library Cataloguing-in-Publication Data
A catalogue record for this book is available from the British Library.

Printed and bound in the UK by CPI Group (UK) Ltd, Croydon, CR0 4YY.

To those I love: Lene, Hedi, Arthur, and Teo.
With you being in it, my life couldn't possibly
be any better than it is.

CONTENTS

ACKNOWLEDGEMENTS

I am grateful to the Leverhulme Trust for supporting me for nine months with a Leverhulme Research Fellowship (RF-2011-108) to give me the time to write this book, and especially to my contact person at the Trust, the fabulous Anna Grundy. I have made use of some previously published material by integrating it, with minor modifications, in some of the chapters. The final part of Chapter 2 appeared as "Enhancement for the Common Good", *AJOB Neuroscience* **1**(3) (2010): 37–9; Chapter 5 as "Prometheus Unbound: Transhumanist Arguments from Nature", *Ethical Perspectives* **16**(1) (2009): 3–20; Chapter 7 as "My Brain, my Mind, and I: Some Philosophical Problems of Mind-Uploading", *International Journal of Machine Consciousness* **4**(1) (2012): 187–200; and Chapter 10 as "Human Enhancement and the Giftedness of Life", *Philosophical Papers* **40**(1) (2011): 55–79. Chapter 6 joins together "Is Ageing Bad for Us?", *Ethics & Medicine* **27**(1) (2011): 25–32, and "Forever Young? Life Extension and the Ageing Mind", *Ethical Perspectives* **18**(3) (2011): 384–404.

Various people have read and commented on parts of this book, and I am grateful for their help, especially Nigel Pleasants, Edward Skidelsky and Rob Sparrow. Thanks are also due to Erik Parens, Carl Elliott and Walter Glannon for their kind support for the project, and two anonymous reviewers for Acumen who were kind enough to express their enthusiasm for the book and to suggest some important amendments. Ann-Sophie Barwich (a walking webcyclopedia) has sent me many useful links to relevant websites, and my wife Teodora Manea has not only contributed various ideas in the many discussions we had about aspects of human enhancement, but also first kindled my interest in the whole topic in 2003 when we first met. Without her this book would not have been written. Finally, special thanks to my daughter Hedi, who knows many things without knowing that she does, and to Arthur for reminding me, every day, how precious first wonders are.

Michael Hauskeller

1
INTRODUCTION

But what do we want in man? Is it physical excellence, mental ability, creative power, or artistic genius? We must select certain ideals
that we want to raise.

(Franz Boas, *Anthropology and Modern Life*)

In 1998, the eminent molecular biologist and Nobel laureate James
Watson challenged critics of non-therapeutic human germ-line
interventions by posing the rhetorical question: "if we could make
better human beings by knowing how to add genes, why shouldn't
we do it?"[1] Indeed, why shouldn't we? Put like this, it seems decidedly irrational to object. It seems quite obvious that there cannot
be anything wrong with making better human beings, for how can
it possibly be wrong to create something that is *better*? Attempts to
make better human beings by means of biomedical interventions
are commonly referred to as "human enhancement". Even when it is
used as an umbrella term covering what are thought to be augmen-
tations of a variety of particular human abilities (such as the ability
to concentrate, to stay awake or to remember), the very use of the
term "human enhancement" in connection with these interventions
gives reason to suppose that it is not only a particular ability that is
meant to be improved, but also, with and through that ability, the
human being as such, that is, the human *as* a human. This interpretation may not strike one as immediately compelling. Perhaps the
term "human enhancement" is just a convenient way to refer to the
enhancement of any capacity that humans may have, and does not
imply that by enhancing one of those human capacities we would
also be enhancing the human as such. However, the way ardent
proponents of human enhancement often speak and write about

1

human enhancement suggests otherwise. Thus when, for instance, John Harris gives his book *Enhancing Evolution* (2007) the subtitle "The Ethical Case for Making Better People", or Julian Savulescu and Nick Bostrom start the introduction to their recent collection of papers *Human Enhancement* with the question "Are we good enough? If not, how may we improve ourselves?" (2009: 1), then they make it quite clear from the start that human enhancement is to be understood as the enhancement of the human *as* a human (or perhaps as a person, but only if being a person is understood as what being human is actually all about). Human enhancement, then, is about making us better than we are, not merely better in this or that respect, for this or that purpose (a purpose that we may or may not endorse), but simply, in some undefined sense, better.

So where does that leave us? Since making things better cannot be bad or undesirable, and since human enhancement is to be understood as the making of better human beings, it appears that anyone who suggested that human enhancement might, by itself, be in any way bad or undesirable could justly be accused of talking nonsense because if it *were* bad, then clearly it would not be an enhancement, and if it truly is an enhancement, then it *cannot* be bad. One might just as well suggest that some water is not wet or that some bachelors are married. So the ethics of human enhancement actually seems to be very simple: all enhancements are, per definition, good.[2] That does not, of course, solve all the problems we would face if we decided to embark on the enhancement project because despite having ascertained beyond doubt that making better humans is *per se* desirable, it is still possible that we do not yet know exactly *how* to make better humans. However, that is commonly thought to be a purely practical problem, which does not affect the desirability of the enhancement project as such. Perhaps it will turn out that "adding genes" does not have the desired effect but, again, that does not mean that we should not at least try. The important question is, if we *knew* how to improve our nature and *knew* that it was safe to do so (that it had no detrimental side effects), then why should we not do it? It seems very clear that there cannot be any such reason. In the absence of any negative side effects, human enhancement is necessarily good and hence desirable.

Let us call this position *meliorism* (Caplan 2006). Watson's question is, of course, designed to silence critics of meliorism by making them appear irrational and foolish. In fact, however, the question effectively conceals at least three problems. The first problem is the assumption that the only knowledge we need in order to realize the meliorist programme is *technical* in nature. It is assumed that we already know the end and we all agree on the desirability of it, so that we only need to discover the appropriate means for achieving it. In other words, even if we do not yet know how to make better humans, we *do* know what would make a better human. But do we really?

The second problem concerns the attitude that the question endorses. Even if we accept that humans can be more or less good, and that better humans are imaginable than the ones we have now, it is not obvious that striving to *make* better humans is a good thing, too.

The third problem arises from the question of how we can *acquire* the technical knowledge that is needed to perform human enhancements safely and with precision. Given that we know what we want, how do we find out about how we get what we want? And can we justify what we need to do in order to find out?

In this book, I am going to concentrate on the first problem by looking into what people actually mean when they talk about "better humans" and what idea of the human good they, often tacitly, apply when doing so. Speaking of "making better human beings" implies not only that humans are different from each other, but also that there are better and worse ways of being human. It only makes sense to speak of better humans if there are, at least theoretically, good humans and not-so-good humans. This means that there must be some standard by which to measure the quality of a human. But is there? And if there is, what might this standard be? The answer to this question is far from obvious: certainly much less obvious than with many other things. Take a car, for instance. When a car company promises to "make better cars" (as the Toyota boss Akio Toyoda announced a couple of years ago) we have a fairly good idea of what they have in mind: cars that are safer, more comfortable, more economical or more elegant. That seems pretty straightforward. However, even with cars, what you regard as better depends on what you regard as important in a car. Whether you think that Japanese cars are better than German cars or the other way round depends on your personal preferences. Perhaps Japanese cars are more economical and German cars are safer. It would be futile,

though, to argue about which car is better as such, that is, *as a car.*
That would be possible only if cars had one and only one purpose
or function, for instance to get us from one place to another as fast
as possible without leaving the ground. If that were the case, then
we would all have to agree that if car A is faster than car B, car A
is clearly the better car. Yet even cars have more than one purpose.
What we expect or want of a car is not always the same.

However, cars are at least purpose-built, so it is not entirely
unreasonable to ask what constitutes a good car (and, hence, what
constitutes a "better" car). Whenever an entity has a clear purpose,
we have little difficulty answering this question. A human-made
tool or instrument usually has a clearly defined purpose, which
is its *ratio essendi*, the reason for its existence. We can say that it
is good, or bad, with reference to this purpose and the degree to
which the tool allows or facilitates the realization of it. A pen, for
instance, is for writing. That is what is has been made for. Consequently, a pen that you cannot write with is a bad pen. Likewise, a
coffee machine is for making coffee. That is what *it* has been made
for. Consequently, a coffee machine that does not make coffee is
a bad coffee machine. Basically, if a thing does its job (i.e. the job
that it is intended to do), it is good. This means that it is good as
the particular kind of thing that it has been designed as, that is,
as a pen, *as* a coffee machine, *as* a car, or whatever. This qualification is important. Each of these things can only be good (or bad)
with respect to the purpose it has. A pen that makes excellent
coffee but is impossible to write with is *not* a good pen. Of course,
in reality it is hardly ever that simple. Imagine a coffee machine
that does make coffee but does it very slowly. In that case we might
say that it is certainly better than a coffee machine that does not
make coffee at all but not as good as one that makes coffee quickly.
Here, speed is obviously used as an additional criterion for coffee-
machine goodness, but that does not prevent us from determining
which of two coffee machines is better than the other. However, it
gets complicated when yet another criterion is applied, for instance
the quality of the coffee produced. If the slow coffee machine produces coffee that tastes better than coffee produced by the quicker
machine, we can no longer say which of the two is better *unless*
we can decide about the relative importance of the two additional
criteria. If we happen to feel that the quality of the coffee produced

4

is more important than the speed with which it is produced, then we will regard the slow coffee machine that produces good coffee as better than the quick one that produces bad coffee. If, however, we find speed more important, we will believe that the quick coffee machine is better despite the poorer quality of the coffee produced. Can we say which of the two criteria we *should* attach more importance to, or which is *in itself* more important? I don't think we can. Importance is not in the object. It entirely depends on our interests. And if you and I do not have the same interest, then we shall also disagree about which aspects of a particular kind of object are more important and which less, and, consequently, when two objects of that kind differ in their properties, which of the two should count as better and which as worse. We may, however, still agree on some kind-specific standard of perfection. Even if you think that, in coffee machines, speed is more important than taste, and I think that taste is more important than speed, we may both find that the *best* coffee machine would be one that makes the best possible coffee in the shortest possible time.

Such an agreement on an imagined highest level of perfection, however, is not possible in the case of human beings, precisely because humans are not purpose-built, at least not yet. Perhaps there are ideal coffee machines, pens and cars but there is no ideal human. Humans can do many things but there does not seem to be anything in particular that they are *meant* to do: some action that they can perform and which is the reason why they have been brought into existence in the first place. Indeed, it is highly doubtful that they have been *brought* into existence at all. Humans come into existence with no particular purpose, which allows them to find their own purpose in life. This would be true even within the framework of an Aristotelian teleological biology, which even today has a lot to speak for it (Hauskeller 2007: 46–60). For Aristotle (as for most of us) it makes perfect sense to speak not only of intrinsic organ-related ends (a human brain is – among other things – *for* thinking, just as much as the wings of a bird or an insect are *for* flying), but also of the ends of whole organisms. Thus a bird, having wings, is *meant* to fly, and a human, having a brain that is capable of abstract thinking, is *meant* to think abstract thoughts. Yet while such a natural teleology allows us to say that it is (objectively) good for a bird to fly and good for a human to think, in the sense that flying is constitutive of a good bird life and thinking constitutive of a good human life, and, consequently, that it is bad for birds if they are prevented from flying and bad for humans if they are prevented from thinking, it does not follow that it would be even better for birds if they could fly faster, or for longer periods of time, or better for humans if they could think more or better. The reason for this is that, while engaging in abstract thinking may be part of the human good, the production of abstract thoughts is not the purpose of our existence. It is not what we are here for (in contrast to a pen, which *is* here for writing, or a coffee machine, which *is* here for making coffee). While we have, among many other things, a brain to think, eyes to see, and a stomach and bowels to digest food, and while being able to use all of these organs according to their purpose may be part of the human good, none of these (nor any of our other abilities) can count as *the* purpose of *our* existence. In that sense, we do not have a definite purpose.

Plants and animals, too, have intrinsic ends but likewise come into being without a definite purpose, although we often assign one to them and then do our best to confound the difference between a living being and a human-made instrument by not only treating them as if their existence had only one purpose, namely to serve human needs and desires, but also by breeding or genetically engineering them so that they are even more attuned to our ends. We then have an external standard for the plant's or animal's "goodness". The assigned purpose allows us to say, for instance, that a cow that gives plenty of milk is a good cow. Consequently, a cow that is genetically engineered to give even more milk (or has the potential to give more milk by being more resistant to, say, mammary dysfunctions), or to produce milk similar to human breast milk and less likely to cause infections when fed to babies, is an even better one. Such a cow would rightly be called an "enhanced cow" (e.g. Wall *et al.* 2005) and would still count as enhanced if the changes that increased milk productivity were also related to increased health problems in the same cow. The cow is "enhanced" with respect to the purpose of giving milk (in the same sense that a car might be called "enhanced" with respect to speed, comfort or safety). It has been "made better" in that particular respect but not necessarily in any other. Only if we identify the animal with the end that we have assigned to it can we identify the improvement of a particular ability with an enhancement *of the cow* as such, which is, of course, exactly what is suggested when a cow with enhanced milk productivity is labelled an "enhanced cow".

In contrast, we are usually far more reluctant to identify humans with particular ends they happen to serve, whether they chose those ends for themselves or had them assigned to them. We routinely distinguish humans from the roles they occupy, although we may sometimes be not much interested in the humanity of an individual or a group of people and may then focus entirely on their role and assumed function. We can, for instance, specify the qualities that a slave must have in order to count as a good slave, but as long as not all humans are slaves (as they may well become to the radically enhanced posthuman), a better slave is not a better human. It is also possible to see everything, including other humans, in relation to oneself and one's own idiosyncratic desires and purposes, in which case anything that serves those purposes will be regarded as an improvement. A nice example can be found in Wilkie Collins's novel *The Woman in White*, originally published in 1860. There, the overly delicate Mr Fairlie expresses his dislike of children by comparing them unfavourably to the ideal child that he finds represented in the cherubs surrounding one of Raffael's Madonnas:

> I sadly want a reform in the construction of children. Nature's only idea seems to be to make them machines for the production of incessant noise. Surely our delightful Raffaello's conception is infinitely preferable. ... Such nice round faces, and such nice soft wings, and – nothing else. No dirty little legs to run about on, and no noisy little lungs to scream with. How immeasurably superior to the existing construction! ([1860] 2009: 46)

In this case the lines are obviously blurred: children are regarded as having only one legitimate purpose, namely not to rattle the speaker's nerves. This purpose defines, or should define, according to Mr Fairlie, their entire existence, which is not as unusual as one should think: most people have their difficulties with children. Just think what exactly we mean when we call a little girl a "good girl!" or a little boy a "good boy!" What we usually mean is that they behaved as we wanted them to behave, that is, we call them good for the same reason we call a dog good when it has fetched the ball we meant it to fetch. Thankfully, at least with adults, we tend to be much better at distinguishing the role from its bearer. Thus a tennis player who wins most of her matches, even against strong opponents, will certainly be seen as a good tennis player, but that does not mean that she will also be seen as a good human, simply because being good at tennis is not commonly regarded as equivalent to being good at being human. Consequently, improving a player's ability to win matches is not really human enhancement in the proper sense of the word, namely enhancement of the human as a human, as long, at least, as it can be plausibly denied that by making them better tennis players we have also turned them into better humans. If human enhancement is understood as the enhancement of human beings not merely as performers of certain tasks, but rather *as* humans – if it is, in other words, understood as the "making of better humans" – then any attempt at enhancing a particular capacity in a person that does not also enhance the human as such must be regarded as a failed attempt. That is why, as Allen Buchanan has pointed out (albeit without fully appreciating the implications), the "attempt to enhance can go wrong in at least two ways …: it can fail to achieve its goal; or it can achieve its goal but make us worse off" (2011: 24).

However, the difficulty is not only that the improvement of certain human capacities does not automatically result in better humans, so that we need to distinguish carefully between those enhancements that can plausibly be seen as *human* enhancements and those that cannot, but also that it is far from obvious which capacity's improvement, if any, would turn us into better humans, and why exactly. When would we be better off than we already are? And when worse off? And how can we tell the difference? Imagine we could turn ourselves into something completely different, for instance into dolphins. Would we be better off or worse off? Doubtless dolphins have abilities that we lack, and vice versa. Clearly dolphins are far better swimmers. On the other hand, although dolphins are reported to be rather intelligent animals, humans are probably better mathematicians. So is it better to be a dolphin or a human? Is there an *objective* answer to that question? Which life we regard as better probably depends on what we value most in humans. Yet if we cannot even agree on what makes a good car, it seems highly unlikely that we will be able to agree on what makes a good human being. And if we cannot agree on that, then we will not be able to agree on what makes a *better* human being either. And in fact we do not agree, even in those cases that seem to be paradigmatic of human goodness. Should Jesus Christ count as a good human being (assuming that he should be counted as human at all)? Most people today would probably admit that he should, even those who are not Christians, but as Alasdair Macintyre once pointed out, "Aristotle would certainly not have admired Jesus Christ and he would certainly have been horrified by St Paul" (1981: 172). Macintyre was right, of course, because Aristotle had a particular idea about what humans should be like, what they should value and what kind of lives are good for them, and the lives of Jesus and St Paul did not go well with that idea. Friedrich Nietzsche, notoriously, rejected both Christian and Aristotelian values (the harmful moderation-pleading "Aristotelianism of morality"; *Beyond Good and Evil* §198, Nietzsche 1966: vol. 2, 654, my translation) in favour of freedom and self-empowerment: "Modest, diligent, benevolent, moderate: that is how you want the human to be? The *good human*? Yet to me that seems to be the ideal slave" (Nietzsche 1966: vol. 3, 691, my translation). Note that there may well be an ideal slave, but not an ideal human unless one wanted to identify the two. In any case, whether we define ourselves as rational animals, or as being corrupted by original sin, or as self-realizing individuals, or as social animals and natural team-players, makes a difference also in practical terms. Different, mutually exclusive ideals come into play and compete with each other, and this conflict can be traced back to mutually exclusive human properties. Thus I cannot be both compassionate *and* permanently cheerful. We can regard both as desirable qualities in a human, but we cannot coherently conceive of the best human as one that is both compassionate and permanently cheerful. A square can be seen as a "good" (symmetrical? aesthetically pleasing?) geometrical form, and so can a circle. But a square circle is not the best geometrical form but an impossibility.

Now what exactly do proponents of human enhancement have in mind when they speak of making better humans? Which human properties do they find so essential to our being that they feel justified to believe that by enhancing them we would also be enhancing the human as such? It is reported, although I am not sure how reliable the source is, that Watson himself had high hopes that, through genetic intervention, we may finally get rid of "stupid children" and "ugly girls" (Brave 2003). So it seems that, according to Watson, making better humans would involve making humans generally more intelligent and more beautiful. Others may think that a good heart or at least socially acceptable behaviour is more important, and would not regard anything as an improvement that does not also improve our willingness to act morally (but what exactly does *that* mean?). Some may argue that, on the contrary, as long as we adhere to old-fashioned moral ideals, which are nothing but prejudices, we will never be truly advanced. Instead, we shall have to free ourselves *completely*. Some will say that it does not matter either way because the only thing that *really* matters is whether or not we are happy. Better humans will be happier humans, and the best humans would be those who get the maximum amount of pleasure for as long as possible. At first glance at least this last suggestion seems to be the most plausible. If there is one thing by which all so-called enhancements can be judged, happiness seems to be a good candidate. It is, after all, the one thing that appears to be intrinsically valuable, whereas everything else that we value is either valuable as a means to the end of happiness or not valuable at all. Or at least that is what a utilitarian would argue.

Happiness or human well-being, however, depends on many factors, and it is not at all obvious what we need to change in human beings to increase their happiness or at least the likelihood of their being happy. Will it help to provide smart drugs for children and students, cosmetic surgery or performance-enhancing drugs that make us faster, stronger and generally more skilful? It does not appear that way. Bostrom (2008) suggests that there are three areas where real enhancement is possible. The first is the extension of life in good health, which, Bostrom believes, everyone desires, if they are honest. The second is the refinement of our cognitive abilities – our intelligence, our memory, our alertness – and the third, the enhancement of our emotions, "eagerly sought by many". Yet even if we conceded that improvements in these three areas were likely to make us happier (which is not at all obvious), it is by no means clear in what way our abilities will have to be changed in order to count as improved. Few will doubt that it would be better for us to have "more life" in the (rather banal) sense of having a longer life, but when it comes to the enhancement of our cognitive abilities and our emotions it is pretty clear that it cannot just consist in having "more" of it. Having a vastly improved memory, for instance, can easily become a burden. Who would want to remember every single detail of their lives? And what about the emotions? Should we be less aggressive, more loving? Will that always be a good thing? Will it make us happier or just shallower? Or perhaps we should transform ourselves in such a way that we generally have deeper emotions that we feel more intensely. But that wouldn't work either, because sometimes we wish for less intensity (to feel anger, envy or pain more intensely does not seem to be generally desirable). A popular solution to these ambiguities is to see the improvement in an extension of human freedom. Emotional enhancement is then understood as increasing the ability to control one's emotions (Bostrom 2005a) and memory enhancement as increasing the ability to "remember important things when you want to" (Savulescu 2001: 420). Those abilities are considered to be "general purpose means", which are useful for any plan of life (Buchanan *et al.* 2000: 167; Savulescu 2001). So it seems that a better human being is one that has more control about things: what they feel, what they remember, when they die (it is argued that if immortality begins to get burdensome we can always kill ourselves). So enhancement basically means more *control*. Control is a good thing: the best, short of the happiness it will ensure. But again, is that really so? Is control always good? It seems not, because at least sometimes the attempt to gain control over a thing is self-defeating. It cannot work because of the nature of what we seek to control. Take, for instance, emotions. An emotion that we can fully control is no longer an emotion, because having an emotion means *being moved* by something: something that is beyond our control. It does not mean making ourselves move, or causing ourselves to be moved. If that is correct, then we cannot possibly be in control of our emotions. If we can choose to be happy or to be sad at will, then happiness and sadness become our own fabrications and will consequently no longer connect us to the external world by providing an adequate reflection of its relevance for us. Perhaps that is also true of other things, such as happiness itself. If it is – that is, if a certain lack of control is a requirement for happiness – then making better humans in the sense of happier humans is downright impossible.

Also, if an increase in subjective happiness or well-being, or indeed becoming "better than well" (Kramer 1994: xv), is the overriding criterion for human enhancement, then we may also have to regard as enhancement, say, the voluntary surgical removal of limbs in order for someone to become what they believe themselves to be. Apparently, most of those who suffer from this surprisingly common type of body integrity identity disorder feel much better after the amputation of the (entirely healthy) limb or limbs that they wanted to get rid of. Rather paradoxically, without them they feel finally "complete", "whole" and "satisfied inside" (First 2005: 5). Should we therefore say that in those cases the surgical removal of a limb is a mental enhancement through physical measures? Or rather medical therapy? Or simply, despite the increase in personal well-being, a case of self-mutilation caused by a particularly perplexing form of insanity? Similar questions arise with regard to gender reassignment: is changing one's sex an enhancement, or a therapy, or what? And on what basis can we hope to answer this question and others like it? That is, in a nutshell, what I would like to discuss in the following chapters. I am going to have a look at the changes and developments of the human condition that are envisaged and proposed as enhancements by those who advocate them, and which enhancement criteria are being (tacitly or explicitly) used when this is done (i.e. what the reasons are for believing that a particular change will in fact be an improvement of the human condition). I will also look into the underlying conceptions of human nature and see how the use of these particular criteria (as opposed to other possible criteria) is being justified by those who use them, how convincing the use of these criteria is and which, if any, criteria are convincing and what concrete changes and developments can be justified on the grounds of those criteria. Let us start with what is commonly called "cognitive enhancement".

2

BECOMING SMARTER

In no walk of civilized life do the intellects of men seem equal to
what is required of them.

(Francis Galton, "Hereditary Improvement")

Cognitive enhancements are, roughly put, all interventions that,
through the manipulation of the human brain, improve the human
knowledge situation by facilitating or accelerating knowledge acqui-
sition, processing, storage, application or range. We can distinguish
between pharmaceutical, neurotechnological and genetic means
of enhancement. While the latter is still largely science fiction, at
least as far as humans are concerned, pharmaceutical and neurotechnological enhancement devices are already being used and
have been shown to have some effect, although in most cases the
improvement is rather underwhelming and seems to reach nowhere
near beyond the normal human range (Sandberg 2011: 79). Ritalin,
which was initially prescribed to treat attention deficit hyperactivity
disorder, or modafinil (designed to treat narcolepsy) are now widely
used (although not as widely as is often assumed) to enhance con-
centration, wakefulness, alertness and short-term memory capacity, which appears to be useful for many cognitive tasks (Turner
et al. 2002). Other drugs, such as Dexedrine or Adderall, can be
used to similar effect, although it is not entirely clear whether those
effects, which are mostly observed under laboratory conditions, can
also be sustained under real-life conditions and whether they are
really owed to the drug itself rather than to the increased confidence that the belief in its efficacy incites (Lucke et al. 2011). Beta
blockers, which reduce anxiety, and mood enhancers such as the

13

anti-depression drug Prozac can also be understood as cognitive enhancers in a wider sense in so far as they make it easier for people to adhere to their tasks and to use their cognitive faculties effectively. Happier and less angst-ridden people are more likely to be alert and to perform well.

In any case, the primary purpose of both pharmaceutical cognitive enhancers and mood enhancers in terms of their actual *usage* is largely the same, namely to boost performance and thus to enhance productivity. This is actually the very reason why they are seen as enhancements in the first place. So it is not because Ritalin improves our ability to concentrate that we see it as an enhancement drug, but rather because by means of improving our ability to concentrate it allows us to *perform better* in situations that involve the completion of certain cognitive tasks. Only in relation to the task that is meant to be performed can the effected change in a person's abilities be seen as an enhancement. In other words, we have become better (if we have) not as human beings, but as performers of a certain task or pursuers of a certain goal. We may have chosen this goal for ourselves or it may have been imposed on us. Either way, whether we think that the enhancement is desirable ultimately depends (or should depend) on whether or not we think the task is worth performing, the goal worth pursuing. That an intervention helps someone to perform better is in itself not a good reason to support and endorse the intervention. We always need to ask what a better performance in a specific context is *good* for and, of course, also for *whom* it is good (sometimes it may only be good for the profits of pharmaceutical companies). Often it will increase our chances to compete with others, which might be good for the individual but not necessarily in the long-term interests of the community in which the individual lives, and for the individual only if they happen to live in a competitive society (and if others do not enjoy a similar enhancement). If the guiding principle were not competition, but, say, cooperation, the situation might be very different, so that other performance requirements would hold. Generally speaking, what change in somebody's cognitive capacities counts as cognitive *enhancement* is highly context-dependent. It depends on what someone wants or what the goal is, and also on what impact the induced change has on that person's other capacities and their general well-being. Thus it has been pointed out that a psychotropic drug designed to enhance the capacity to process information and consequently to increase one's perception of choices might actually be harmful to people who suffer from certain pathological conditions such as anxiety/panic disorder because they would feel unable to cope with the many choices that are now available to them (Glannon 2011: 25). Yet even for perfectly normal people an increase in the number of perceived choices might not lead to more satisfaction (Lane 2000). It may be good to be able to tell oneself that one has more than one option and to be able to freely choose between them, but that does not mean that the more choices we have the better we feel, or the better we perform. This is in fact not so, the reason being that too many choices may lead to uncertainty and indecision, which is both frustrating and disabling (Nagel 2010).

Any intervention intended to change our cognitive capacities must be assessed with regard to its context. The context determines whether a change is, overall, an enhancement or not. That is why forgetting can be as much an enhancement as remembering, low intelligence as much an enhancement as high intelligence. This is quite obvious when you look at the intervention from the perspective of the individual and with regard to their desire, not to perform well, but to be reasonably happy. It is frequently argued, though, that general intelligence is as an "all-purpose good", which under normal circumstances will indeed improve individual well-being because "cognitive capacities are required for the deployment of any kind of instrumental rationality – the capacity to reliably identify means to one's ends and projects", and this seems to be highly relevant to our well-being because people "need to exercise instrumental rationality in order to obtain pleasure and avoid pain, in order to fulfill their desires, and in order to realize objective goods" (Savulescu *et al.* 2011b: 10). This sounds plausible enough, but only as long as we do not look too closely at the assumptions that are being made here. The idea seems to be that we need to be smart in order to figure out how best to get what we want, what is pleasurable and what is objectively desirable, and getting what we want, what is pleasurable or what is objectively desirable makes us happy. Thus the smarter we are, the more likely we are to figure out how to get what we want or need, and hence the more likely we are to be happy or have a good life. If only it were that easy! Finding the right means to achieve our ends is certainly useful once you know what you want, but it is not always clear what you want, especially if there are too many options. Moreover, it is not always good for you to get what you want. Although you may believe that what you want is good for you, you may be mistaken, and if you happen to want something that is not good for you, then being very good at figuring out how to get what you want is not exactly in your own best interest. It does not increase your well-being. If your goals are misguided, being a good rational decision-maker will not get you very far. But what if you are not mistaken and what you want is really good for you? In that case, enhancing your ability to choose the right means to get what you want might indeed enhance your chances of having a good life. Yet while it is comparatively easy to know what you want, it is much harder to know what is really good for you. And there is not the slightest evidence that people with above average general intelligence (the kind of intelligence that is measured by standard IQ tests) tend to have a clearer understanding of what is good for them, nor, if they do, that they are more likely to act in a way that is beneficial to them. Nor do they seem to be, on average, more content with their lives (Diener & Lucas 1999).

Many intelligent people smoke (or used to in the old days, when that was still socially acceptable), knowing perfectly well it is bad for their health and that they should quit if they want to remain healthy. Many intelligent people also do not exercise a lot, although they know they should. They also know that certain eating habits do not exactly increase their chances to live a long healthy life, but still refuse to pay too much attention to what they eat. This is not so much because they are weak of will or biased towards the present (although this may also be the case), but because health, although valued by all, is only one good among others: one thing, albeit an important one, that contributes to a good life. Even if I do value my health and am smart enough to know that being very careful about what to eat and what not, and how much when, might gain me a few additional life years in good health, I might still feel that gaining those additional years is not really worth paying the price of keeping a strict diet for the rest of my life, or even engaging in the kind of all-considering "longevity program" advocated by determined life-extensionists such as Ray Kurzweil (Kurzweil & Grossman 2005). I also know that regular exercise might keep me healthy for a while longer but I may still decide that I prefer spending my time reading instead. And that is not because I have certain goals to the achievement of which reading is more conducive than exercise, but simply because I enjoy reading. It is what I like to do, what makes *my* life go well (which is not to say that it cannot go well in many other ways that do *not* involve reading).

If someone's life does not go well it is not usually because they are not (instrumentally) clever enough. People are unhappy for all sorts of reasons but few of these reasons have anything to do with a lack or deficiency of instrumental reasoning capacities. Some people are unhappy because they are alone and have no one to talk to. Others find themselves trapped in a dysfunctional relationship and do not see a way out. But that is not because they are not quite smart enough to think of the right means to either end the relationship or make it good again, but because there is no simple solution: no way not to get hurt and to get the better of the situation. In such situations instrumental rationality simply does not cut it. It can even be counter-productive. Others are unhappy because they feel unfulfilled and their existence seems pointless to them. They do not know what to do with themselves and their lives. It is not that they lack the ability to conceive of the right means to achieve their goals; rather, they cannot find any goals worth pursuing. Others have suffered losses, have seen loved ones die or get seriously ill, or have seen their business fail through no fault of their own. Their problem is not an inability to determine correctly which means to choose. There is no straightforward recipe for happiness, or well-being, or a well-lived life. One needs a lot of luck and, more than cognitive, performance-facilitating capacities, certain emotional dispositions. Gratitude (Emmons 2008; Visser 2008), modesty, or an open and caring nature and what is frequently referred to as emotional intelligence (Goleman 1996) seem to contribute more to subjective happiness than IQ (both directly and indirectly, through, for instance, their effects on one's social relations), and it is easy to see why. Clearly it is not always good for a person to be an entirely rational decision-maker.

However, cognitive enhancement is often likened to the effects of education and traditional learning. It is argued that since we seem to attach great value to the latter, we should also value and support the former (Harris 2007: 2). Yet although the purpose of education is manifold, its purpose is not usually to render people more intelligent. Rather, its purpose is to teach them how to *use* their intelligence to acquire a certain knowledge and certain skills that the educators regard as useful and therefore worth acquiring. It is about preparing people for life and for the tasks and challenges they are likely to face in the kind of society they happen to live in. To the extent that education is goal-oriented, preparatory for the performance of certain tasks, there is no reason why we should not expect cognitive bioenhancement to be similarly useful, if not as something that can replace education, then as a welcome complement or facilitator, as long, that is, as we support the performance goals in question. Education (just like any other form of enhancement, bio or otherwise) is not intrinsically (i.e. independent of all context) good. The pragmatist philosopher John Dewey believed that the main objective of education was the integration of new members into an existing group by communicating "habits of doing, thinking and feeling" and initiating them "into the interests, purposes, information, skills, and practices of the mature members" (Dewey 1916: 3). It is rather obvious that on this account not all education is unequivocally good or desirable. It very much depends on whether we approve of the habits that are being transmitted through any particular education process. There is no education *as such*, but only many different kinds of education. Because education is not only form, but also content, there is no education that does not deliberately or inadvertently instil certain values and create a sense of what is important and what is not, which is actually the whole point of it. At its best, education aims to develop human potential, and to help people find out who they are and become the best they can be. At its best it aims to open a world, without regard to utility and the requirements of the job market, focusing on truth and virtue while leaving room for the individual to expand and develop, in accordance with Wilhelm von Humboldt's ideal of education or *Bildung*, which for a long time informed the self-conception of Western universities, but has now increasingly come under threat by an impact-crazed political agenda. General intelligence, let alone instrumental rationality, plays only a minor, subordinate role in this process.

It cannot be denied, though, that being smart makes it a lot easier to get a good job and to succeed in a competitive, largely knowledge-based society such as ours. So given the conditions of modern society, intelligence might have some effect on well-being.

But even if intelligence is useful to acquire certain (material and immaterial) goods that we (rightly or wrongly) tend to value, it does not follow that *more* intelligence – that is, intelligence that exceeds what is currently possible for humans – is always good and contributive to even more well-being. There may well be a threshold above which any further increase in intelligence does not markedly increase our general competence, if that is what is required, nor our overall (subjective or objective) well-being. It is certainly hard to cope with the demands of a competitive society when you are stupid, but not when you are *reasonably* intelligent (Tännsjö 2009a: 424). You don't have to be super-intelligent to have a good life in our world and, from the (contestable) fact that being intelligent helps in having a good life, it cannot be inferred that being more intelligent will allow us to have an even better life. The evidence that we have is either inconclusive or suggests rather the opposite. Often outstanding cognitive abilities go along with social and emotional disorders. Thus it is well documented that children with Asperger's syndrome, while on the one hand suffering from an impaired ability to socially interact, restricted stereotypical behaviour patterns and narrowly focused, very intense interests, on the other hand often exhibit superior abstract reasoning abilities (Hayashi *et al.* 2007; Landeweerd 2011: 209). This is surely not a mere coincidence. Abstract reasoning requires the suppression of concrete reality, which is eternally changing, eludes complete conceptualization and tends to thwart our expectations, especially when humans are involved, by insisting on radical individuality. Life is messy and stands in the way of abstract reasoning. It must first be reified and neutralized before it can be properly processed. Human relations, and everything that needs to be invested into them, are, for the purpose of abstract reasoning, a dispensable distraction. Therefore it should not surprise us if an overdeveloped ability for abstract reasoning turned out to be accompanied by a diminished and damaged capacity to engage with the world of particulars. G. K. Chesterton once remarked that it is not imagination that breeds insanity, but reason, and there is some truth in that: "Poets do not go mad; but chess-players do. Mathematicians go mad, and cashiers; but creative artists very seldom" (1908: 27). Chesterton reminds us that mental insanity often goes along with exceptional abstract reasoning abilities, a fact that he explains like this:

> If you argue with a madman, it is extremely probable that you will get the worst of it; for in many ways his mind moves all the quicker for not being delayed by the things that go with good judgment. He is not hampered by a sense of humour or by charity, or by the dumb certainties of experience. ... The madman is not the man who has lost his reason. The madman is the man who has lost everything except his reason. *(Ibid.*: 32)

Of course, we do not know for sure what it might be like to be cognitively enhanced to such an extent that our capacities exceed that of any human currently living. Most of us probably have no idea what it is like to have the cognitive capacities of those among us who excel in certain cognitive tasks. It is likely, though, that any enforced one-sided development of one particular capacity such as abstract reasoning will be detrimental to other, complementary capacities. Moreover, it is probably even impossible *not* to be one-sided, but instead to do equal justice to all sides, considering that some capacities seem to balance each other out. Thus it seems that we are capable of abstract reasoning to the extent that we are capable of forgetting or pushing aside the radical individuality of every concretely existing thing. Conversely, we are capable of attending to the manifold details that individualize the world (an attention that seems to inform artistic creativity) to the extent that we are capable of refraining from the generalizations that abstract, conceptual reasoning requires. It might well become possible for us to enhance either of those capacities, but in neither case would we have created better humans, just, say, better artists or better mathematicians. And most likely those better artists would be worse mathematicians, while those better mathematicians would be worse artists. There is always a price to be paid, always a trade-off to be made.

So, to sum up, as far as I can see, there is no reason to assume that our lives would improve in proportion to (some of) our cognitive capacities, as is often assumed. And it does not matter whether the capacity in question concerns instrumental reasoning, or abstract reasoning, or any other cognitive activity. Sometimes the promised advantages are entirely speculative: "Human beings with cognitive capacities far beyond those available to existing people may ... have access to far higher pleasures than those accessible to existing humans" (Savulescu *et al.* 2011b: 10). I don't quite see why this should be so but, yes, for all I (or for that matter any of us) know, they may. But then again, they may not. It is really hard to tell, especially since the very concept of "higher pleasures", which we owe mostly to John Stuart Mill's botched attempt to rescue the new ethical creed of utilitarianism from the charge that it was a "philoso- . phy for swine", is, to put it mildly, rather murky (Hauskeller 2011). And when we start talking about higher pleasures *that no existing human has ever experienced*, the claim borders on the nonsensical.

Another cognitive capacity that is often put forward as an area in which enhancement seems both possible and desirable is memory: that is, the ability to store and retain information. There are various biopharmaceutical companies (such as Memory Pharmaceuticals and Helicon Therapeutics) that specialize in the development of drugs to treat the impairment of memory function that comes with certain neurological conditions such as Alzheimer's or vascular dementia, from which roughly 180 million people suffer world-wide. Partial successes with such drugs have given rise to hopes that they could also be used to enhance the memory capacities of those who do not suffer from any disorder or disease. But just how much more memory capacity would it be good for us to have? Before we can answer this question we first need to clarify what *kind* of memory we are talking about. There is clearly a difference between long-term memory and short-term or working memory, both in terms of the underlying neurological processes and with regard to their purpose and function. Working memory is the ability to retain information for as long as it is needed to perform a certain task that requires the use of this information, for instance when we try to remember a phone number that someone has given us until we get a chance to make the call or write it down. It allows us to work with the information we receive. Usually it lasts only for a few seconds and is limited to a fairly small number of (four to seven) elements. Can working memory be enhanced? Certainly! Practice helps, as does the use of mnemotechniques. It has also been shown that working memory can be improved in healthy individuals by influencing the dopamine system in the brain through administration of psycho-stimulant drugs such as amphetamine or methylphenidate. However, the extent of the improvement seems to depend very much on the baseline level, such that a real improvement could only be observed in individuals whose working memory was rather poor. People who already start with a good working memory do not show any improvement after being treated with the drug. On the contrary, their performance tends to gets worse (Barch 2004).

However, for those whose working memory falls short of the demands that the performance of certain tasks puts upon them, treatments like the above may be useful. It may enable them to catch up with those who have a better working memory and to successfully face the task at hand. However, although we may describe this as an individual enhancement in the context of certain performance requirements, it is not a *human* enhancement in the sense of being an enhancement of the human, let alone of the human *as* a human. Improving short-term memory may well be beneficial for the performance of certain tasks, but it will not change our lives in any significant sense. This seems more likely when it comes to the improvement of long-term memory, which is constitutive of our identity as particular persons. To a large extent we are what we remember, and to be able to connect with the past through vivid memories gives our lives depth and a certain satisfying completeness. However, it should be quite obvious that simply having more long-term memories is not always desirable. There are, after all, some things we would rather forget and some things that we do not need to remember, that we have no use for. The fact is that not all memories are valuable (either intrinsically or instrumentally) and that some things are actually good to be forgotten. Treatments designed to enhance memory could have the unintended side effect of preventing us from forgetting those things (Carlezon *et al.* 2005: 439). Thus having, for example, an artificial hippocampus that boosts memory capacity need not be a blessing at all. It may equally well be experienced as a burden. But if that is so, how can we make sure that we only remember what we want to remember or what is good for us to remember?

Also, the sheer number of memories might turn into a problem. In his story "Funes the Memorious", the Argentinian writer Jorge Luis Borges describes a man who, as a result of an accident that left him paralysed, found himself equipped with perfect memory and perfect sensuous perception. Funes, as the man is called, meets the definition of a transhuman, defined by Bostrom as "a being that has at least one ... general central capacity greatly exceeding the maximum attainable by any current human being without recourse to new technological means" (2008: 108), one of these general central capacities being memory. As it happens, the story's narrator refers to Funes as a predecessor of Nietzsche's overman. In spite of this, Funes appears to be severely disabled, not because of his physical impairment but rather because of his vastly improved memory and perception. Both present and past are to him "almost unbearably rich and clear". We ordinary humans can see the sun rise and perhaps spot some details that are unique to this specific sunrise, but the posthuman Funes "knows exactly the forms of the clouds during the sunrise of 30 April 1882" and in fact any detail of anything he has ever perceived in his life. He is said to have "more memories than all other human beings together". But this means that his memory is, in his own estimate, "like a garbage bin". It is anything but a blessing. His unerring perception and memory make it difficult, almost impossible, for him to abstract from the differences in things and to see what they have in common. He does not understand generalizations. For him everything is what it is and nothing else. Each moment in time is different, and nothing is ever the same as anything else. Not only are two dogs so different from each other that he cannot understand how we can call both of them by the same general name, but also he even has trouble to accept that a dog at a certain time is given the same name as that *same* dog one minute later. The narrator comments that Funes was not very talented at thinking, for thinking requires forgetting differences; it means to generalize, to abstract. But "in Funes's stuffed world nothing existed but singularities".

We can take this story as a thought experiment that illustrates the possible dangers of single trait enhancements. But it is more than just a thought experiment. There is also some empirical evidence that Borges's account of the price one would have to pay for improved memory was surprisingly accurate. The Russian neuropsychologist Alexander Romanovich Luria's account of his patient S. from the late 1960s could have been taken directly from Borges's imagination. Luria's S. was able to remember the minutest details of events even years after the event occurred, but had great difficulty forming general concepts and recognizing voices or faces. According to Luria, S.'s memory was "a junkheap of impressions" (Luria 1969: VIII). S. himself was very much aware of the disadvantages

23

of his superior memory: "I frequently have trouble recognizing someone's voice over the phone ... because the person happens to be someone whose voice changes twenty to thirty times in the course of a day" (*ibid*.: 25). Paradoxically, because of all the details he remembered he had trouble recognizing faces:

> They're so changeable. A person's expression depends on his mood and on the circumstances under which you happen to meet him. People's faces are constantly changing: it's the different shades of expression that confuse me and make it so hard to remember faces.   (*Ibid*.: 25)

The ability to "remember" (or, more precisely, to recognize) faces is impaired because in order to "remember" faces we need to forget or overlook those changes that S. found so confusing. In order to recognize a face we do not have to remember it exactly as it was the last time we saw it, but we have to remember only those general features that usually do not change over time and "forget" all others. This means not simply that forgetting can be as important for us (and for the ability to perform well in certain contexts) as remembering, but rather that forgetting is *itself* an integral part of memory, at least for that kind of memory that connects the past to the present. It is one thing to remember singular events in the past, like the colour of the shirt you wore last Christmas, and quite another to recognize persons or things, which requires identifying the present image with a past image or, more precisely, identifying what the past image represents with what the present image represents. Material things, but particularly living things, exist through and in the changes they undergo. A person stretches, as it were, from the past to the present and stays the same despite those changes. Both recognition and abstract thinking require that one be able to distinguish between the relevant and the irrelevant and to disregard the latter. The brain, just like a computer, has only a limited storage capacity, so it makes sense to erase images that are no longer needed. There is an art of forgetting, just as there is an art of remembering, and remembering too much is not an enhancement but a disease. In a more recent case, a woman, "AJ", found herself so overwhelmed by detailed memories of every aspect of her personal life (apparently remembering exactly what she did on every single day during the past twenty-five years) that she found it difficult to concentrate on anything else:

> Whenever I see a date flash on the television (or anything else for that matter) I automatically go back to that day and remember where I was, what I was doing, what day it fell on and on and on and on. ... It is non-stop, uncontrollable and totally exhausting. (Parker *et al.* 2006: 35)

This particular disorder, which is constituted by the effects of a superior autobiographical memory, was first described in 2006 and dubbed *hyperthymestic syndrome* (meaning super-memory syndrome). More cases have been reported since. Now, the main problem with AJ's superior memory condition seems to be that she lacked control over her memories. If she had had *access* to all events in her past and could have recalled them at will, instead of being haunted by memories that forced themselves upon her without her consent, then it would seem that her situation would not prevent her from getting on with her life and hence would not compromise her well-being. Yet for one thing that might simply not be possible, and for another it might still undermine our ability to distinguish what is important (or good) to remember from what is not.

But what if we had complete control over our memories and could decide which things to remember and which not? What if we could change ourselves in such a way that we remember only the good things and forget all the bad ones? Wouldn't that be a real improvement? Perhaps, except that a completely controlled memory no longer seems to be memory at all. It is the sheer involuntariness of our memories that gives us identity over time. If we could control our memories we would in effect control our past, and controlling one's past is for all practical purposes the same as inventing it. However, an invented past is no past, as the invented identity that is based on such an invented past is no real identity (which is beautifully illustrated in Christopher Nolan's 2000 film *Memento*). Apart from that, it is also by no means clear which memories would be good for us to keep. Remembering the good things and forgetting the bad ones is far too simple. Sometimes we suffer from remembering the good things that happened to us (namely when the good times are over), in which case it might be better for us not to remember them. At other times we suffer from remembering the bad things, in which case it might be good for us to forget them. On the other hand, if we forgot all the bad things that happened to us, then we would never be able to learn from our experience. As Leon Kass has pointed out (2003: 27), some things *ought* to be remembered, even though it might be painful to do so, not only because remembering them helps us protect ourselves from harm, but also because it allows us to develop and exercise our moral conscience and responsibility.

There are, of course, severe cases where people find it hard to cope with memories of certain traumatic events. Although there is no way yet to completely erase those memories, it is already possible, through the use of beta blockers such as propranolol, to weaken their emotional impact, thus making them less painful. As a consequence, factual recall of those events is also dampened (Kolber 2006: 1562). Interventions designed to blunt certain memories – what is aptly called "therapeutical forgetting" – could thus be useful to counter or prevent post-traumatic stress disorder (PTSD), and is indeed desired by many who suffer from it: "I have severe PTSD and would sell my soul to the devil himself to be rid of 24/7 hellish flashbacks and night terrors", remarks a participant in an online discussion on the topic (*ibid.*: 1565). However, there are also those who do not want to get rid of their memories, despite the pain they cause them. In a letter to the *New York Times Magazine*, a woman wrote:

> Six years ago, I watched both of my teenage boys die, several hours apart, after our car was struck by a speeding patrol car. ... I don't mean to judge the way in which others should treat (or be treated for) their own personal tragedies. But for me, I needed to retain every detail of my memory, not only for the manslaughter trial that followed a year and a half later but also for my own well-being. ... Although it's painful to relive that night and its aftermath, doing so helps me feel that I am doing something positive with this tragedy. As for erasing the memories of that night, I would never want to take a chance that even an iota of all the positive memories of my wonderful sons would disappear along with the painful ones. (Spicer 2004: 66)

So retaining those memories, painful as they are, might not only be necessary (or at least helpful) in coming to terms with the past by "actively integrating them into the narrative" of their lives (President's Council on Bioethics 2003: 227), but those memories may also be so intertwined with memories we would not want to lose that we cannot cut ourselves off from them without thereby also giving up the ones dear to us. Often the good and the bad, the beneficial and the harmful, hang together, so we cannot separate them. We take either the whole package or nothing at all.

This complexity is also the reason why it is so hard to take a particular functional enhancement for an enhancement of the human as such. Often an improvement in one area makes other things worse, and what appears to be a weakness that ought to be alleviated is a strength when looked at from a different angle. As the American psychologist Daniel Schacter has pointed out, what we tend to regard as memory's sins are in fact "by-products of otherwise adaptive features of memory, a price we pay for processes and functions that serve us well in many respects" (Schacter 2001: 184). Schacter identified seven such sins: persistence, transience, blocking, absent-mindedness, misattribution, bias and suggestibility. *Persistence* links back to what we discussed above. It is the fact that we are often haunted by painful memories. Yet remembering "life-threatening events persistently – where the incident occurred, who or what was responsible for it – boosts our chances of avoiding future recurrences" (*ibid*: 187). *Transience*, the fact that we forget many things over time, can certainly be a nuisance but, given limited storage space, it is in fact an advantage. Another familiar problem is *blocking* – the inability to access a piece of information that we know we have (e.g. when we try to remember someone's name, but cannot quite get hold of it) – but blocking protects us from data overload and potential chaos. Imagine:

> that the word "table" brought forth all the memories that you have stored away involving a table. There are probably hundreds or thousands of such incidents. What if they all sprung to mind within seconds of considering the cue? A system that operated in this manner would likely result in mass confusion produced by an incessant coming to mind of numerous competing traces. (*Ibid.*: 190)

The other "sins" can be explained in a similar manner as useful adaptations, or parts thereof.

The lesson to learn from this example is that, generally speaking, whatever we try to enhance there may be unintended consequences that show themselves only when it is too late to do anything about them. And it once again underlines the importance of context for the evaluation of any particular change. Whether a drug that partially erases (or dampens) one's memory is an enhancement or not depends on so many aspects of the situation that we can only decide the question by focusing on particular aspects and ignoring others. Thus if we suffer from the haunting memory of a traumatic experience, a drug that helps us forget may be seen as an enhancer, and the successful, chemically induced forgetting an enhancement, but only if we ignore everything else and look only at the specific suffering that has now disappeared. If, instead, we took into account the possible (or perhaps even inevitable) distortion of our self-image and our relation to reality, we would perhaps be more hesitant to call the effected change, all things considered, an enhancement.

As there is no human enhancement as such, neither is there cognitive enhancement as such. There can only ever be enhancements of particular functional capacities, and we need to be very careful not to conclude from the fact that the augmentation of certain capacities may appear useful and desirable in *some* contexts, that it will be useful and desirable in *all* contexts, or that a further-reaching augmentation of those capacities in the same contexts will be as useful and desirable as a moderate augmentation. Some, like Bostrom, may want to be a posthuman when they grow up, but perhaps if they got what they want they would, like many adults today, find themselves wishing they were children again. And why would we *want* to radically enhance ourselves and become posthuman in the first place? Being a little more intelligent is perhaps imaginable (and desirable), but being vastly more intelligent is not imaginable and might have implications that are extremely undesirable. Do we really want to comprehend everything? Can one never have enough knowledge? Will our lives become better and better the more knowledge we acquire? I don't think there is an obvious answer to these questions, but it seems to me that it is rather unlikely.

But perhaps we are not interested in the perspective of the individual at all, but want to base our assessment on the consequences an intervention has for society as a whole. Many advantages seem to beckon from wide-scale cognitive enhancement. Thus it is claimed that if we were only smarter and more creative we would be able to solve all those nasty problems that we face today, from climate change to political unrest (Buchanan 2011: 2; Sandberg 2011: 84). Given that our survival might depend on finding a solution to those problems, improving human cognition is more than just an option. Instead, it is "a matter of life and death" (Savulescu *et al.* 2011b: 15). But that again assumes that the only reason we have not yet solved those problems is that we are simply not smart enough to do so, which is a huge assumption to make. We need to consider the possibility that some of those problems cannot be solved at all. Others may be solvable in theory, but the reason we have not yet solved them is not that we are not smart enough to find the solution, but that we are unwilling to do certain things that appear to be necessary to tackle the problem efficiently and to prevent the worst. If, for instance, we can halt climate change only if we *radically* change our lifestyle (and that means changing not just individual behaviour, but the very foundations of our civilization), which we all know we are extremely reluctant to do, then we must either find a way to get people to implement the required radical change, or find out how to halt climate change without making any drastic changes at all to the way our societies work. It may well be that the latter is impossible – it simply *cannot* be done – in which case becoming a lot smarter would not help us one bit. The other option, changing people's behaviour to the required extent, may be possible in theory, but is not something that seems likely to be achievable through cognitive enhancement. So it is rather doubtful whether we need cognitive enhancement to solve the "big" problems.

We may also want to take into account what people are actually going to do with improved cognitive abilities. Will they use it for the good of society or will they, on the contrary, use it to harm other people? Ingmar Persson and Julian Savulescu (2008) have recently drawn attention to the "perils of cognitive enhancement" and demanded that we find ways of morally enhancing people in order to make sure that they do not abuse their enhanced cognitive powers. Interestingly, this proposal prompted Harris (2010), who is usually in agreement with Savulescu, to write a surprisingly sharp response, in which he basically attacks Savulescu for his lack of trust in the self-purifying power of cognitive enhancement and, of course, for his apparent willingness to sacrifice human freedom for more security. We shall have a closer look at "moral enhancement" in Chapter 3. Yet we can already see – and this is something the argument between Persson and Savulescu and Harris shows nicely – how what we are willing to regard as an enhancement does not depend merely on the overall context, but also on the value system we happen to endorse. If we value human freedom more than anything else, then we shall see certain changes as enhancements that we would not regard as enhancements if we valued security more. However, even if we are pretty clear about our values, the essential contextuality of every concrete biomedical intervention, cognitive or otherwise, makes it difficult, perhaps impossible, to decide, once and for all, whether an intervention should, ultimately, count as an enhancement or not. If I value individual freedom, I should, it seems, welcome interventions that help me and others get more control over their lives. But the trouble is that whatever manipulation of my body, including my brain, helps me gain more control, is likely to be usable by others to gain more control over *me*. As C. S. Lewis (1955: 68–70) pointed out more than fifty years ago, every power that "we" acquire is a power that can equally well be used against us (just think of the atomic bomb). If we can construct brain–computer interfaces that, say, allow army pilots to control their machines by thought alone, then the possibility of manipulating the soldiers' minds directly by means of the same device is never far away – not to mention the danger of allowing people to set in motion deadly devices by a purely mental act, which may make killing other human beings even easier than it already is. None of this is probably in the interest of the individual. Is it in the interest of society instead? Is it, as some have argued, for the common good? And if it was, would that make it permissible or even desirable?

To answer this question, let us look at a concrete example. In a paper published recently in *AJOB Neuroscience*, Anton Vedder and Laura Klaming (2010) argue that the neurotechnological improvement of eyewitness memory through transcranial magnetic stimulation (TMS) would be an enhancement "for the common good" and that many of the objections commonly raised against cognitive enhancement in general would cease to apply if we looked at it from the perspective of the common good rather than from that of the individual. So let us see how convincing this claim is.

Unfortunately, Vedder and Klaming say very little about what, in their view, *constitutes* the common good, except that an enhancement for the common good would be one that is "neither primarily self-regarding nor self-serving and potentially benefits society as a whole" (*ibid.*: 6). It is not immediately clear, though, what kind of enhancement should count as beneficial for society, and for what reason exactly. Nor is it clear whether and under which circumstances common good should take precedence over individual good. The authors discuss the neurotechnological improvement of eyewitness memory as a paradigmatic example of an enhancement for the common good. They do not explicitly argue their case, which suggests that they believe the connection to be obvious and undeniable. However, we can reconstruct their *implicit* argument as follows:

1. Eyewitness testimony "plays an important role in the apprehension, prosecution and adjudication of criminals" because the decisions made by law enforcement officials rely heavily on it.
2. Relying on eyewitness testimony can be justified only if it can be trusted, that is, if there is sufficient reason to believe that it is accurate.
3. The accuracy of an eyewitness's testimony depends on the accuracy of their memory, which, however, is notoriously malleable and hence unreliable.
4. Therefore, any means of improving the accuracy of memory is desirable with respect to the purpose of apprehending, prosecuting and adjudicating criminals.
5. Since it is in everybody's interest that criminals are found out and get convicted (and innocents do not), improving eyewitness memory is beneficial for all of us (except perhaps for criminals), that is, for society as a whole.

The crucial step of this argument is, of course, the last one, where the interests of a particular societal subgroup (i.e. law enforcement officials) are identified with the interests of society as a whole. The problem with this step is that there are all sorts of possible technical and legal innovations that appear good for law enforcement officials (the police, prosecutors, lawyers and judges) by allowing them "to do a better job" (*ibid*.: 22), but which we would be very hesitant to regard as good for society as a whole.

It would arguably be a lot easier to apprehend and convict criminals if the doings of all citizens and visitors were permanently monitored by the police. For the sake of the common good we should therefore strive to make state surveillance as widespread and thorough as possible. "Enhanced interrogation techniques" no doubt also help the police and prosecutors do a better job, as does the right to detain suspects without trial for as long as needed to ascertain their guilt or innocence. In general, individual legal rights often present an obstacle to law enforcement, which makes it appear immensely desirable to be permitted to suspend them. Although all these measures are clearly in the interest of law enforcement, and all upright citizens presumably have an interest in seeing the law enforced, many people would still disagree with the proposition that they are all "for the common good". This indicates that there must be something wrong with Vedder and Klaming's reasoning. The fault lies in the assumption that just because we all share a certain interest (e.g. that crime be prevented) we must also have a derivative interest in whatever serves that first interest. The reason why this is not so is that we have various interests, which cannot all be fully satisfied because they are, to a certain extent, mutually exclusive. We may have a strong interest in being protected from crime, but we also have a strong interest in having our privacy and autonomy respected (so we are facing once again the conflict between the value of security and the value of freedom that I pointed out earlier). However, since we cannot be *fully* protected from crime without accepting a drastic infringement of our privacy and autonomy, the best we can hope for is a compromise that allows *both* interests to be satisfied to the greatest possible extent. Thus we can never infer from the fact that one of our interests is served by a particular practice that this practice is for the common good, that is, in our own best interest, unless we know for certain that none of our other interests are violated or threatened by it. For the common good is nothing if not the individual good of all people.

Although Vedder and Klaming concede that "the protection of privacy and autonomy of individuals seems important" (*ibid*.: 18), they leave it open whether eyewitness memory improvement by means of TMS should be made mandatory or remain voluntary, that is, whether or not we should allow eyewitnesses to refuse the enhancement: and this despite the fact that admittedly TMS may cause "unpredictable responses such as unwanted or even traumatic memories" (*ibid.*: 17), which is surely not in the interest of the witness. The authors' willingness even to *consider* forcing people, in the name of the common good, to undergo a treatment that is not entirely without risks shows clearly enough how dangerous it can be to adopt the perspective of a presumed "common good", which Vedder and Klaming recommend we *always* adopt when we look at "cognitive enhancement in general" (*ibid.*: 23). There is a tendency here to view the common good as something absolute that exists irrespective of what is good for the individuals concerned, that is more important than the latter, and that therefore occasionally requires that the merely individual good be sacrificed.

Now, if that is not regarded as entirely out of the question with respect to innocent bystanders of a crime, it would appear that we are even more justified to make sure that law enforcement is assisted as best as possible when we know or suspect that the witness was not innocent at all, but in fact actively involved in committing the crime. When Vedder and Klaming highlight the importance of accurate eyewitness testimony, they disregard the fact that eyewitness reports are often unreliable not because the witness forgot what really happened, but rather because they, for one reason or another, choose to *lie* about it. In that case memory enhancement would do nothing to secure greater accuracy. Instead we would need to apply some kind of truth serum. (That truth serums have proved unreliable in the past is of no account because, first, we may develop better ones in future and, second, because TMS is not entirely reliable either.) After the Mumbai massacre in November 2008, in which more than 170 people died, Indian officials were planning to use such a truth serum on the sole surviving gunman, Azam Amir Kasab, to make him disclose the details of the attack (Borrell 2008). I don't know whether they really did and, if they did, whether they succeeded, but the point is that if we accept the argument proposed by Vedder and Klaming then we must conclude that such a "veracity enhancement" would clearly be for the common good and hence desirable. It also appears reasonable to say that, given the circumstances, we would be more justified to administer the drug by force.

For that is what the advancement of the "common good" seems to require. And why stop here? It is no doubt in the public interest that perpetrators are found out and punished, but surely it would be even better if they did not commit any crimes in the first place. If that is the case, developing and distributing a pill that prevents people from committing crimes (in accordance with Persson and Savulescu's suggestions for moral enhancement) would clearly be an enhancement for the common good in Vedder and Klaming's sense.

Now I am not saying that improving eyewitness memory in the way proposed by Vedder and Klaming is such a bad thing. Perhaps it is, and perhaps it isn't. What I am worried about is the *argument* that the authors use to support their claim that the use of TMS would be an "enhancement for the common good", and the *suggestion* that we generally look at enhancement proposals from a "common good perspective". Any notion of common good that is worth its salt must be informed by what is good for the individual, and the connection must always be borne in mind and properly reflected. The concession that even common-good enhancements must always be voluntary is not sufficient. Once memory enhancement (TMS), veracity enhancement (truth serums), or morality enhancement (no-crime pills) are available it is going to be very hard to refuse them. For why would anyone refuse to assist the law unless they had something to hide? And this means, of course, that from a certain liberal perspective all those particular enhancements are not really enhancements at all.

3

MAKING BETTER HUMANS BETTER

You are to be made into a good boy, 6655321. Never again will you have the desire to commit acts of violence or to offend in any way against the State's Peace.   (Anthony Burgess, *A Clockwork Orange*)

Quite often we find descriptions of already available or merely envisaged cognitive enhancement technologies, both in the popular media and in scientific journals, informed by the assumption that those technologies will eventually be used to benefit humanity. Fairly common are statements such as the following from an article that appeared a few years ago in *Time*:

> Indeed, it would be hard to argue against promoting the use of an intelligence enhancer if it were risk-free and available to everyone. Imagine a legion of cancer researchers on smart drugs, racing toward a cure. Or how about a better class of Wall Street executives, blessed with improved thinking and wiser judgment?   (Szalavitz 2009)

That would be very nice indeed. But how likely is it really that things will turn out that way? Legions of extremely smart cancer researchers racing toward a cure? Seems rather too good to be true. Wise Wall Street executives? Sounds more like a contradiction in terms. It appears far more likely that the latter will use their improved brains to find even more effective ways to enrich themselves, and the former may also feel that they have far better things to do than spending all their time and energy on finding a cure for cancer. The assumption that improved cognitive abilities will naturally be used for the common good is hardly convincing. It ignores human self-ishness, which we have little reason to believe is less common or less articulated among the more intelligent than it is among the cognitively less fortunate. Or is that merely because even the most intelligent among us are still not smart enough? What if we cognitively enhanced people to a superhuman level? Would that change the situation? Or perhaps even make it worse?

There is a passage in Jonathan Maberry's futuristic novel *The Dragon Factory* (2010), where the genetically designed twins Paris and Hecate discuss who and what they are, and what it means for them to be the way they are. Both have blue eyes and perfect eyesight, have never had cavities and are a lot stronger and faster than other people. They are also (in Hecate's own words) "gorgeous and really fucking smart" (*ibid*.: 225), at least smarter than anyone else, except for the occasional "freak". Their father, the brilliant geneticist Cyrus Jakoby (who later in the novel turns out to be the enhanced and now negligibly senescent Josef Mengele) not only designed them but also raised them in the belief that they are "elevated beings" or, alternatively, "gods or aliens or the next phase of evolution" (*ibid*.: 226). In other words, they are fully aware that they are no longer entirely human, that, whatever they are, they are *significantly* different from the rest of us, a "separate species". Therefore, on the basis of Bostrom's well-known definition, which requires a posthuman to have at least one posthuman capacity, that is, a "general central capacity greatly exceeding the maximum attainable by any current human being without recourse to new technological means" (Bostrom 2008: 108), we are probably justified, although they do not use the word themselves, to call Paris and Hecate *posthumans*. However, contrary to what posthumans are commonly imagined to be like, at least by those who promote radical enhancement with a view to transcending the human condition and creating, or paving the way for, a new race of superhumans, Hecate and Paris are not exactly good persons. In fact, they are so convinced of their superiority over everything merely human that they have never felt any scruples to use people as mere means to help them get whatever they desired. But at least one of them, namely Paris, is beginning to doubt himself. He asks his sister whether the fact that, for all practical purposes, they belong to a separate species can justify what they do: "Is that why we can kill and steal and take without remorse? Are

36

we above evil because evil is part of the human experience and we're not quite human?" His sister, however, does not share his doubts and replies brusquely:

> Listen to me, sweet brother. We *are* gods. ... And, yes, we're evil. ... We're evil because evil is powerful. We're evil because evil is delicious. ... We're evil because evil is strong and everything else is weak. Weak is ugly; weak is stupid. Evil is beautiful.

Although Hecate is a fictional character, this does not diminish the force of her argument. Since posthumans do not exist yet, they are all fictional in the sense that we have to imagine what they will be like and what it is going to be like to be one. Yet even philosophers occasionally assume without much argument that posthumans will, naturally, be morally good, too. Thus Bostrom (2008: 112) ends one of his imaginative accounts of the splendid lives that the advanced humans of the future will no doubt enjoy with an almost comically improbable description of their moral engagement:

> You are always ready to feel with those who suffer misfortunes, and to work hard to help them get back on their feet. You are also involved in a large voluntary organization that works to reduce suffering of animals in their natural environment in ways that permit ecologies to continue to function in traditional ways.

In fact, however, it is pretty obvious that we have little reason to expect even radically enhanced humans, or posthumans, to be morally good in a sense that we are familiar with and can relate to, rather than morally bad. There are several reasons for this.

First, there does not seem to be any intrinsic connection between cognitive enhancement and moral enhancement. Academics do not seem, as a rule, to be morally better people than non-academics. If you are quick in resolving mathematical problems that others are unable to crack no matter how long they work on them, you may still be a sleazebag. If you can concentrate better than anyone else on a given task and are able to remember all the stuff you have ever learned and is relevant to your task, you may still be a homicidal lunatic who eats babies for breakfast. High intelligence is not an indicator of moral goodness. Neither is how much one knows. Of course, if being a morally good person depended merely on the theoretical knowledge of right and wrong, and if that knowledge could be acquired in the same way as knowledge about natural facts can be acquired, then we would have some reason to believe that by enhancing people cognitively we will also make them better in the moral sense. However, it is highly doubtful whether there really are moral facts that can be discovered just as natural facts can, for instance the exact chemical composition of a human being. If there really are moral truths, as some (including some proponents of human enhancement)[1] believe, in the sense that some actions are wrong in themselves so that they would be wrong even if nobody felt they were, then it seems that the intelligence needed to discover those truths is different in kind from the practical intelligence that is required to figure out how a steam engine works or the theoretical intelligence that we need to understand quantum mechanics, non-Euclidian geometry or string theory. But how likely is it really that we shall one day figure out whether, say, abortion actually is morally permissible, as a liberal education has taught most of us to believe, or whether, on the contrary, all those pro-lifers have been right all along and abortion is in fact tantamount to murder? And what kind of cognitive enhancement should we perform to help us settle the argument once and for all? It is not clear at all where we should look for an answer to the question whether abortion (or anything else for that matter) is right or wrong.

It is, of course, conceivable that we shall find a way to make people *believe* (or make them more likely to believe) that abortion is permissible, or the opposite, that it is not permissible, but that would not enable us to know whether it *really* is. Rather, we would have to assume that it is permissible (or not permissible): in other words, that the facts of the matter have already been confirmed and it already is clear who is right and who is wrong. As long as that is an open question, the induction or boosting of a belief, be it the one or the other, cannot be seen as a genuine moral enhancement. If an intervention caused us all to believe that abortion was morally permissible while in fact it was morally wrong, or that it was morally wrong while in fact it was morally permissible, then in neither case would we have become morally better people. We would not be morally enhanced (although we may well *think* of ourselves as morally enhanced). So our moral beliefs, in order to count as morally good, must be true. That is, they must correspond to, and reflect, moral truth, and it is unclear how such truth should ever be ascertained, always assuming that it exists in the first place.

Yet even if we do make the assumption that there really are moral facts, and also believe that we can, in principle, know what these facts are, simply knowing those facts might not be sufficient to make us morally good (or better) persons. We often know (which in this case means that we do not doubt) that some action we are about to perform is morally wrong, and then do it anyway. People lie, knowing perfectly well that they should tell the truth. People cheat on their spouses while being fully aware that this is not the way they ought to treat the person they love and spend their life with. We all behave like scumbags at times, and often we know it. The problem is that mere knowledge (or belief) that something is the case does not necessarily motivate us to act in any particular way. I may willingly do what I know is morally wrong, just as I may willingly declare something to be true knowing that it is false. That is another reason why we have no reason to believe that cognitively enhanced humans will be morally good just because they are much cleverer than we are.

Furthermore, we also need to consider the enormous increase in both social status and sheer manipulative power that superior intelligence paired with physical strength and attractiveness is likely to give a person. One can easily imagine how finding oneself fitted with such a power will prompt the average person to abuse it. With great power comes, as Spiderman has taught us, great responsibility, but also great temptation. And why should a radically enhanced human, one that is far superior in intelligence and sheer physical strength to others, *not* think of themselves as a *better* kind of being? After all, the whole point of using human-enhancement technology is the deliberate creation of better, or, in Maberry's words, "elevated", humans. Why should the same rules apply to them as to the rest of us? Aren't the better also *better* in the sense of being more worthy and, if not exactly that, then at least more to be trusted in their judgement of what is right and what is wrong? Should those enhanced humans, or posthumans, coexist with ordinary humans, they are likely to feel entirely justified to subject them to their will, just as we feel justified to control the lives of those we consider

39

incapable of making rational decisions for themselves, be it non-human animals, children or the severely mentally impaired.[2] Even if their attitude will be, by and large, human-friendly, humans in a posthuman society may well end up having the status of pets rather than being viewed as equals equipped with the same rights as posthumans.[3] In that case posthumans may feel entirely justified to sacrifice mere humans if that is thought necessary to safeguard or advance posthuman existence or well-being, just as we tend to feel justified to sacrifice non-human life in the interest of humanity. They may be wrong, of course,[4] but they may not know that. Or they may be right, in which case we should perhaps even agree with them and be willing to give up our own interests and even our lives for theirs, as some have seriously argued.[5] How posthumans actually will, or would, feel about and behave towards humans can, of course, be merely speculated, but if they are anything like humans the worst is to be expected. As Buchanan has pointed out:

> Much would depend upon whether the enhanced were merely stronger and smarter or were also morally enhanced, with greater capacity for empathy, a clearer understanding of the real basis of moral status, and more impressive powers than we possess for resisting the temptation to exploit others. (2009: 371)

Even if we imagine a posthuman society in which all citizens have been radically enhanced and no ordinary humans are left, so that the issue of two different classes of people, one of which is in many respects far superior to the other, no longer arises, it is not clear whether those posthumans would feel any kind of solidarity with each other. It seems that human solidarity and fellow feeling partly depend on the realization that none of us are immune to suffering, disease and death, that even the virtuous can fall and become miserable, and even the rich and mighty may become poor and weak. A radically enhanced human may no longer have reason to share this view. Their superior cognitive skills and sheer physical strength are likely to make them far less vulnerable than us ordinary humans, and thus less inclined to give much attention to the needs of others (which, of course, would hardly be necessary any more since those others will be far less likely to need them).[6]

There is yet another reason why we should not expect radically enhanced humans to be morally good, and that is that the very *absence* of moral scruples and remorse can itself, as Hecate's above argument shows, be seen as a human enhancement. From a certain point of view, morality is a weakness: something that needs to be overcome if one wants to gain full advantage of improved cognitive, emotional and physical powers. Morality certainly is a limitation, and as such a danger to the value of boundless expansion that some transhumanists, whose commitment to the idea of human enhancement is particularly strong, affirm as the basis of their philosophy. Max More, in a seminal essay first published in 1990, urges the reader to endorse "the values of Boundless Expansion, Self-Transformation, Dynamic Optimism, and Intelligent Technology, and Spontaneous Order" (More 1996). He denies the existence of intrinsic values, urges us to adopt values that are objectively conducive to our survival and flourishing, and ends with a passionate appeal to wipe the slate clean and make a radically new beginning: "No more gods, no more faith, no more timid holding back. Let us blast out of our old forms, our ignorance, our weakness, and our mortality. The future is ours" (*ibid.*). If we take this really to heart, then it seems that we should also try to get rid of our moral feelings, feelings of compassion and solidarity and fellow feeling, and of everything that might hinder our progress to the desired liberated condition of the posthuman.

Of course, the more prominent advocates of human enhancement show little or no desire to break with traditional morality. They all see themselves as (in the ordinary, human, sense) good persons, and indeed they are (or at least not worse than the average philosopher). In their majority they even appear to be motivated by a genuine moral impulse, the desire to "make the world a better place", as both Bostrom (www.nickbostrom.com/papers/2index.html) and Harris (2007: 4–5) claim for themselves. This self-image is also conveyed in the mission statement of the former World Transhumanist Association (now humanity+), according to which the organization "advocates the *ethical* use of technology to expand human capacities", thus committing itself to accept the practical restrictions imposed by traditional morality. Whether this is entirely consistent with many transhumanists' commitment to "boundless expansion" is doubtful. It is interesting in this context to compare the latest version of the Transhumanist Declaration on the humanity+ website (http://humanityplus.org/learn/transhumanist-declaration) with the previous one, which was replaced only recently. Whereas formerly the declaration foresaw "the feasibility of redesigning the human condition, including such parameters as the inevitability of aging, limitations on human and artificial intellects, unchosen psychology, suffering, and our confinement to the planet earth", thus focusing on various limitations and the need, or desirability, to overcome them, the new version is more moderate in its aims and no longer conveys so strong a sense of oppression and a longing for complete autonomy. The new declaration envisages "the possibility of broadening human potential by overcoming aging, cognitive shortcomings, involuntary suffering, and our confinement to planet Earth". Only the last bit remains unchanged. Whereas formerly the goal was to (completely) redesign the (whole) human condition, the mere broadening of human potential is now thought sufficient. It is no longer *all* suffering that is to be overcome, but only *involuntary* suffering: not *any* cognitive limitations, but only such that may reasonably be seen as *shortcomings*. Most importantly, there is no mention any more of our "unchosen psychology", which presumably includes our moral intuitions, our sense of right and wrong. So apparently those who drafted the new declaration have come to terms with their (moral) psychology and are now willing to accept it for what it is. However, the question is, is there any good reason to accept it? C. S. Lewis (1955), whom I cited before, pointed out that the logic of the conquest of nature (i.e. of all boundaries and constraints and generally everything that eludes our control) envisaged by eugenicists in Lewis's time and many proponents of human enhancement today, also demands a reconsideration of our own *values*. If values can be manipulated, why should we then manipulate them in such a way that they accord with conventional morality? Have those who, like Bostrom, want to "make the world a better place" perhaps misunderstood the implications of their own project? As Lewis says:

> at first they may look upon themselves as servants and guardians of humanity and conceive that they have a "duty" to do it "good." But it is only by confusion that they can remain in this state. They recognize the concept of duty as

the result of certain processes which they can now control. ... One of the things they now have to decide is whether they will, or will not, so condition the rest of us that we can go on having the old idea of duty and the old reactions to it. How can duty help them to decide that? Duty is itself up for trial: it cannot also be the judge.   (*Ibid.*: 75)

In our own day, proponents of human enhancement also tend to see themselves as servants and guardians of humanity who, despite having recognized the concept of duty as the result of certain processes that they can now control, hang on to the old idea of duty and propose to condition the rest of us in accordance with that idea. Thus Persson and Savulescu, the latter of whom is clearly one of the most prominent promoters of human enhancement in the UK (and always good for a surprise), have recently begun to warn the public of "the perils of cognitive enhancement" and to demand that research into, and development of, cognitive enhancement be complemented by an exploration of the possibility "of biomedical means of *moral* enhancement" (Persson & Savulescu 2010: 667), whereby moral enhancement is to be understood as "an enhancement of our motivation to act morally" (Persson & Savulescu 2008: 167). According to Persson and Savulescu, "biomedical moral enhancement, were it feasible, would be the most important biomedical enhancement.[7] Without moral enhancement, other techniques of biomedical enhancement seem likely to increase global injustice" (2010: 668). And not only that: it would also make the world a far more dangerous place, with super-smart terrorists being in a much better position to successfully follow through on their evil schemes: "We may not have yet reached the state in which a single satanic character could eradicate all life on Earth, but with cognitive enhancement ... we may soon be there" (2008: 167). And because it is so important – indeed, our very survival may depend on it – the authors suggest that not only do we have a moral duty to explore all possibilities of enhancing our motivation to act morally, but also that, once we have discovered how to do that, moral enhancement should be made compulsory for everyone, or at least for everyone "in need of improvement" (*ibid.*: 168). The whole thing is simply too important to allow anyone to escape the procedure and remain morally unenhanced.

Yet how exactly is moral enhancement supposed to work? Persson and Savulescu take it that our moral dispositions have a basis in our biology. Consequently, we should be able to change the former by changing the latter. As the *core* of our moral dispositions they identify, first, a (biological) disposition "to *altruism*, to sympathize with other beings, to want their lives to go well rather than badly for their own sakes" (*ibid.*) and, second, "a set of dispositions from which the sense of *justice* or *fairness* originates" (*ibid.*: 169), which include gratitude and anger, remorse, feelings of guilt, shame, pride, admiration, contempt and forgiveness. If we take all this to be the core of moral goodness, then, the authors conclude, "moral enhancement will consist in strengthening our altruism and making us just or fair, i.e. properly grateful, angry, forgiving, etc." (*ibid.*). This might not be easy, of course, but there is some evidence that the feat may still be accomplished.

So what evidence is there? Frankly, not much. Persson and Savulescu cite experiments with monkeys that suggest they have a sense of fairness, even though it does not seem to be quite as developed as that of humans. In the ultimatum game,[8] chimps regularly accept an unequal share while humans tend to reject offers that they regard as unfair, even though this means they get nothing at all. This is usually taken to show that, at least in this kind of experiment, chimps are "blind to unfairness" (while in fact it could just mean that they are, in this particular instance, more rational than humans). In any case, the fact that identical (human) twins behave very similarly in the ultimatum game, suggests that there is a genetic basis to our sense of fairness. What else? Apparently the hormone oxytocin is somehow connected to trust behaviour, so that by increasing the amount of oxytocin we may be able to make people more trusting, and selective serotonin re-uptake inhibitors (SSRIs) that are commonly used as antidepressants may, by increasing the serotonin level in the brain, promote a willingness to cooperate and an aversion to aggression. And that is all the evidence cited. One problem with this is the unsupported generalization of situation-specific experimental findings. Thus it is by no means clear that SSRIs will increase aversion to aggression in all possible, or even most, settings as opposed to doing so in those particular settings that the experimenters chose to use. And the increase in trusting behaviour through oxytocin seems to be limited to the trusting behaviour of *investors* in a particular game scenario (Kosfeld *et al*. 2005). The main problem, however, is that it is not at all obvious that by making people more trusting (be it as investors or otherwise), or aversive to aggression, or less inclined to accept a smaller share in the ultimatum game, we transform them into morally better persons. Someone who is generally more trusting than another is not therefore a better person, at least not in the sense that it is advisable for people to be. Surely it depends on whom they trust and in what context. If you trust Hitler to do the right thing, then this does not seem to have much moral merit, nor is it in any other way advisable.

Likewise, aggressive behaviour is not always bad, to be avoided or to be condemned, just as the willingness to cooperate is not always good and to be applauded. If you feel very much inclined to cooperate with the henchmen of an oppressive regime, few would say that this makes you a good person. Good cooperators are just that: good at cooperating. Whether this is morally good or bad depends on the situation: on the where, the when and the who with. Clearly there are situations where it is good (i.e. both prudent and morally justified, if not obligatory) *not* to trust, and *not* to cooperate. Sometimes it is good to be aggressive and to refuse all cooperation. Even altruism, which Persson and Savulescu identify as at the core of our moral dispositions, is not unqualifiedly good, as they admit themselves: "there is an evolutionary reason why altruism does not extend indiscriminately to strangers: such an indiscriminate altruism would expose altruists to a too great risk of being exploited by free riders or to direct harm from out-groups" (2010: 661).

What about fairness? Well, that may be a desirable moral quality but the willingness to retaliate in the ultimatum game by rejecting any proposal that is thought unfair is not in any obvious sense morally better than the willingness to accept one's share even if the other gets more. This is partly due to the fact that to expect that one be treated fairly by others does not necessarily mean that one treats others fairly. One would have to see whether those who tend not to *accept* an unequal share as the responder in the ultimatum game, are also more willing to *offer* an equal share when they are in the role of the proposer. That this may not be the case is suggested by experiments carried out by Molly Crockett and colleagues (2010) at Cambridge, which have shown that SSRIs make people not only more aversive to aggression and less willing to accept harm to others, but also, for this very reason, more willing to accept "unfair" distributions in the ultimatum game. After all, the decision not to tolerate the first player's "unfair" behaviour is at the same time a decision to inflict harm on them by letting them go away empty-handed. So rather ironically, a less aggressive behaviour, that is, an increased unwillingness to harm others, may come along with a diminished sense of fairness or, more precisely, an increased unwillingness to punish unfair behaviour. This suggests that it may, in fact, be impossible to make people both less aggressive and (in Persson and Savulescu's sense) "fairer" and, in more general terms, that morality is multidimensional, so that perhaps it makes as little sense to try to make people more moral as it would make sense to try to make people more "emotional". What experiments have shown so far is merely that by changing the "biology" of a person one can influence the way they feel about certain actions and events and, as a consequence, how they behave and how they judge those actions and events morally. But this is a far cry from showing that by changing a person's "biology" we can morally enhance them, that is, make them morally better.

For instance, it has been demonstrated (Young & Saxe 2009) that TMS can be used to change the way test subjects feel and think about the moral blameworthiness of actions. Consider whether an action that causes harm, but was never intended to do so, is more blameworthy or less blameworthy than an action that was intended to cause harm, but which failed to achieve its object. Am I, for instance, to be blamed if I *plan* to poison you by giving you tea that I think is poisoned while in fact it isn't, so that you remain unharmed? Am I also to be blamed if I make you a cup of tea, not knowing that it is poisoned, thus unintentionally causing your death? Most people would probably say that someone who intends harm without success is more blameworthy than someone who accidentally, without intention or foreknowledge, harms another. Apparently TMS can change that, so that test subjects become more inclined to hold people responsible for the consequences of their actions even if they had no way to foresee them, and more inclined to exculpate those who, despite having the intention to harm, in fact caused no harm. So their moral judgement appears to be different from what it used to be. However, it is, once again, not at all clear whether that is a change for the better or for the worse. Is it wrong to blame someone for something they did, but did not want to do? In what sense would it be wrong? Do they overlook or misinterpret the facts of the case? Do they commit a logical error? None of these seem to be the case. What we have instead are two different moral frameworks, one of which is more prominent in our culture than the other, and for this reason has the appearance of being more reasonable. Yet objectively, accidental harm is not less blameworthy, nor more blameworthy, than the intention to harm.

Other experiments that attempt to manipulate people's moral judgement are similarly ambiguous. Crockett and colleagues (2010) used the SSRI citalopram to augment serotonin neurotransmission in test subjects who were then presented with classic trolley problems, in which they had to decide whether or not it would be morally justified to actively bring about the death of a single person in order to save the lives of several others. It turned out that those with augmented serotonin levels were less inclined to push a fat man on to the tracks (and thereby kill him) in order to divert a trolley that would otherwise kill five innocent bystanders. Crockett and colleagues concluded that blocking serotonin uptake made subjects "in emotionally salient personal scenarios ... less likely to endorse harming one person to save many others" (*ibid*.: 17437). Whether that is seen as a moral enhancement obviously depends on whether we think it is better not to get personally involved in any killings of innocent people, even if that means that more people will end up dead. From a utilitarian point of view this is clearly not so. Rather, the *right* thing to do would be to sacrifice the one if there is no other way to save more than one other. To refuse would just show that one does not think clearly enough or that one is too weak or too emotionally immature to accept responsibility also for the lives that one could save and then to act accordingly. So for a utilitarian, the serotonin-induced neuromodulation of moral judgement and behaviour would clearly not count as a moral enhancement. On the contrary, the change would be seen as a *corruption* of moral judgement. Would they be right or wrong? There is no *objective* way to decide that. There are simply two different ways of looking at the situation, and no matter what decision we actually make, it is never obvious that it is the right one. Should we torture the terrorist if there is no other way to find out where he has hidden the bomb that is likely to kill thousands of innocents? Jack Bauer in the American television series *24* would not hesitate and simply do "what is necessary", but we may still feel that it is morally wrong and perhaps that some greater good is at stake here. There is no straightforward answer, but many would feel inclined to say that yes, in the case described above, torture would be morally permissible. Some would even say it is morally required. But what if we had to torture not the terrorist, but the terrorist's innocent daughter, to persuade them to tell us where the bomb is hidden? We probably would feel much less comfortable with that but, then again, what about all those innocent lives that we might save? Can we just ignore them? Wouldn't that be wrong, too? It seems to me that it is impossible to decide this question one way or other and once and for all. We can only *act* in the situation, because we must, and thereby make a decision that is not to be misunderstood as a generalizable answer to the *theoretical* question whether it is morally wrong, permissible or required in a situation like this to torture, but merely an answer to the *practical* question what *we* (or rather *I*) should do here and now. It is, in other words, *our* decision in a particular, concrete situation in which we happen to find ourselves, with no safety net and no guarantees. So when exactly would we have achieved the, according to Persson and Savulescu, urgently required moral enhancement of human nature? When people have become *less* utilitarian in their judgement and behaviour, which might be accomplished by lowering the serotonin level in their brains or simply by damaging their ventromedial prefrontal cortex (Koenigs *et al.* 2007), or when they have become *more* utilitarian?[9]

The researchers who conduct such experiments are usually well aware that all they can show is that our moral judgement can be *influenced* by various interventions, but not that it can be *improved* by those methods. No scientific experiment can ever show that because in order to regard a change as a moral improvement, we need a moral framework, which necessarily lies outside the scope of the experiment. Although Crockett and colleagues are occasionally a bit careless in the way they present their findings – thus they initially seem to claim that serotonin "promotes prosocial behavior" and "harm aversion" (cf. also Crockett 2009), which can easily be interpreted as a claim about a successful moral enhancement – they later, and very wisely, qualify that statement by distinguishing between personal and impersonal harms and different levels of prosocial behaviour, which allows them to describe the serotonin-induced bias in moral judgement as "prosocial at the individual level", but as "antisocial at the group level". In the same way, rejecting unfair offers in the ultimatum game is prosocial at the group level (because it enforces fairness norms) but antisocial at the individual level (because it involves personally harming others). So how do we want people to be: prosocial at the individual or at the group level? And which group are we talking about? Every human being? All sentient beings? Only those that share our nationality?[10] Only white people? There is no such thing as *the* group. Hence, even if we agreed that it is better for people to be "prosocial at the group level" than "prosocial at the individual level", we would still have to decide *which* group our attitudes and the resulting actions should ideally benefit. Presumably we do not want people to be racists, but do we want them to be personalists (respectful of the lives and well-being of all persons), humanists (respectful of the lives and well-being of all humans, including human embryos), or sentientists (respectful of the lives and well-being of all sentient beings, including animals), to name just a few possibilities.

Substantial moral disagreements make it difficult to decide what needs to be changed in what way. Moreover, it seems that there is hardly any action that is *always* wrong, or *always* right, independent of the context and the individual circumstances in which every concrete action is embedded. Even the worst that we can imagine, say, the torture and killing of an innocent child, can, as we have seen, appear justified or permissible in certain situations. Tom Douglas (2008) argued that we could avoid such difficulties by concentrating on clearly counter-moral emotions, but the two examples he provides – (a) a "strong aversion to certain racial groups" and (b) "the impulse towards violent aggression" – are not very convincing. While it is hard to see racism as anything but morally pernicious, it is far from clear that the main component of racism is, as Douglas suggests, a particular emotion and not instead a certain set of misguided beliefs (cf. Harris 2010: 105). And the "impulse towards violent aggression" can, as Douglas himself admits, be exactly what is needed in some circumstances. We may indeed be able to identify certain emotions "such that a reduction in the degree to which an agent experiences those emotions would, under some circumstances, constitute a moral enhancement" (Douglas 2008: 231), but the problem lies in the qualifying parenthesis "under some circumstances". If the emotion is not always bad, we need to specify when it is bad and when not. And even if we could do that for all possible situations, which is rather unlikely, we would still not know how to change people in such a way that they are more able to respond under *all* circumstances in the proper manner. For what we need in order to decide what, in any given situation, is the right thing to do is not a particular kind of disposition or emotional attitude, and not even a rule that guides our actions, but rather what Aristotle called *phronesis*: a kind of practical reason (cf. Jotterand 2011).

Phronesis is the ability, acquired through experience, to find the proper response to the situational challenges that we face due to the sheer variety and complexity of the world in which we live. And since very often it is simply not possible to know what is the right (or best) thing to do before the situation arises and we actually find *ourselves* in that situation and in need of acting one way or another, we cannot engineer morality. An aversion to aggression, greater compassion or a "prosocial attitude" (on whatever level) is not going to do the trick. It is all about, as even Persson and Savulescu acknowledge, being "*properly* grateful, angry, forgiving, etc." (2008: 169). It is, in other words, about finding Aristotle's middle, which is in the habit of changing from situation to situation. That is the reason why freedom, understood as moral agency, is absolutely essential to morality, because there cannot be a moral judgement without (the supposition of) freedom. One may also argue, as Harris (2010) did, in his surprisingly harsh response to Persson and Savulescu, that the freedom to do evil (or wrong) is *in itself* valuable, so that if moral enhancement consists in making people less capable of doing wrong – with the ultimate goal of making them completely *in*capable of it (Persson & Savulescu 2011a) – we would have lost more than we would have gained. That is, of course, also a question of what we value most and how we understand ourselves as humans. Would it be better if we were all constituted in such a way that it was impossible for us to harm or even kill each other (similar to the way robots are to be constructed in accordance with Asimov's first law of robotics,[11] which effectively prevents robots from ever harming a human)? Would the loss of freedom be a price worth paying for a world in which humans no longer hurt each other? Persson and Savulescu seem to think that it would, claiming that even though more effective methods of surveillance might turn the liberal state "into something uncomfortably like the totalitarian state depicted in George Orwell's novel *Nineteen-Eighty-Four*", "the gain in security against terrorist attacks might be held to be worth this cost" (2010: 666; cf. Persson & Savulescu 2011b: 443). They also, in their reply to Harris, argue that the apparent loss of freedom would be morally unproblematic because the morally enhanced person's inability to do evil would not be different from the inability of the (naturally) good person to do what they see as morally wrong. We do not normally require of a good person that they are capable of the worst crimes, but have voluntarily decided against them: "People who are morally good and always try to do what they regard as right are not necessarily less free than those who sometimes fail to do so" (Persson & Savulescu 2011a: 5). This sounds reasonable enough. However, I am not quite convinced, not merely because I am probably enough of a Kantian to believe that moral behaviour that is based entirely on our inclinations and not on any conscious decision that this is the right thing to do has little or no moral merit, but also because the very fact that we would be *engineered* to feel and think a certain way would deprive us of our humanity and turn us into mere puppets hanging from strings that are being moved by those who have decided not only that we are in need of enhancement, but also what kind of enhancement we are to be subjected to. We would lack freedom not so much because we were incapable of evil, but rather because others – the "conditioners", as Lewis called them – would have decided *for us* what is evil and what is not and would then have programmed us accordingly. This raises not only the issue of "moral arrogance" (Hanson 2009), but also that of the consequences in terms of the way such a morally enhanced person will see herself in relation to her moral dispositions.

I think Jürgen Habermas (2003) was quite right to emphasize the importance of what we may call existential contingency (i.e. the perception of ourselves as grown, rather than made) for our ethical self-understanding both as individuals and as a species. It might be a fiction that we are autonomous beings and that it is ever, as Habermas says, "the person *herself* who is behind her intentions, initiatives and aspirations" (2003: 57), but if it is, then it is a *necessary* fiction, a fiction without which we could no longer regard ourselves as moral agents. We would allow ourselves to be turned into mere means to serve the end of morality, and would cease being an end in ourselves, becoming, as it were, a mere shadow or simulacrum of a good man (or woman), not unlike the juvenile delinquent and sociopath Alex in Anthony Burgess's novel *A Clockwork Orange* (1962) after being conditioned to have a strong aversion to aggression in any form. Alex is forced to watch violent films while being given a drug that makes him sick, until the very thought of violence produces nausea in him. Thus cured from his antisocial dispositions, he is released and, unable to defend himself, becomes the helpless victim of various assaults. The behaviour-modification treatment called the Ludovico technique that Alex was forced to undergo should count as a successful moral enhancement along the lines suggested by Persson and Savulescu. Yet it is also the destruction of a human being, which is not only a sad sight, but also ultimately undermines the whole idea of morality. For if people have become mere means to the end of morality and are no longer ends in themselves, what then is the point of morality, of being moral in the way we treat each other? Why should we, as Kant would have us do, treat others always as ends in themselves and never merely as means, if they in fact *are* nothing but means?

Another problem is that developing efficient methods of moral enhancement might be just as dangerous as developing methods of cognitive enhancement, since both "could be put to both good and bad uses" (Persson & Savulescu 2008: 174). The same technology that would allow us to improve people's morality is likely to also enable us to manipulate them in the opposite direction. If we can make people less aggressive, we can also make them more aggressive. If we can make them less a danger to others, we can also make them more of a danger; and at certain times maybe that is exactly what we want. The *morally* best person is not always the best person for the purpose at hand. Not all purposes are moral purposes. It is also unclear whether the greatest threat comes from thoroughly evil people – that is (presumably) people who have no moral convictions whatsoever – or rather from people who have strong moral convictions that just differ from ours and that happen to include the necessity of killing lots of us.[12] Did the terrorists responsible for the 9/11 suicide attacks on the World Trade Center in New York really have a diminished moral sense? Shortly after the attacks Osama bin Laden declared: "Terrorism is an obligation in Allah's religion". Since for the devout Muslim the only moral obligation is to do God's will, any religious obligation is *ipso facto* a moral obligation. This suggests that it is far too simple to think of morality in terms of morally good people and morally bad people. We need to acknowledge the fact that there are different moral frameworks, so that what appears to be right, good or desirable in one framework may appear wrong, bad or undesirable in another. I am not saying that all these different moral frameworks are equally valid or that we should "tolerate" moral beliefs that differ substantially from ours (for instance that it is right, and indeed a moral duty, for parents to kill a daughter who has had the misfortune of being raped). My point is merely that what counts as moral enhancement will depend entirely on the moral framework that one happens to endorse, and we cannot be certain that we all share the same moral framework.

4

FEELING BETTER

A man who is master of himself can end a sorrow as easily as he can invent a pleasure. I don't want to be at the mercy of my emotions. I want to use them, to enjoy them, and to dominate them.

(Dorian Gray, in Oscar Wilde, *The Picture of Dorian Gray*)

The proposal to make people morally better by manipulating the way they feel about certain things is fraught with difficulties pertaining to the very nature of morality. Yet even if we cannot make ourselves or others morally better by the suggested methods of biological enhancement, we might at least make ourselves and others *feel* better, and that seems in itself a worthwhile goal, perhaps ultimately even the only worthwhile goal. Many people are not entirely happy with their lives and very few are happy most of the time. Almost everyone is unhappy sometimes, and many are frequently unhappy. This is not only because bad things happen to us – "into each life some rain must fall" – but because even when there is nothing particularly worrisome happening in our lives, it is hard to sustain an emotional high for a longer period of time. Arthur Schopenhauer, the nineteenth-century German philosopher, argued that happiness must remain the exception because it is nothing but the experience of a fulfilled desire, while the desire itself is the felt awareness of a want, and as such painful. As soon as the desire is fulfilled, he argued, it is either replaced by a new desire that, as such, is equally painful to endure, or it is not replaced, in which case we shall soon sink into a state of boredom, which is by no means better and in fact just a different form of suffering (2008: 364). So if Schopenhauer is right, then unhappiness is, owing to the way we are constituted, pretty much unavoidable.

Of course, as experience teaches us, it is not quite as bad as that. We can enjoy periods in which we do not desire anything at all or, which is the same, do not desire anything but what we have, so there is no potentially painful gap between a desire and its fulfilment. We can also enjoy periods in which we *do* desire things that we do not have, but without suffering in any way from the fact that we do not have them. Many desires carry their own satisfaction, so it is often just as pleasurable, or even more pleasurable, to desire a thing than to get what one desires. And even though a life of perpetual highs may not be possible, that is not what we normally mean by happiness. As John Stuart Mill has pointed out, a happy life, as it is commonly understood, does not consist in:

> a life of rupture; but moments of such, in an existence made
> up of few and transitory pains, many and various pleasures,
> with a decided predominance of the active over the passive,
> and having as the foundation of the whole, not to expect
> more from life than it is capable of bestowing.
> (Mill 1998: 60)

However, even if we accept this as an adequate account of happiness that is both real and humanly achievable, it seems that there is still much room for improvement. Aside from the fact that few are lucky enough to enjoy that kind of happiness, we may also wonder how much *more* happy we could be if we did not have to suffer any pains at all, if our pleasures were even more varied and more plentiful, and if life were only capable of bestowing more of what we tend to expect from it. Unfortunately, it seems that each of us has our own default level of subjective well-being to which we return no matter what happens to us. Whether we win the lottery or lose a loved one, we are likely, after a short period of euphoria or mourning, to get back to roughly the same level of happiness (Bok 2010: 145). This level seems to vary from individual to individual, each of whom has their own base mood, dependent on their genetic constitution and their brain chemistry. Accordingly, changing our environment in ways that appear to be conducive to subjective well-being can achieve only very little in terms of enhancing well-being. If we want a major improvement in this area, it seems we have to start changing ourselves, our very own nature. This radical solution to the problem of imperfect happiness has been forcefully advocated by the transhumanist David Pearce, principally in his internet manifesto *The Hedonistic Imperative* (1995). Pearce imagines a future in which all suffering has been eradicated, a "naturalised heaven" and "engineered paradise", in which there are no longer any obstacles to perfect happiness. Numerous developments, such as the increasing availability and use of chemical mood enhancers, the ongoing medicalization of everyday life, the progressing pharmacogenomic personalization of medicine, and the creation of technologies of "neuroscientific mind-making" as well as virtual reality software, justify the hope, or indeed the prediction, that human suffering is not here to stay. "Over the next thousand years or so, the biological substrates of suffering will be eradicated completely." Once this is achieved, the "states of mind of our descendants ... will share at least one common feature: a sublime and all-pervasive happiness" that we currently cannot even dream of:

> our descendants ... will have the chance to enjoy modes of experience we primitives cruelly lack. For on offer are sights more majestically beautiful, music more deeply soul-stirring, sex more exquisitely erotic, mystical epiphanies more awe-inspiring, and love more profoundly intense than anything we can now properly comprehend. (*Ibid.*)

By then it will also be commonly acknowledged that we are in fact *entitled* to lifelong well-being "in this world, rather than the next". It will, in fact, be regarded as a basic human right.

Whether all this is a real possibility or mere wishful thinking I don't know. If I had to bet I would put my money on the latter. However, more important is the question whether a world devoid of suffering is actually desirable. Would we have truly enhanced ourselves if we had managed to render ourselves incapable of suffering: if nothing that happened to us could ever mar or diminish our happiness? Would a non-suffering human be a *better* human? It may well seem that way. If there is anything that is *intrinsically* bad, surely it is suffering, *any* kind of suffering, however mild, however short-lived. There does not seem to be anything good about it. Admittedly, the ability to feel pain is in general highly useful in an environment that can harm or even destroy us. Our survival, as well as our well-being, depends on our ability to distinguish the harmful from the beneficial or indifferent. Pain is a message that our body sends to our brain: this is dangerous stuff! You are hurt! Next time avoid! However, the value that pain has seems to be entirely instrumental, and if its instrumental value is the only reason why becoming incapable of feeling pain appears not desirable, we can always try to find another and less painful way to serve the same purpose that pain serves now. Why should it not be possible to reconfigure the human body in such a way that it, when in danger or harmed, issues warning signals to the brain that are not subjectively felt as painful? We are highly trained in interpreting and following the guidance of conventional symbols that, in themselves, do not mean anything. What we need is a painless equivalent of a stop sign or a red traffic light. If we can engineer the body to be immune to pain, then it may also be possible to equip it with a different warning system. In that case we would no longer need pain. We are, after all, not dumb brutes, but human beings capable of exercising our rationality and of deciding not to do certain things for the simple reason that we *know* them to be harmful or to have harmful consequences. Or so we like to think. This sounds plausible enough, but only as long as we focus on physical pain. However, our happiness is more often compromised by mental pain, by sorrows and worries, frustration, sadness, discontent and grief, rather than by physical pain. So in order to be as happy as Pearce wants us to be, we would have to lose our ability to feel any of those, too. But then, why should we bother at all? Why should we trouble ourselves with paying attention to a warning system that is designed to help keeping us alive? What does it matter really if we die or suffer some harm? Why should we care? Or rather, how *can* we care if it is no longer in our nature to do so? The problem is that if we are truly incapable of suffering, *any* suffering, then it is hard to see how we could ever care about anything any more, including our own life and well-being. The reason why we do not want our bodies to come to harm is that such harm usually results in pain at some stage. Or it will kill us. Yet the reason why we do not want to be killed is that we are, if not downright scared of it, at least prejudiced against dying. If we did not *mind* dying we would have no reason to protect and defend ourselves against it, and it is hard to see what it can mean to mind dying if not that the prospect of dying is, for us, not a happy one.

Yet it is not only the care for one's own life and well-being that must disappear with the ability to suffer, but also the care for other things and people. To care for something or somebody, to value them and hold them dear, to feel attached to them and love them, all require that suffering be still possible. Far from standing in the way of happiness or well-being, so-called contrast experiences might even be necessary for happiness (Berghmans *et al.* 2011: 161), not only in the sense that there cannot be any mountains without valleys, but also in the sense that some forms of happiness are inherently linked to at least the possibility of unhappiness. We cannot really love someone if the idea that they may come to harm does not in the least worry us. We cannot love them if it does not make us sad to see them harmed, or if we do not feel grief when they die. Yet love, that is, loving and being loved, is something that we would not want to sacrifice despite it being a major source of human suffering, because it is also an important part of human happiness. So is the experience of great beauty, which is often mixed with a particular kind of sadness that acknowledges the fragility, vulnerability and ephemeral nature of the beautiful object. Whenever we admire the beauty of a living thing, the fact that it only exists for a short while and will some time soon disappear forever is essential to its beauty. This is what August von Platen meant when he said that "he who hath set his eyes on beauty has already committed himself to death".[1]

We may also want to consider what the elimination of all suffering might do to the human character. Almost a hundred years ago, Franz Boas, in his critique of the eugenics movement, pointed out that although ending all suffering may be a "beautiful ideal", its realization would destroy society by weakening the individual beyond recognition. There would no longer be any motivation to undertake anything remotely strenuous, to try to overcome hurdles, and no more room for anything but self-indulgence. The smallest discomfort would be seen as intolerable, and much that has been achieved and achievable in the past would be beyond our reach: "Many of the works of sublime beauty are the precious fruit of mental agony; and we should be poor, indeed, if the willingness of man to suffer should disappear" (Boas 1916: 477). In that sense, the happier human is not necessarily the better human. Also, happiness is not all we seek, and perhaps not even anywhere near the top of the list. You are probably not currently reading this book in order to be happy. You are not reading it because doing so makes you happy, nor are you doing it because you expect that reading it will in some way contribute to your happiness. As an activity, you may not even find it particularly pleasurable. So why are you doing it then? Whatever the reasons may be (and I am sure there is more than one), ultimately you are doing it because you want to: because you find yourself wanting to do it. The topic happens to engage your interest, and reading about it is the kind of thing that people like you do when they are interested in a topic. The desire for happiness has nothing to do with it. Generally speaking, people do not want to be happy, certainly not in the sense that they want to have as many pleasurable experiences and as few painful experiences as possible. This is not to say that they want to be unhappy, but simply that to be happy is under normal circumstances not one of their goals. Instead, they want to *do* certain things in or with their lives and, if they are lucky, doing those things will make them happy (or at least not unhappy). And even though we normally prefer to be happy rather than unhappy, there are situations in which feeling good simply is not an option for us. If a loved one dies or otherwise comes to harm we cannot be happy, and if we could we would not want to be because we would feel that being happy in the face of their death or misery would be a betrayal of our love to them. If the pain we feel is sufficiently strong, we may of course be tempted to end it, because some pain is hard to bear, but to yield to the temptation and to reinstall a happy mental state, what Alexander Pope called the "eternal sunshine of the spotless mind", would also be a decision to forget (because suffering itself is a kind of remembrance) and as such a declaration of indifference. It is an act that says "what happens to you does not affect me: you are nothing to me". It is an act of separation, a denunciation of community. In this sense a happier human would not be a better human, but a diminished human. As Leon Kass put it, an "untroubled soul in a troubling world is a shrunken human being" (2003: 27). I don't want to suggest that all suffering is good and that it should under no circumstances be alleviated. There is nothing wrong with treating patients with, say, major depressive disorder with fluvoxamine or other SSRIs that have been found to reduce symptoms considered to be harmful to the patient, but it is one thing to use a drug to help people cope and go on living their lives and quite another to promote the use of similar devices to create a race of happy human or posthuman beings. It can certainly be useful, and helpful, to make people care less through the application of SSRIs (Hoehn-Saric *et al.* 1990; Elliott 2003: 74), but increased indifference can hardly be seen as an enhancement of human nature. And while caring less may help people function better in certain contexts, caring for nothing at all is not even likely to boost performance.

Happiness, it seems, is not always appropriate, and for this reason not always desirable. If life's a piece of shit when you look at it, then it won't do to always look on the bright side of life, unless one does not mind going AWOL from reality and living in a dream world of one's own making. But perhaps this is an exaggeration and a misunderstanding of what mood enhancers actually do. Perhaps the reason why we are happier after having taken the drug is not that we have become blind to the bad, but rather that we have become open to the good. It is not that the drug makes us see things that do not really exist, or see them in a way that distorts their true nature, but rather that it makes us see a side of things that we have previously overlooked and see them in a way that does them full justice. So, as Guy Kahane has argued, while a drug that cut us off completely from the reality of things could justly be accused of corrupting our emotional lives (Kahane 2011: 169), this might not be the way that mood enhancers work. Instead of directly causing us to feel better by stopping us from properly responding to the reality of our circumstances, they may simply enable us to appreciate the good things in our lives, which, in the clouded state of our misery, we have failed properly to respond to. In other words, far from no longer being able to respond to the world, the drug would allow us to respond to it better than before. Mood enhancers might actually *increase* responsiveness; responsiveness, that is, to the *right* reasons. Right reasons, for Kahane, are those that are "in favor of orienting our lives around the good" (*ibid.*: 173). This is supposed to be right because the good has moral and ontological priority over the bad, which has no reality in itself, but is merely a privation: the mere absence of good. Thus by taking a drug that helps us see the positive side of things (of which there always is one), we do what we ought to; namely, refuse "to grant evil equal standing". This is certainly an interesting argument, but its plausibility heavily depends on the metaphysical (Neoplatonist and Augustinian) assumptions on which it rests. While it is true that in most cases not *all* is bad and we do not exactly distort reality when we manage to direct our attention to what is *not* bad, taking a drug that helps us do so still seems like an easy way out that does *not* do justice to the situation (say, of having lost a loved one), simply because the bad stuff is not only equally real, but also demands, for the time being, greater attention. It is true that for "everything there is a season, and a time for every matter under heaven", and sometimes it is simply not the season to be happy. Sometimes it is the season to mourn, to be sad, perhaps even to hate. Kahane makes it sound as if we had a moral obligation to always look for the silver lining no matter how dire the situation or the prospects, but I don't see why we should believe that. There is no moral obligation to be happy. "Cheer up!" and "Look on the bright side!" are not the kind of encouragement we appreciate when we have just lost somebody or suffered some other great harm. It is inappropriate because the cheerful mood it is suggested we have would be inappropriate in that kind of situation. That might change after a while, and a time may come when it is no longer appropriate to be fully absorbed with one's own loss and pain, but that does not mean that it *never* is.

Yet if what counts is not so much that we are always happy, no matter what we do or what happens, but, rather, that we have the kind of feeling that the occasion demands, then we can perhaps make ourselves better by enhancing the *appropriateness* of our emotions. To feel better would then not mean to be always happy, but to be happy when appropriate, sad when appropriate, angry when appropriate, forgiving when appropriate, and so on. Clearly, we do not always feel the way we should be feeling, not even according to our own standards. We know we should be happy – everything is working in our favour and nothing seems to be missing from our lives – but strangely we are not. Or we know we should be angry about an insult, but somehow cannot summon enough energy to actually be. In view of this discrepancy, Matthew Liao and Rebecca Roache have argued that being:

> able to regulate or induce certain feelings in appropri-
> ate circumstances can help us in several ways. We might
> feel better just by being able to experience emotions that
> should come naturally. It can be frustrating not to be able

to experience joy when one knows one should, and when
all those around one seem joyful.

(Liao & Roache 2011: 246)

However, there are several problems with this proposal. For one
thing, there is the curious notion of the "natural" being employed to
give direction to our emotional self-creation. On the one hand we
are encouraged to take full control of our emotions, which implies
that, if we choose to, we can feel any way we want and that in *that*
sense there is nothing natural about the way we feel; on the other
hand we are asked to use our control to make us feel the way we
should, "naturally". Certain emotions, we are told, should be there
and, if they are not, we take a pill to assist nature, as indeed we
should. Thus the natural assumes a normative role (which we shall
explore in greater detail in the next chapter). Yet why exactly should
we want to have the kind of feelings that allegedly should come naturally? Because it can be *frustrating* not to be joyful when others
are, and we do not want to be frustrated. The same holds, presumably, for situations in which emotions other than joy are required;
it can also be frustrating not to feel grief when grief should "come
naturally", that is, when it is what others expect you to feel and what
they would in all likelihood feel themselves if they were in your situation. So again, by being linked to what is natural, happiness, in
the form of an absence of frustration, is being presented to us as
an ethical obligation: the default state of mind to which we should
always aspire. Yet clearly, what is being described here as natural
is in fact a *social* norm, one that demands conformity of feelings.
We feel the way we "naturally" should when we feel what others
feel or would feel in our situation. And we are frustrated only if it
is important to us to feel as others do, if being different and for this
reason being potentially regarded with disapproval by others makes
us uncomfortable.

Also, because there is no (in any normatively relevant sense) natural way to feel about certain things, and social expectations are
often flexible with regard to our emotions, it is not always clear what
is appropriate in a particular situation. How sad exactly are we supposed to be when our pet cat dies? How long should we mourn for
a loved one? How long and how deeply should we bear a grudge
against someone who did us wrong? Should we seek revenge or be

forgiving? Should we love someone or not? There are substantial decisions to be made here, once all this is under our control. And even if the social and cultural norms about how to feel in certain situations are comparatively clear-cut, what counts as appropriate in our own culture may well be seen as inappropriate in other cultures. The same situation might require very different emotional responses. Accordingly, a lack of social inhibitions may be applauded and advantageous in the United States, but rather less so in a more guarded culture (Elliott 2003: 76). So if the very notion of what is appropriate is socially and culturally determined, then the enhancement of our emotions can only ever be understood in relation to the culture and society we happen to live in.

Despite this limitation, Liao and Roache seem to believe that we can, for many situations (if perhaps not for all), clearly say which emotional disposition is the right one. For instance, one ought to love one's children, not only in the sense that it is "natural" to do so, but also in the sense that loving them is a moral obligation we have: "in being able to induce parental love that one does not feel spontaneously, one may also be able at least partially to fulfill a duty to love a child" (Liao & Roache 2011: 246). Love is something we *owe* to a child or a partner. Particularly children have a (human) *right* to be loved, from which it follows that "all able human beings in appropriate circumstances", which in most cases means their parents, have a corresponding duty to love them (Liao 2006a: 431). But is that really so? Immanuel Kant ([1786] 1974: 25–6) famously distinguished between pathological love and practical love. Pathological love is the kind of love that we actually *feel* for someone. Practical love, on the other hand, is independent of how we feel. Rather, it describes the way we *act*. What we owe to our children is not that we have certain feelings towards them (Kant's pathological love), but that we look after them, protect them from harm, provide them with opportunities for self-development and allow them to prosper, give them an education and teach them what is important in life and what is not (Kant's practical love). It may be easier to do all that when you feel deeply for a child, but it can certainly be done without. More importantly, you can love your child madly and not do any of the things that are required by what you owe to them. Social workers have described their surprise at finding that even the most abusive parents, who are grossly negligent in their duty of

care, seem to "love" their children in the sense of being emotionally attached to them (Moorhead 2012). It might not be incoherent to stipulate a "duty to love" (as Kant believed), since there are
already various ways of actively bringing about certain emotions in
us, including love (Liao 2006b), and a love-inducing drug will make
this kind of self-manipulation even easier, but it does not follow that
there actually is such a duty. The fact that love is (or may be about
to become) commandable does not mean that we ought to com-
mand it. This is plausible only if children *need* to be loved in order
to thrive. They certainly need more than food and shelter – human
affection, bodily contact, kindness, being listened to – but not necessarily the kind of exclusive love that most people happen to feel
for their own children. Liao cites studies about children who developed anaclitic depression and other illnesses when being raised
in institutions where they "did not receive love but only adequate
care", as well as studies about "infant monkeys raised in maternal
privation settings" (Liao 2011: 489). Yet merely "adequate" care in
an institution might lack various things besides (pathological) love,
and the monkeys in question were in fact deprived of *all* social contact and raised in social *isolation*, which constitutes a far more serious deprivation than merely being raised without a mother. What
is important is how children are being treated, namely with respect,
attentiveness to their needs and the willingness to be there for them.
In other words, parents, and much less care workers, do not have
to "feel lovingly" towards the children in their care, but to "behave
lovingly". Loving behaviour is not in any way false or merely pre-
tended love. When one behaves lovingly to a child without feeling
the exclusive love that a mother might typically feel for her child
one is not merely pretending to love them. In important respects it
is more real than the warm glow and attachment that most parents
feel toward their own children. So we may want to think about ways
to improve the care that children get from their parents and others
who have a mandate to look after them, but I doubt that this can be
achieved simply by increasing the level of oxytocin in their brains
and generally making them more loving.

This is, of course, an empirical question, but even proponents of
the idea, such as Liao, suggest that all the celebrated "love hormone"
might do is "make individuals more susceptible to a wide range of
emotions and attitudes associated with parental love" (*ibid*.: 493).

This does not mean that it cannot be used effectively to further certain goals. Savulescu and Anders Sandberg (2008) have suggested that in the face of ever-increasing divorce rates on the one hand, and the considerable value of close relationships for personal happiness and development on the other, it is clearly desirable to find ways to reverse the trend and help couples to stay together. Since the main reason for the break-up often seems to be a dwindling sexual interest in one another and an erosion of mutual attachment, both of which can be explained by a human biology that was shaped at a time when sexual relationships did not have to last long to fulfil their purpose, and conventional methods of helping relationships have proved to be only moderately successful, it is imperative to explore new avenues of preserving or rekindling sexual interest and attachment. Thus we could try to use pheromones to stimulate sexual appetite and attraction, and oxytocin or vasopressin to bond couples together, which is just a different (though perhaps more efficient) way of doing what we have been doing all along to keep relationships alive. "There is no morally relevant difference between marriage therapy, a massage, a glass of wine, a fancy pink, steamy potion and a pill. All act at the biological level to make the release of substances like oxytocin and dopamine more likely" (Savulescu & Sandberg 2008: 37). In other words, we are already in the habit of manipulating ourselves to feel in certain ways that we regard as desirable. Again, such a self-manipulation may well be a moral duty, not only when it comes to loving our children, but also when it helps us to stay faithful to our partner. Savulescu and Sandberg deny that this renders what we feel as a result any less original or authentic than what we feel spontaneously, that is without manipulation, at least when it is not used to create an entirely new relationship out of the blue, but instead to sustain an existing relationship (which is based on a certain compatibility between the partners: on shared values and experiences and an appreciation of what the other is, and not merely on the feeling of love). Yet whether we think that a deliberately created emotion is authentic or not also depends on our idea of authenticity (Parens 2009) or, more precisely, on our idea of the self, in relation to which we consider an action or the result thereof as authentic or inauthentic. If being authentic means something like staying true to oneself, then we first need to know what we truly are before we can answer the question of an action's authenticity.

For Savulescu and Sandberg and many other advocates of human enhancement there cannot be anything more authentic than self-creation because that is what defines us as human beings. We stay true to what we are by becoming what we want to be. From this perspective, there is no question that the suggested neuroenhancement of love and marriage is absolutely authentic.

The concept of authenticity and the underlying notion of the true self has often been invoked both in support and in defiance of particular enhancement proposals as well as the whole project of human enhancement. In his influential book *Listening to Prozac* (1994), Peter Kramer claimed that the anti-depressant Prozac can make us whole (again). It can help us restore or find our "true self". He discusses the case of Julia, whom he describes as pleasant, well spoken and comfortable with herself. She is married with children, and works part-time as a nurse. What is her problem? She is overly concerned about keeping an orderly home, without being really obsessive about it: "she just disliked it when things were left messy". However, "her style, her preferences, her sense of propriety, her perfectionism were so pronounced that she was continually angry at her children and husband and ... stalemated in her career" (1994: 24). After taking Prozac she became more relaxed and more tolerant of messiness and her life became better. Kramer recognizes that Julia's problem arises from certain cultural expectations (*ibid.*: 39). If those expectations were different, the problem would cease to exist. So it is pretty obvious that medication works here in the service of certain societal values. It is a social enhancement in so far as the improvement is an improvement with respect to those (variable) values. Kramer celebrates Prozac as a feminist drug: empowering and liberating. Only the outcome counts. *Why* someone is not as happy or does not perform as well as they should is irrelevant. Another case presented by Kramer is Lucy, whose mother was murdered when she was ten years old. This event did not seem to have any immediate negative consequences on her development: she remained productive, responsible and caring. However, as an adult she became prone to putting herself at risk, falling in love with the wrong men and demanding constant attention out of fear of losing them. Again, Kramer insists that the reasons for this behaviour are of no interest. All that matters is that certain characteristics of her behaviour cause her more pain than is usual or good for her. They should, accordingly, be treated as symptoms to be targeted directly, like loss of appetite or insomnia. If Prozac can get rid of the symptoms, then that's fine.

Carol Freedman (1998), however, has objected that by changing the way we feel in such a mechanical manner, we cease to be responsible agents; we are treating our emotions as if they had no cognitive dimension, no meaning beyond their immediate effect on our well-being, while in fact emotions often carry an insight. If Lucy did not feel devastated by her mother's death, she would fail "to see how really devastating it is to lose the person who has been the center of her world. In this way, emotions are like beliefs" (*ibid.*: 139). Hence Lucy's rejection-sensitivity is not just a kind of pain (like a tooth ache) but reflects a genuine *insight*. Similarly, Carl Elliott makes the point that often it is appropriate to feel empty, confused, sad or lonely: "Some societies seem to call for a response of alienation" (1998: 180). To know that all is not well is better than to believe that all is well while it is not: "It would take a moron not to be depressed" (*ibid.*: 183).

Others, such as David Degrazia (2000) have insisted that using Prozac can be an authentic part of the project of self-creation. We determine what we are, and this way we are staying true to ourselves. Self-enhancement is thus authentic, and it is an enhancement (an enhancement of the human as a human) precisely because it is authentic. The enhanced human is then simply the authentic human. There is, however, an interesting ambiguity here concerning the locus of the authentic self. Is the authentic self the one *resulting* from the self-manipulation (the happy and better-functioning self) or is it the self-manipulating self? Am I enhanced because I have finally attained my "true self" in the form of a particular new mindset and set of emotional dispositions, or am I enhanced simply because I have created and transformed myself, no matter what it is that I have transformed into? Neil Levy (2011) has argued that whatever one's preferred view of authenticity – whether one sees it as self-discovery or rather as self-creation – enhancement technologies can function as tools to attain or increase authenticity. Either they help us become what we truly are or they help us be what we have been all along, namely self-creating beings. In practice, however, both conceptions lead to the same outcome. Both agree that we are, as Levy puts it, "most human", "live most meaningfully", not by "accepting our distinctive natures", but by "transcending limitations" (*ibid.*: 312). So in either case, realizing one's true (human or individual) self demands self-transformation.

Elliott has pointed out that the idea of authenticity is "a crucial part of modern identity" (2003: 29). It is indeed, and that is why, for many of us, it is not enough to feel good; we must also feel like ourselves. Kramer's Prozac achieves both at the same time because happiness and authenticity are thought to go hand in hand. The idea is that we feel more like ourselves because we feel good, and we feel good because we feel more like ourselves. The unhappy life is therefore *ipso facto* inauthentic. By tying the idea of happiness (or fulfilment) to the idea of authenticity we legitimize our efforts to enhance ourselves. We don't quite trust our right to be happy, but we never doubt our right to be ourselves. In fact, it is not only a right, but also a duty. Nobody should be forced to live a lie, and everyone should aspire to live a truthful life (i.e. a life true to what they are). Thus the pursuit of happiness gains in both dignity and moral urgency. That is why the use of existing enhancement technologies as well as the development of new ones is so often described as morally obligatory. It cannot be other than good to become what one really is. The idea of authenticity drives the human-enhancement movement, echoing ancient models of human self-development such as Plato's tripartite soul (*Phaedrus*), whose human part is in a constant struggle to control, with the help of the lion-like part, the "multiheaded beast" of the lower passions (*Republic* 588), or Aristotle's organismic teleology, according to which every living thing has its function, which determines not only what it is, but also what is *good* for it.

However, is there really such a thing as the true self that can be found or restored? And if there is, is it necessarily identical with the happy, well-functioning self? If there is a true self, could my true self not be that of a misanthrope and pessimist? And would I then have enhanced myself (namely with respect to authenticity) if I had found a pharmacological means to make myself hate other people even more and find the world an even worse place than before? So again, as long as we do not assume that happy is what we are meant to be and that our true self is the happy self – and there does not seem to be any good reason to do so – we must allow for the possibility that different people choose different moods or emotional dispositions to reflect best what they feel they are. Thus we still have not rid ourselves of what Rein Vos calls the "mood-state selection problem" (2011: 201). It is pretty clear that there are no good or bad mood states as such. In other words, a "good mood is not good *as* a mood" (*ibid.*). Moods are only good or bad with respect to certain purposes, which may differ from individual to individual and from situation to situation. We should also bear in mind that while it is often *useful* (for various purposes) to be in a certain mood, that does not mean that it is, overall, *beneficial* (either for the one who is in it or society as a whole). So whether an intended manipulation of a person's mood works or not, it is not human enhancement: a contribution to the improvement of the human as a human. At best it is an aid: a useful device to facilitate the attainment of certain goals, such as the preservation of a marriage. But perhaps we do not want to preserve our marriage because we realize it is bad for us, but unfortunately we still feel affection for our spouse. In that case we should get rid of our affection. Or a marriage can be saved only if one of the partners dampens their sexual interest. Whatever we look at, it seems that there is no general answer to the question how we *should* feel. Should we rejoice at the sight of a newborn? Should we feel grief when someone dies? When a loved one dies? (We may well argue that if we do not grieve for a loved one, then it is not a loved one, but that still does not mean that we *should* grieve.) If there is no general answer to such questions, then we can only solve the mood-selection problem on an individual basis, and that means by staying flexible and being able to respond to any situation in the way we think we should respond. In other words, we need to gain complete control over our emotions, and that is indeed the direction in which most of the proposals for mood enhancement that we have discussed are heading. Savulescu and Sandberg make this quite clear when they conclude their discussion of the various possibilities of neuroenhancing love and marriage with the confident assertion that "chemical and other biological manipulation of our emotion … represents an important move towards 'biological liberation,' that is, to us being liberated from the biological and genetic constraints evolution has placed on us" (2008: 41).

Yet the idea of the liberated self does not replace the idea of the true self; rather, the liberated self is thought to *be* the true self. The answer to the question "What are we?" is that we are the kind of being that chooses to be what it is. Thus in order to be what we (truly) are, we need to be able to turn ourselves into whatever we choose to be. The enhanced human is the true human is the (biologically) liberated human is the happy human. The goal of biological liberation sets the standard for what counts as human enhancement and what not. The individual is seen as enhanced if they have become closer to the ideal of the fully liberated human, which is the true human self in the sense that it is what we, as humans, have always been meant to be. And what we have been meant to be is in control of our destiny, which requires, among other things, being in control of our emotions. Yet when we have achieved that kind of control, when we can make ourselves feel this way or that way, how do we then decide what to feel? Why should we feel this rather than that? Because it is more appropriate? Because it is more natural? Or for no reason at all? The paradox of complete control is that it makes us goalless. The only thing that is left is the extropian goal of boundless expansion: of change for the sake of change.

5

BECOMING TRULY HUMAN

I am searching for a human being.
(Diogenes, DL vi. 41)

In his *Abolition of Man* (1955), C. S. Lewis attacked those who thought that humankind had finally reached a stage where the ancient dream of conquering nature might actually come true to such an extent that even our own human nature could be controlled and changed at will. Lewis was, for various reasons that we do not need to discuss here, opposed to the idea of changing what we are, but he also thought that it was actually logically impossible to gain complete control over nature and that the underlying attitude of mastery was eventually self-defeating. What is usually called nature is in fact anything and everything that limits, or threatens to limit, our freedom of choice. In other words, the term "nature" signifies the absence of human autonomy.[1] Thus "nature" always begins where human control ends. The word refers to something we have not yet been able to control and that, consequently, to a certain extent controls us. But, as Lewis pointed out, at the very moment we rid ourselves of nature entirely and thus became totally autonomous, there would be nothing left that could guide us in our decisions, so everything we did from then on would no longer be grounded in our particular being and would thus be completely arbitrary. The question "Why should we choose this rather than that?" would no longer be answerable. In order for our decisions to be *our* decisions, we need to maintain an individual self that is not itself a product of our decisions. In other words, it must be given, not chosen. This individual self, precisely because it exists[2] prior to all conscious decision-making, provides us with a secure foundation for all our decisions and the actions that result from them. Yet it can only do so if it consists of more than just a set of individualizing properties. Since it needs to give direction to our decisions and actions, it must instead comprise a set of values. Those values define what each of us is. In the absence of such values our decisions would be groundless and the result of whatever impulse came over us in that particular moment. "Nature, untrammelled by values, rules the Conditioners and, through them, all humanity. Man's conquest of Nature turns out, in the moment of its consummation, to be Nature's conquest of Man" (Lewis 1955: 80). The problem to which Lewis draws our attention here is that values, without which there cannot be any rational, that is, non-arbitrary, decision-making, cannot be chosen. They have to be found or, rather, they have to choose us. A value that we picked for ourselves, one that we were free to endorse or not to endorse, would be no value at all. Values are uncontrollable and in that sense belong to the realm of nature. Hence there must always be something that we do not control, something we accept as a given, in order for us to remain the authors of our own decisions and actions. There is, in other words, no way to get rid of nature entirely.

What interests me in this argument is its implication for the debate on human enhancement and the inherent normativity of human nature (or some particular concept of it). Looking at the present debate it may seem that it is carried out between two opposing camps whose disagreement about whether or not we should try to "make better people" is mainly due to different views on whether or not human nature, as it is, is in any way relevant to the question of what we should do. In the first camp there are those who are suspicious of the promises that are frequently made about the fabulous opportunities that biotechnology will create for us, and of all the talk about "lives wonderful beyond imagination"[3] that our descendants will allegedly enjoy if we just go along with the tide of scientific progress instead of clinging to the past and irrational taboos. Those "bioconservatives", as they are derisively dubbed by their more adventurous opponents, apparently want to protect human nature and along with it the status quo of what human life is now. The other camp is formed by people who profess to think little of human nature, who deny its moral relevance, urge us to remould it, and do not seem to make any assumptions about it in their arguments. What Lewis's argument suggests, though, is that, contrary to initial appearance, in fact both camps need to presuppose certain values, which means to assume certain things as natural or given, the only difference being that they cannot seem to agree on *which* values are to be left alone and unquestioned. So the disagreement is not really about whether or not we should, or want to, leave nature alone but, rather, *what* nature. Nor does one camp believe that human nature has moral authority and the other not. Rather, they assign moral authority to different conceptions of human nature and see different things as valuable. For no matter how "rational" and "objective" one claims to be, there are always some values in the equation on which the plausibility of one's position depends. As Lewis pointed out:

> [A] great many of those who "debunk" traditional or (as they would say) "sentimental" values have in the background values of their own which they believe to be immune from the debunking process. They claim to be cutting away the parasitic growth of emotion, religious sanction, and inherited taboos, in order that "real" or "basic" values may emerge.   (1955: 41–2)

Of course, those values are not more real or basic than the values they reject. They are just different. And just as this was true for the eugenicists that Lewis had in mind, it is also true for today's "conditioners": those who claim that we should, perhaps even have a moral obligation to, use biotechnology in order to create better humans. Some of these call themselves "transhumanists"; others resent the name but nonetheless promote views that are very similar, and I shall here take the licence to call them transhumanists too.

A transhumanist is someone who believes, or professes to believe, that we should do everything we can to leave the human condition behind and to evolve into something better than human. Transhumanists are convinced that what we are now, even when we are at our best, is not good enough. We could do far better than that: become vastly more intelligent, live much longer, perhaps indefinitely, and experience as yet unimaginable pleasures (e.g. Pearce 1995; More 1996; Bostrom 2008). Being a transhumanist in spirit, if not by name, Harris makes a strong case for "enhancing evolution" and the "making of better people". He believes that it is our duty to "make the world a better place",[4] and that for that reason we need to take "control of evolution and our future development to the point, and indeed beyond the point, where we humans will have changed, perhaps into a new and certainly into a better species altogether" (Harris 2007: 4). Those who are less enthralled about the prospect of controlling evolution and human enhancement, such as Leon Kass, Michael Sandel or Francis Fukuyama, are ridiculed as "contemporary gurus" who believe:

> that there is something special about themselves and that their particular sort of being is not only worth preserving in perpetuity, but that there is a duty not only to ensure that preservation, but to make sure that neither natural selection nor deliberate choice permit the development of any better sort of being.   (*Ibid.*: 16)

Put like this, it sounds as if these critics just suffered from too much self-love and vanity and clearly thought that surely there can be nothing better than themselves. In reality it is, of course, not quite that simple. What is true is that Kass, Sandel and Fukuyama all seem to believe that on the whole human nature is not that bad after all. There is much that is worth preserving, and the real or apparent deficiencies we tend to bemoan are often the flipside of things that make life valuable and precious to us, so that by trying to improve on human nature we might lose just as much as, or even more than, we will gain.

However, they are not completely indiscriminate in their acceptance and defence of the present human condition. Kass seeks to preserve not everything about us but rather "aspects of our given humanity that are rightly dear to us" (2003: 20) and Sandel seeks to protect "the gifted dimension of human experience" (2007: 89), which contrasts sharply with the transhumanist attitude of mastery and the "Promethean aspiration to remake nature" (*ibid.*: 26). But what exactly is human nature? Fukuyama takes it to be "the sum of the behaviour and characteristics that are typical of the human species, arising from genetic rather than environmental factors" (2002: 130). In other words, everything we are and do by virtue of being human (as opposed to what we do by virtue of living under conditions that are not the same for all humans) belongs to human nature, such as (presumably) playing, having sex, sleeping, eating, digesting, laughing and crying, talking, arguing, fighting and many other things. Some of these activities we share with (other) animals, some are unique to us, but all of them are part of human nature and define our being.[5]

Now it is not immediately obvious why this should be particularly relevant for making a decision on whether or not and in what way precisely we should try to change what we are. Fukuyama maintains that we need to protect the "full range of our complex, evolved natures against attempts at self-modification" (*ibid.*: 172) in order to preserve the basis of human dignity and rights. According to him, there is something unique about the human race that entitles "every member of the human species to a higher moral status than the rest of the natural world" (*ibid.*: 166). We cannot exactly say what it is, but it must be something that we all have in common by virtue of being human and which serves as the basis for our mutual respect. This "factor X" "is the human essence, the most basic meaning of what it is to be human" (*ibid.*: 150). Yet, Fukuyama holds, this human essence cannot be found in any particular property such as language, conceptual thinking, self-consciousness or the ability to act in accordance with moral principles. If it were, then we could just hold on to this particular property, change the rest and still preserve the human essence (always assuming that this is a priority for us). But humans are, in fact, what they are as complex wholes, that is, because of the particular way all those properties and activities that define human existence work together. They form a unity, and it is that particular unity that makes us special and deserving of being treated with respect and care.

Now this is, of course, a highly controversial claim. More important, it is a claim that we have no means to verify or to refute. It is about what it means to be human, but meanings can change and obviously being human does not mean the same thing for everybody. You and I may disagree about what makes humans particularly worthy of moral respect, and some may even think that there is no such thing as human dignity, at least not *in re*, so that it is futile to look for its foundation in human nature. And there is no way we can decide the question once and for all. It is ultimately a matter of how we want to define ourselves. Also, not even Fukuyama would want to claim that what is less appealing about our behaviour, such as, for instance, our obvious fondness for the torturing and murdering of other human beings, is a necessary condition of human dignity. "There is too much that is thoroughly unrespectable in human nature (along with much that is admirable), for the mere fact that X is a part of human nature to constitute any reason, even a prima facie reason, for supposing that X is good" (Bostrom 2008: 131). So it seems that we cannot really get around determining what is valuable about what we are, since this is, as Jonathan Glover has pointed out, the only thing we have a good reason to preserve (2007: 83–7). Human nature as such, whole or not, has no moral authority. It cannot tell us what to do. To presume otherwise is to commit a naturalistic fallacy, as Fukuyama is frequently accused of having done (e.g. Agar 2004: 90–97).

But for the transhumanists, Fukuyama's alleged failure to avoid the naturalistic fallacy is only a minor defect. As we shall see, they are perfectly willing to commit the same fallacy when it serves their purposes. The real problem transhumanists have with Fukuyama's position, and likewise Sandel's and Kass's, is the underlying belief or suggestion that it might actually be a good thing that not everything is subject to our will, that there are some things we cannot (yet) control and that some things simply *happen* to us. That is what Sandel means when he talks about the virtue of staying open "to the unbidden". The so-called "bioconservatives" have respect for nature in the sense that they want to keep some areas and facts of our lives free of human control. But from the transhumanist point of view, control is *always* desirable, and that is why nature needs to be fought and overcome wherever we encounter it. Consequently, ageing, death and all the usual partial incompetence and inability that characterize our existence are all perceived as expressions of "nature". They are part of our natural human condition. Nature is associated with inevitable decline and failure. Thus Gregory Stock speaks reproachfully of "life's natural ebb" (2002: 9) that we need to counter. Nature is what binds us: what sets limits to our aspirations. In short, nature is clearly the enemy. Accordingly, the extropian transhumanist Max More (1996) casts nature as entropy, that is, a tendency to dissolve order and destroy information and usable energy, and consequently those who try to protect it from human

intervention as entropy-promoting forces. Whereas, in More's telling of the story, the transhumanists defend reason and hence continue the tradition of European Enlightenment, their opponents rely
on faith only, which means that they are in the grip of indefensi-
ble dogmatism and irrational beliefs, which of course we need to
shed as soon and as rigorously as possible: "No more gods, no more
faith, no more timid holding back. Let us blast out of our old forms,
our ignorance, our weakness, and our mortality. The future belongs
to posthumanity" (More 1994). Nature, for the transhumanists, is
mostly that – ignorance, weakness and mortality – and it is hard
to see why we should cling to these properties if we do not have to.

Yet despite their professed contempt for nature, transhumanists
often seek support for their own goals in a particular understanding of human nature. It is true that some transhumanists consist-
ently deny that anything follows from human nature regarding the
desirability or undesirability of human enhancement or becoming
posthuman. Many, however, do at least implicitly assume that what
we are is relevant for what we ought to do, in the sense that it provides the justification for the transhumanist plan of action and even
contains an obligation to follow it. In other words, they presuppose
a normative conception of human nature. A good example is More
himself. He urges us to get rid of "old conceptual structures and processes which act as a drag on progress" (1996), to discard all dogmas
and all religion, which allegedly keep us on our knees and only allow
us to look up but not to walk forwards. Radical self-transformation
is what we should strive for. But why? The answer is that this is our
nature and we ought to stay true to our nature:

> Humanity must not stagnate to go backwards to a primitive
> life, or to halt our burgeoning move forward, upward, out-
> ward, would be a betrayal of the dynamic inherent in life
> and consciousness. We must progress on to transhuman-
> ity and beyond into a posthuman stage that we can barely
> glimpse. (*Ibid.*)

It is obvious that when More says that we "must" not stagnate and
we "must" progress on, he does not mean to say that the latter will
happen anyway: that the process that will eventually turn us into
posthumans is inevitable. On the contrary, he is saying that the

future lies in our hands and that it is our *duty* not to stagnate or even go backwards. To do that, even to allow it, would be a "*betrayal* of the dynamic inherent in life and consciousness". What we would betray, according to More, is our own human nature. But calling some course of action a *betrayal* is using a moral category. We *must not* betray is a self-evident moral imperative (because this is part of the *meaning* of the word "betrayal"), so that if we did betray by choosing not to progress we would be *morally* to blame. From this we can infer that there is a value in progressing that we are not supposed to question. It is what we are *meant* to do by virtue of what we are. This is clearly an argument from nature, by which I mean an argument that proceeds from a claim about what some being's nature is to a conclusion that tells us what this being ought to do (or, sometimes, how it ought to be treated). So it appears that nature, after it has been expelled from the transhumanist paradise with a great show of indignation, is immediately invited back in through the backdoor, just as Lewis thought it would.

More is certainly not exceptional in this respect. Other transhumanists use similar arguments from nature when it suits them. Savulescu, another transhumanist in spirit although not by name, defends the use of performance-enhancing drugs in sport as a perfect expression of human nature and distinctiveness. Far "from being against the spirit of sport, biological manipulation embodies the human spirit – the capacity to improve ourselves on the basis of reason and judgment. When we exercise our reason, we do what only humans do" (Savulescu *et al.* 2004: 667). So manipulating our bodies in order to improve ourselves is an exercise of reason, which, as far as we know, we alone of all living creatures are capable of. The ancient definition of the human animal as *zoon logon echon* or *animal rationale* is being evoked and given a peculiar twist by putting the emphasis on practical reason or, more precisely, a reason that is directed towards self-improvement. Thus it is suggested that what makes us human is not the ability to reason as such and certainly not the ability to think about and contemplate the world (Aristotle's *theoria*). What is supposed to make us human is rather a particular goal-oriented *use* of reason: "To choose to be better is to be human" (*ibid.*: 670). This, however, is clearly not intended to be a purely descriptive statement (although it might be intended to *look* like one). It is not just claimed that choosing to be better is what humans typically do. Thus it belongs to a different category than similar-sounding statements such as, for instance, "To get together and chat about the weather or other trifles is to be human". Neither is the statement apologetic, like the statement "To err is to be human" (*errare humanum est*). It is not intended as an excuse. Rather, it is an expression of pride. In the language of speech acts we could say that as an illocutionary act it is an encouragement (i.e. to encourage is its *function*), and what it encourages us to do (its intended perlocutionary effect) is to live up to our nature. We are *invited* to identify with that particular description and expected to *accept* the invitation by acting accordingly. Savulescu is telling us that choosing to be better is what being human is all about: what it *means* to be human. We are being asked to *define* ourselves in that particular way: to take it as an instruction on how to become truly human. The message is that if we want to stay true to ourselves we must approve of, defend, promote and especially use not only performance-enhancing drugs in sport but all enhancement techniques in general and in all areas of life.

My impression is that this message pervades a good deal of the transhumanist literature. Occasionally even mythical images are employed to convey it. Stock for instance, in his book *Redesigning Humans*, cites Prometheus in order to support his claim that not only are we about to "seize control of our evolutionary future" (2002: 2), but that this is going to happen whether or not we want it to happen. We can, Stock explains, have as many well-founded objections as we like; it won't change a thing, because Prometheus's stealing fire from the gods is "too characteristically human". Prometheus is here clearly introduced as the paradigmatic human: as an embodiment of the human essence. What is being said, then, on one level, is that biotechnological progress cannot be stopped because being humans we will always "steal fire from the gods", that is, continue to find and take possession of new means to increase our power and control. In theory, one could agree with that diagnosis and still deplore the fact: alas, we are thieves by nature! But the image, as it is being used here, does not really permit that option. For we are not being told that we are like a common thief but rather like Prometheus: a mythical figure who was willing to sacrifice himself for the good of mankind. It is the same Prometheus that Percy Shelley described in his play *Prometheus Unbound* as an altruistic and

81

peace-loving version of Milton's Satan, who, like Prometheus, is distinguished by his "courage, majesty, and firm and patient opposition to omnipotent force". We are also told that using biotechnology in order to redesign ourselves is a primary instance, not of stealing, but of "stealing *fire* from the *gods*". In other words, it is a noble, heroic act: an act of resistance against tyrants who, for no good reason, like Shelley's Jupiter, withhold from us what we urgently need for our survival. The gods in Stock's simile are close relatives of More's entropic forces. They represent nature as an obstacle to human freedom, as everything we have not yet conquered. So it is not only our nature to steal fire from the gods (a descriptive, although metaphorical statement), but it is, in fact, for that very reason, our holy mission (an implicitly prescriptive statement).

Not surprisingly, Prometheus was also cited as the paradigmatic human by Pico della Mirandola in his *Oration on the Dignity of Man* (Pico [1486] 1985). Pico declares him to be an apt symbol of humanity "by reason of our nature sloughing its skin and transforming itself" (*ibid.*: 5). I said not surprisingly because the first few pages of Pico's *Oration* strike me as the *locus classicus* of transhumanist thought. In a sense Pico was the first transhumanist because he provided transhumanism with its paradoxical normative anthropology by describing man as an animal whose nature it is not to have a nature. In an attempt to promote this anthropology, Pico invents his own myth of origin, which is a variation of the one Plato tells in his *Protagoras*. According to Plato, Prometheus (again!) and his brother Epimetheus were given the task to assist in the creation of the mortal races by giving them their powers and abilities. But Epimetheus persuaded his brother to let him do it on his own, which turned out to be a mistake. Since, as his name already indicates, he was not given to *pronoia* (foresight), he forgot to save some powers for us humans, who had the bad fortune to come last. Through Epimetheus's fault we ended up with nothing and could only survive because Prometheus and Zeus stepped into the breach, the one getting us fire and the wisdom of how to use it (that is to say, technology), and the other giving us political abilities and moral emotions that enabled us to live together and support and help each other (Plato, *Protagoras* 320d–322d).

Pico's telling of this tale is quite different. What Plato described as an initial defect that makes us dependent on technology and on each other, Pico describes as our greatest advantage and highest virtue. In his version of the story, the short-sighted Epimetheus is replaced by God himself, who, being the "best workman", although initially committing the same blunder of giving out all the archetypes and having none left for us humans, immediately knows how to turn the apparent failure into an opportunity to create his masterpiece. For, he reasons, each animal that has been given a particular nature is thereby also confined. The very fact that it has a nature means that it is also bound by it. It cannot go beyond what its given nature allows it to be. But humans, since they are of "indeterminate form" and have no nature of their own, can be anything they want, anything they decide to be. Thus God addresses man with the following words: "In conformity with thy free judgment, in whose hands I have placed thee, thou art confined by no bounds; and thou wilt fix limits of nature for thyself" (Pico 1985: 4). Man is here being defined as the unbound animal, a being for which no limits exist except those he sets for himself. Our nature is that we have no nature. We can have whatever we choose and be whatever we will. "Thou, like a judge appointed for being honourable, art the molder and maker of thyself; thous mayest sculpt thyself into whatever shape thou dost prefer" (*ibid.*). But again, this has to be read not as a mere description of what we, in fact, are, but as a statement about what we ought to be and do. Not all choices are equally fitting. This becomes apparent when God continues: "Thou canst grow downward into the lower natures which are brutes. Thou canst again grow upward from thy soul's reason into the higher natures which are divine" (*ibid.*). Although we are free to choose between the higher and the lower, it is clear that we would abuse our God-given freedom if we chose the lower. For the likes of us, only the sky is the limit. We can be brutes and stay within the bounds of nature (or what we have persuaded ourselves to accept as nature) or free ourselves from these bounds[6] and become like the angels or even God himself, not only potentially free but actually free, and that is precisely what we are meant to do in virtue of what we are:

> as Asaph the prophet says: "Ye are all gods, and sons of the most high," unless by abusing the very indulgent liberality of the Father, we make the free choice, which he gave to us,

harmful to ourselves .... Let us spurn earthly things; let us
struggle toward the heavenly.   (Pico [1486] 1985: 7)[7]

There are echoes here of the Genesis story, which also, beneath
the pious Christian surface reading that we are all familiar with,
contains the idea that rising above our present condition to a God-
like existence is our birthright. Unlike Pico's God, the Hebrew God
of the Old Testament is jealous and determined to prevent us from
becoming like him, which we could have. When Adam and Eve still
lived in the Garden of Eden, they were neither immortal nor did
they know themselves. But the tree of knowledge and the tree of
life were always there, and with them the possibility of wisdom and
eternal life. And once they had eaten from the tree of knowledge
it was only a matter of time before they would also eat from the
tree of life and become like God himself. In order to prevent this,
and for no better reason, God expelled them from the garden. This
story can easily be given a transhumanist reading. God is the tyrant
who unjustly denied to us what was rightfully ours and drove us
away from our home, for which we have been looking ever since.
Countless other myths about the Golden Age that once was, about
Kingdoms of Far Away where there is no death nor sorrow nor
toil and where we truly belong, all convey the same message: that
home is somewhere else – and, as Dorothy knew, "there's no place
like home". These fantasies of a lost home, that is, a place where we
truly belong and where we can live the life that we are, by our very
nature, meant to live, have haunted human imagination for millen-
nia and nourish the soil from which transhumanism grows. Hence
the conviction that we are all potential, even teleological, immortals. That we are *in fact* not immortal does not show that we are not
meant to be immortal, that immortality is not our destiny. We only
have to overcome some obstacles that Nature has put in our way.
In the Genesis story, Nature is represented by God, who deliberately stands in the way of human perfection. God, in other words, is
acting like a true bioconservative. There is also a transhumanist in
the story, namely the serpent, who urges Eve to move on, to improve
herself. The serpent promises knowledge and, despite his reputation
for being a compulsive liar, speaks nothing but the truth. He is the
real hero of the story and deserves his punishment by God no more
than Prometheus deserved his.

However, my claim that transhumanism (as a philosophy that is essentially prescriptive, arguing for and demanding a particular kind of practice) presupposes a normative conception of human nature does not rest on the sporadic occurrence, within transhumanist literature, of mythological allusions or argumentative passages that seem to imply such a conception. My claim is, in fact, more general, namely that *all* proponents of radical human enhancement implicitly appeal to human nature. First, it is not true that there are *no* aspects of humanity that, in Kass's favourite phrase, "are dear to them", but only that what is dear to them seems to be different from what is dear to their opponents. If there were nothing that was dear to them, they would no longer be able to state their case for human enhancement (this is a version of Lewis's argument introduced above). Enhancement is, by definition, good. An enhancement that leaves us worse off than we were before is no enhancement, or at least no human enhancement in the proper sense. Hence, in order to decide whether a proposed or already achieved change of our qualities or abilities is, or is not, an enhancement, we need a standard by which to measure this change. The obvious standard is subjective well-being. If we are happy then we are well. If we become even happier as a result of taking a particular drug or undergoing a genetic intervention, then we are better than before or, indeed, "better than well" (Kramer 1994: xv). But subjective well-being is not independent of the creature whose well-being it is. It is species specific. What is constitutive for the well-being of a human is different from what is constitutive for the well-being of a chicken. So all proposals for specific enhancements need to take our human nature into account. Only what increases *our* well-being as human beings can qualify as an enhancement.

Now, the connection between human well-being and human nature can perhaps be acknowledged without assuming a *normative* conception of human nature. Yet it is notoriously difficult to predict what will, in fact, increase our well-being. For instance, as we have seen, high general intelligence is not obviously more conducive to our well-being than low intelligence, and neither is enhanced memory or changed emotional capacities. We can easily imagine circumstances in which all of these diminish subjective well-being. If subjective well-being were all that counted then high intelligence would not necessarily be an advantage, and we would have no reason to promote it. Low intelligence could be very helpful indeed for maximizing the enjoyment of the simple pleasures of life. I am quite positive that we would enjoy typical television programmes more if our intellectual demands were lower. So perhaps when we think about enhancing human traits with a view to well-being, we should attempt to make people less intelligent rather than more.

In an attempt to avoid this unwelcome conclusion, proponents of human enhancement usually prefer to cut the link between subject-ive happiness and objective good. They either understand the term "well-being" in such a way that even when we *feel* well we could, in fact, be not well – that is, as objective well-being – or use a differ-ent term entirely that is more apt to convey the intended objective meaning, such as "quality of life" or "human flourishing". In other words, they want to follow John Stuart Mill rather than Jeremy Bentham. Poetry, they claim, is indeed better than pushpin. Like-wise, reading and being able to understand and appreciate Proust is better than reading Tom Clancy. But why and in what sense would it be better? In what sense would we have a higher quality of life, or would we flourish more? If, as it is assumed, we would not necessar-ily *enjoy* ourselves more, would we then have a more *refined* kind of enjoyment? What exactly would we have gained?

I do not mean to say that there is no gain. Like most trans-humanists I would rather be a happy Socrates (and perhaps even a disgruntled Socrates) than a happy pig, but the question is how this preference can be justified. It seems to me that the only possible justification is an appeal to some idea of what it means to be human. Human flourishing (just like quality of life, or objective well-being) is a concept that can hardly be understood without an assump-tion about what humans are supposed to be like, that is, without some normative conception of human *nature*. Most people do in fact prefer Clancy to Proust but we like to think that they *ought* to like Proust better because that would be more befitting humans. Being content with books by authors like Clancy or happily watch-ing game shows on television is an insult to their human nature, to their inherent possibilities. Humans are *thinking* beings so they had better think in order to live up to what they are. Human enhance-ment is thus proposed as a way of eventually turning us into what we are meant to be. So despite the fact that whenever human nature is invoked by "bioconservatives" such as Fukuyama and Kass, proponents of human enhancement deny that there is such a nature, or that, if there is, it has any normative significance; they themselves constantly rely on some implicit understanding of human nature to give sense to the idea of human flourishing and the claim that we have a moral duty to promote it. It might be a different understanding of human nature but it is just as value-laden and normative as that of their opponents.

6

LIVING LONGER

Caelum, non animum mutant, qui trans mare currunt.
(Horace, Epistle 1.11)

Fuelled by recent scientific advances in biogerontology,[1] the prospect of slowing down or even arresting the process of ageing and thus indefinitely extending our maximum lifespans has led an increasing number of writers to jump on the bandwagon of life extension and to argue that virtual immortality is a good thing and we should do everything in our power to attain it. It is assumed that any significant extension of our lifespans would turn us into better humans, in the sense that we would be better off than we are now. The reasoning applied here is relatively simple and intuitively plausible: we all appreciate being alive, and no one wants to be dead (unless something bad has happened to them or nothing good is likely to happen ever again, so that life has lost its meaning or worth). We do not normally care very much for the idea of dying, and try to hold on to our lives as long as possible. So all things considered, we tend to regard life as a good and death as an evil. Given this universal and strong preference for life over death, how could we not regard indefinite life extension and virtual immortality as a good thing? How then could we not see it as an improvement of human nature? It would seem irrational not to do so.

However, this argument, plausible as it may seem at first sight, is misleading, because it is based on the premise that we (normally) do not want to die, which is then taken to imply that we *do* want to live forever (i.e. have an implicit desire for indefinite life extension). Yet this conclusion is in fact not warranted. If you ask people whether they want to die, most of them will indeed deny it. However, if you ask the *same* people whether they want to go on living forever, you may find that most will deny this too. Admittedly, this contention is based on anecdotal evidence, tested with various groups of students and colleagues. I am not aware of any sociological surveys that would directly support it. Nor, however, is there sufficient evidence to support the opposite claim, namely that most people *do* want to live forever. Rather, this is often taken for granted. As Jayne C. Lucke and Wayne Hall have pointed out, "there is, as yet, no coherent picture of public beliefs and attitudes towards real life extension strategies" (2005: 101). However, it does not really matter how many people, despite valuing their lives, actually do not want to live forever (that is, how many prefer living forever to dying at some time), or indeed whether there are any such people at all. Nor does it matter much what exactly those people who reply that they would not want to live forever imagine their unending lives to be like. The point I am trying to make is not empirical, but rather logical. What I am asking is whether we can, as is often suggested (see e.g. Bostrom 2008: 113–16), legitimately conclude from the fact that people do normally appreciate being alive and accordingly desire not to die that they also have an (implicit) desire to have their lifespans indefinitely extended, that is, to live (potentially) forever. It is quite possible that a person does not want to die and still does not want to live forever. On the face of it this seems to be a blatant contradiction. How can we at the same time not want to die *and* not want to live forever? Obviously, if you do not die you will live forever and the only way to avoid living forever is to die. The one entails the other. However, there are many situations where there are only two options open to us and we do not like either of them. We can wish to avoid illness and at the same time wish to avoid doing the things necessary to maintain our health as long as possible, such as keeping to a strict diet or exercising regularly. There is no contradiction in *wishing* both of these things, only in achieving both. Perhaps we cannot have our cake and eat it but there is no difficulty at all in *wishing* we could both have *and* eat it. My point here is that it is entirely possible, as well as consistent, that for many people living forever is an idea they find just as abhorrent as the idea of dying, so that we cannot infer from the fact that they do not want to die that they *do* want to live forever. It just does not follow. Note that I am *not* saying that indefinite life extension is a bad thing, morally wrong, or undesirable. I am simply pointing out that we cannot *assume* the desirability of indefinite life extension simply on the grounds that (to many of us) the prospect of our own death is rather unappealing. Even if life is a good, death need not be an evil.

Advocates of radical life extension are often puzzled about the fact that relatively few people are willing to embrace and support wholeheartedly the "crusade against aging" (de Grey & Rae 2007: x), which they themselves regard as *self-evidently* of the utmost importance and as something we simply cannot afford not to engage in. From their point of view, it is plainly irrational to have any reservations about the project, and the only explanation they can see for people having such reservations, despite its obvious irrationality, is that they are caught in some kind of "pro-aging trance" that has its roots in a psychological need to regard what is unavoidable as, to some extent at least, good and desirable (*ibid.*, 10–11).[2] Yet, it is argued, now that we are on the brink of understanding why we age and of using this knowledge to arrest or even reverse the process, this trance has lost its use and we should wake up, see ageing and the resulting death as the evils they are, and fight them with all our strength and all available means. Ageing, writes Aubrey de Grey, "is just like smoking: It's really bad for you. It shortens your life …, it makes the last several years of your life rather grim, and it also makes those years pretty hard for your loved ones" (*ibid.*: 10). Although ageing has some unpleasant concomitants (those grim last years), for de Grey it is clearly the fact that ageing eventually leads to death that makes it such a "curse" (*ibid.*: 14). For this reason, and this reason alone, ageing must be understood as a "humanitarian crisis", taking a "toll of tens of thousands of dead every day". De Grey regards this situation as intolerable and is determined to put "an end to the entire horror show" (*ibid.*: 36). This view of death is shared by many other convinced life extensionists. Max More already demanded in 1990 that "science, technology and reason … be harnessed … to abolish the greatest evil: death" (More 1996). More recently, Bostrom even published a colourful "fable" in a respectable journal, in which he represents death as a thoroughly evil, giant dragon that tyrannizes the planet: "The dragon stood taller than the largest cathedral, and it was covered with thick black scales. Its red eyes glowed with hate, and from its terrible jaws flowed an incessant stream of evil smelling yellowish green slime" (Bostrom 2005b: 273). Just as in real life, the people in Bostrom's fable are at first reluctant to accept the moral necessity of killing the dragon until a small boy – and, as we all know, small boys always tell the truth – points out what should have been obvious to everyone all along: "The dragon is bad!" (*ibid*.: 275). The object of the fable is obviously to convince us that the boy is right and that therefore searching for a cure for ageing is "an urgent, screaming moral imperative" (*ibid*.: 277).

Now let us have a closer look at the assumption, which life extensionists tend to regard and present as a self-evident truth, that ageing (and what it leads to, namely death) is "really bad for us". Is it really? Before we can answer this question we obviously need to know what it is we are asking. That, however, is not at all clear. Neither is it clear what "bad" means and in what sense ageing and dying might be considered bad, nor who the "us" is for whom it is supposed to be bad. We also need to differentiate between ageing and dying because, although, as yet, ageing inevitably results in death (as its principal cause), in theory we could age and not die, just as we can now avoid the process (or, more precisely, processes) of ageing altogether and die young (or die old, but from other causes than ageing, such as a car accident). So let us first look at death and ask whether *dying* (that is, the loss of life, or death) is really bad for us. This question can be understood in at least two different ways. First, we can ask whether each person's own death is bad for them. In other words: is *my* dying bad for *me*, and *your* dying bad for *you*? Second, we can ask whether each person's death is bad for everyone else: is *my* dying bad for *you*, and *your* dying bad for *me*?

Philosophers occasionally deny that death is an evil on the grounds that nobody is able to experience their own non-existence. If death is real and is indeed the non-existence that it is commonly imagined to be, at least among non-believers, then we do not suffer at all from being dead. As Epicurus was the first to argue, our fear of death (and the implicit conviction that death is an evil) rests on a conceptual confusion: when we imagine ourselves as being dead we tend to imagine ourselves as at the same time being aware of our condition, that is, as somehow being both dead and alive. Yet in fact we will not experience anything at all. Properly speaking, we will not even *be* dead, because there will not be anyone left to be anything at all. "Death, therefore, the most awful of evils, is nothing to us, seeing that, when we are, death is not come, and, when death is come, we are not" (Diogenes Laertius 1958: 651).

Those who are not convinced by Epicurus' argument think that he rather misses the point because it is precisely the expected absence of all experience that makes death such a terrible thing. Thus the poet Philip Larkin, in his poem "Aubade" (1977), complains about philosophers who argue that what cannot be felt should not be feared but fail to realize that what we fear is not feeling, that is, not being able to feel (or see, or hear) anything at all. But that only shows how right Epicurus was to suspect a fallacy. Larkin invites us to imagine how terrible it would be to be completely deprived of our senses and thus of the means to relate to the world, unloved, unloving, immersed in utter loneliness. But we will not be alone and disconnected from the world. We will not *be* at all. Sure enough, what we fear most in death is probably nothingness itself, but we mistakenly fear it as something that will happen to us.[3] And it is the same nothingness that lies behind us and the same nothingness that would have been if we had never been conceived in the first place. And we would not if things had been only slightly different. Would that have been bad for us? I do not think it makes sense to say that it would.

Admittedly, it seems that people can be harmed even when they are not aware of it. I can, for instance, be deceived without knowing it, and we may want to insist that my being deceived is bad for me, even if I never learn of the deceit and never suffer any negative consequences from it (although it is rather difficult to explain why that should be so). But my point is not so much that I will not experience my death and hence it cannot be harmful to me, but rather that there will no longer be an I that can be harmed.[4]

However, although this is a beautiful argument that, as I find, does much to dampen our fear of death, it seems to have the disadvantage of proving too much. If there is no harm whatsoever in death, why do we regard taking someone's life as a serious offence and having one's life taken one of the worst harms that can befall an individual? If death is not bad for us, then it seems that killing someone can only be wrong to the extent that it involves suffering for the victim or third parties. There should be nothing wrong, then, with taking someone's life if they are not aware of it and nobody minds their being gone. Yet most people would not accept this. Neither would they agree that in cases where there *is* suffering involved, it is *this* aspect that makes the act of killing bad and not the fact that somebody is dead as a result of it. But again, why should we regard death itself an evil for the one who has died or is about to die? The fact that we do does not necessarily show that we also have a good reason for it. The answer that immediately springs to mind is that normally people do not *want* to die. In fact, to most people at most times, that seems to be their strongest, most fundamental desire, in the sense that when their lives are in obvious and imminent danger there is little that they would not sacrifice to avoid death. The desire to stay alive is deeply ingrained in our minds and perhaps even more so in our bodies, which will fight death even when our minds have already given up all hope. Sometimes, of course, we will sacrifice our own lives if that seems necessary to protect something that is even dearer to us: perhaps the life or well-being of a loved one, our own personal integrity or a project we identify with. However, that does not show that we no longer regard our death as bad for us, but only that we regard something else as even worse than that.

On the other hand, we do not have to regard death as an evil in order to understand why we should feel strongly about killing and erect robust legal and moral barriers against it. Take the case of personal property. Being robbed of what belongs to us is certainly something we deeply resent, and we do so even if we might in fact be happier without it. In other words, having what we own taken away is not necessarily always bad for us. But the fact that I might be better off without my television or my car does not invalidate my right to them and does not make it less of an injustice to have them taken away from me without my consent. John Stuart Mill defined a right as "something which society ought to defend me in the possession of", for the sake of "general utility". He argued, very convincingly I think, that the reason why we feel so strongly about these rights is that this utility is a special one, namely the "extraordinarily important and impressive kind of utility" that is attached to the protection of *security*, which is something "no human being can possibly do without" and "the most vital of all interests" (Mill 1998: 98), in the sense that it is absolutely essential to human well-being (*ibid*.: 103). In other words, we need to have some assurance that we shall be allowed to hold on to what we have worked for (right to property), and we need to be fairly certain that we are not killed when we meet other people (right to life), that is, we need to have reason to believe that it is rather unlikely that they will harm us. If that were not so we would not be able to live in community with other people. Being what we are – social beings who need and seek each other's company – our well-being depends on it. Hence the killing of a member of the community needs to be sanctioned. None of this would be necessary, of course, if we did not value our lives. But from the fact that we do, it does not follow that having our life taken away from us is in any way bad for us. We can value a thing, demand that it be protected, and feel insecure and hence unhappy when it is not, without being the least worse off when it is taken away from us. Nothing is good or bad for me when I am dead but, as long as I am alive, I have good reason to want to stay alive and to applaud institutions, such as moral inhibitions, that help me achieve this. Thus we cannot infer from my preference for life over death, and my desire to put death off as long as possible, that my dying is bad for me.[5]

However, one may object that perhaps it is not so much my death itself that is bad for me, but rather the fact that I have no choice: I *must* die, whether I want to or not. The inevitability of death as a result of ageing is what makes it bad for us. We want to make our own choices, and whether or not my dying is bad for me, the mere fact that it is being *forced upon me* is already sufficient reason to resent it and declare the whole process of my ageing (as the gradual deterioration of my body leading to its final breakdown and disintegration) bad for me. Yet this alternative interpretation is hardly convincing. If it is not death itself that is bad for me but rather the fact that it comes unbidden – the sheer involuntariness of it – then we should expect other things that we cannot avoid doing or prevent from happening to us to be considered at least equally bad. That is not the case, though. There are many things that come unbidden without this fact worrying us too much. We do not only have to die, we also have to eat, or breathe, and we would normally not say that eating or breathing, or having the impulses that make us eat and breathe, is "really bad for us". At worst we will think of it as a minor inconvenience. The reason for that is quite obvious, namely that we do not normally regard eating or breathing itself as bad, and hence nor the need for it. So if death is not bad for me, the inevitability of death does not seem to be much of an evil either.

Now let us assume that, contrary to what I just argued, my dying really was bad for me. Would that be sufficient to justify the claim that dying is really bad for *us*? Not necessarily. Even if we had a good reason to believe that our own death is bad for each one of us, that is, my death is bad for me, and your death is bad for you, we could still deny that, all things considered, my death is bad for you and your death bad for me. If it is far from obvious that we suffer any harm by dying, it is even less obvious that other people's deaths harm us. On the contrary, in a very real sense we benefit from the fact that other people die. Of course, there are people whose death is harmful to us because we depend on them in some way, or care for them. But in general, we need other people to die so that we can find ourselves a place in this world, just as they need us to die to make room for them. If people did not have to die, it is extremely unlikely that we would have been born in the first place, and, in the unlikely event that we were born, that we would have found a partner or a decent job. While it may not be strictly necessary that in a world populated by potentially immortal humans the birth rate would dramatically decrease, it is for several reasons a probable outcome. There would be much less room for new people and no gaps in the social fabric that they could fill. There would also be much less need for them. Nobody would have to take over, nobody would have to pay for our pensions, and no other being would have to satisfy our longing for continued presence in this world. If it is likely that once we have discovered how to stop ageing and thus extend our lives indefinitely, having children will become the exception rather than the rule, then it is also likely that if scientists had made this discovery a century ago, we would not exist. A Kantian might consider this already a sufficient reason for judging the attempt to abolish ageing with its resulting death to be unethical. If we test the maxim that guides the attempt by applying Kant's categorical imperative (cf. Kant [1786] 1974: B 53–8), we shall find that this maxim can never become a universal law, nor can we ever desire for it to become one. If the maxim of our course of action is that if we can abolish death and thus become virtually immortal, we will do so, and if we then try to turn this maxim into a universal law so that *everybody* (including, as complete universalization demands, those who lived before us) followed it, we find that this is not possible since it would remove the grounds of our own existence. If everyone chose to be immortal, then we could not. In fact, we could not exist at all (that is, most of us could not, although some might). Hence, seeking to end ageing and the resulting death is, from a Kantian perspective, morally wrong.

The same result can be derived by applying the golden rule, according to which we ought to do to others what we would like them to do to us. As Richard Hare has argued, the internal logic of morality compels us to prescribe every action as universally binding that we approve of when we are affected by it. In other words, the golden rule is a, if not *the*, fundamental principle of morality. According to Hare, the rule entails, as its "logical extension", that we ought to do to others what we appreciate they *did* to us. Since we do appreciate being alive and that our existence has not been prevented, we must also abstain from preventing the existence of others (Hare 1993: 153). Hence, if putting an end to human ageing prevents the existence of other people (namely all those that would have been born otherwise), then it is clearly morally wrong.

Yet even if we do not accept this kind of ethical reasoning, the fact remains that if the people who went before us had not aged and died it is unlikely that we would exist. If we consider our own existence a good, then whatever was a necessary precondition for it must also be regarded as a good, or at least cannot be plausibly regarded as bad for us. Hence, to the extent that my existence requires the death of others, their dying (or having died) is not at all bad for us.[6] And if ageing is the process by which nature ensures that people die if other circumstances fail to kill them, neither is ageing.

But what if we separate the issues and look at the process of ageing itself, ignoring for the moment its outcome, death? Would we then still be able to deny that "ageing is really bad for us"? Obviously we are talking here about biological ageing and not chronological ageing. Biological ageing can be defined as "the inexorable increase in molecular disorder" (Hayflick 2002: 419), which results in a gradual loss of function and physiological capacity. It does not seem that there is anything good in that. It is hard to doubt that getting old is generally not fun and often comes with plenty of discomfort, pain and constriction. In ageing, we experience the gradual disintegration of our bodies and, often enough, our minds. Taken by itself this really is bad for us: that is, your ageing is bad for you, and mine for me. And even though *your* ageing is not in any obvious sense bad for *me*, it is, other than your dying, not particularly good for me either. I might benefit from your growing too old to continue doing your job when I am keen to do it myself. Yet there is also the downside that I might have to look after you or pay for your subsistence. Since there is no clear advantage to any of us it is probably fair to say that, on the whole, ageing itself (disconnected from death) is bad for us.

However, in reality ageing does not occur without subsequent death. It is a process that leads to death, and we cannot ignore this when we answer the question whether ageing is bad for us. When ageing leads to death, ageing functions as a kind of attunement to our mortality: a slow, gradual dissolution of the body that exemplifies our, to use Heidegger's term, "being-toward-death" and familiarizes us with the idea that one day we will no longer be.[7] The transition between life and death seems less incisive when death is preceded by ageing. To be torn from life in the midst of youth is commonly regarded as a tragic event,[8] not only because there was so much life still to be lived, but also because neither the one who dies nor the ones who survive them have had time to get accustomed to the idea of their passing. Ageing makes dying easier, both in the sense that it helps us to cope with the inevitability of it and in the sense that it gives death ample opportunity to strike. Without ageing, death would occur far less frequently, resulting in the problems outlined above. Ageing, as a prelude to death, is a precondition of our existence. So to the extent that ageing leads to death, it is, on the whole, *not* bad for us: neither my ageing for me and yours for you, nor ageing as a general feature of human life (i.e. that we *all* age and die) for the community of humans. Ironically, ageing would only be bad for us if it did *not* result in death. So if we managed to abolish or indefinitely postpone death without arresting the ageing process, then ageing would indeed become bad for us. But as long as that is not the case, ageing is not really bad at all.

I have argued that despite the apparent plausibility of the claim that "ageing is really bad for us" there is little reason to believe this. Death does not seem to be an evil from the perspective of the individual (i.e. it won't be bad for *me* to be dead), nor from the perspective of the community (i.e. it isn't bad for me that other people die).

The same holds, although for slightly different reasons, with respect to ageing. Ageing coupled with death is, all things considered, not bad for us: neither for the individual nor for the community. Ageing is only bad when it does not lead to death. Thus far from being "the greatest evil", it appears that death is no evil at all, and neither is ageing. And if that is the case, then finding a cure for ageing is not an "urgent, screaming imperative" after all.

Yet even if we should decide that death is indeed an evil, non-death (or living forever) need not be a good. From the fact that a person does not want to die it follows neither that (a) death is an evil to them, nor that (b) living forever is a good to them. If this were a valid argument, which it is not, then we could just as easily conclude from the fact that a person does not want to live forever, that, to them, (a) life is an evil and (b) dying is a good. The logical error of deducing a desire to live forever (or indefinitely) from a desire not to die is what I call the *immortalist fallacy*. A similar point was made by A. W. Moore (2006). There is, Moore argues, a logical gap between always wanting something to be so and wanting that thing always to be so. I may at any particular time wish not to die, but that does not mean that I, at that or any other time, wish never to die. As Moore puts it: "I might never want to die, without wanting never to die" (*ibid.*: 313). To repeat, none of this tells us anything about whether or not indefinite life extension is desirable (let alone whether *moderate* life extension is desirable). The argument just shows that it is not at all *obvious* (because implied by our appreciation of being alive) that indefinite life extension is desirable or at least commonly desired.

However, can we think of any good reason why anyone should *not* want to live forever? We may suspect that the reason why some people claim that they do not is simply that, when they think of a never-ending life, they imagine themselves becoming old and frail and burdened with various ailments (rather like Swift's pitiful immortals, the struldbrugs, or the unfortunate Tithonos, who, at the request of his lover, the goddess Eos, was granted immortality by Zeus, but not eternal youth), and then going on existing in that condition without any hope of ever improving, or mercifully ending, their miserable lives. Yet this is arguably a complete misunderstanding of what convinced life extensionists such as de Grey are trying to achieve. The aim is to stop the ageing process at an ideal age, say at thirty-five, or, if one is already past this age, rejuvenate the body and bring it back to that stage, in which we are supposed to be at the height of our powers. In other words, the aim is not the preservation of life as such, but rather the preservation or restoration of *youthful* life. So the reason why not all people are exactly crazy about the idea of living forever is perhaps simply that they imagine it as different from what it will in fact be like. Perhaps we do not all want to live forever if that means being condemned to an everlasting senility. But what we really do want, and cannot possibly or with good reason *not* want, is to be *young* forever. And that is precisely what anti-ageing science is going to get us: not merely eternal life, but, in the words of de Grey, "an endless summer of literally perpetual youth" (de Grey & Rae 2007: 335). But is it really? Is it even *conceivable* that our youth lasts forever?

I do not wish to take issue here with the scientific evidence that suggests that engineered negligible senescence – the complete obliteration of all physical symptoms of ageing – can be achieved for humans. This may, or may not be so. For all I know, in twenty years' time science will have found a way to defeat human ageing. So let us assume that we shall sometime in the not too distant future fully understand the mechanisms that govern human ageing and be able to use this knowledge to stop or even reverse the ageing process. We shall then be able to conserve our bodies at a biological age of, say, thirty-five, that is, retain the body of a healthy thirty-five-year-old even when we are seventy, 120, or still older. However, it is not at all obvious that once we have achieved this we have also gained what we intended to gain, namely eternal youth, because youth might be not merely a condition of the body, but also, and perhaps even more importantly, a condition of the mind, which is a possibility that is generally overlooked by proponents of radical life extension.

A nice example of this common oversight is provided by the science-fiction author and prolific writer of well-informed popular science books Ben Bova, who, in his book *Immortality* (1998) quotes the last stanza from Lewis Carroll's poem "Solitude" (1856):

> I'd give all wealth that years have piled,
> The slow result of life's decay,
> To be once more a little child
> For one bright summer-day.

According to Bova, Carroll has in these lines summed up "what most of us feel ...: We would pay anything we have to avoid aging and inevitable death" (1998: 212). However, it is clear that what Carroll is saying here is something rather different. What he would pay anything for is to be *once more*(!) a little child, for *one*(!) bright summer day. Thus he does not express a longing for eternal life or a fear of death. Rather, he deplores the irretrievable loss of youth, which, by its very nature, cannot be retained and, once lost, cannot be retrieved. Neither Carroll nor, for that matter, anyone else can ever be a child again, not even for one single summer day, and the reason for this is not that science has not yet discovered how to rejuvenate the body, but rather the impossibility of erasing the accumulated weight of all the experiences that make up our lives while at the same time preserving our personal identity. Carroll could not become a boy again because in order to do so he would have had to stop being Carroll, the young man (he was only twenty-one when he wrote the poem) and aspiring mathematician and poet. What Carroll, in the same poem, calls the "fairy-dream of youth", the "golden hours of Life's young spring, of innocence, of love and truth, bright, beyond all imagining", is by necessity transitory. One cannot be innocent forever, cannot live in the world, take it in and engage with it, and yet remain untouched by it, unchanged, unharmed, unless, perhaps, one is severely mentally disabled. That is *not* to say that staying innocent and childlike forever would, on the whole, be desirable, that is, preferable to mentally growing up (i.e. becoming more experienced and world-wise). We may, occasionally, envy those who, owing to some developmental disorder, are like children throughout their lives, but more often we deplore their fate because we feel that their lives have not fully blossomed: that some development that should have taken place has been cut short and that they have been harmed by that. They have been prevented from living a full human life. But that does not change the fact that growing up has its own regrets, that we lose as well as gain by it. My point is not that it would be better for us to stay childlike throughout our lives, but that mentally growing up always incurs a loss and that that loss is in fact *inevitable* in the sense that we can only avoid incurring it by not growing up, which would be an even greater loss. Under the conditions of experienced time, "eternal youth", in Carroll's sense of an eternal childhood, is therefore an oxymoron, a contradiction in terms.

Yet it is not only the experiential innocence of childhood and the particular kind of enjoyment that comes with it that cannot be preserved over time. Even for an adult, living one's life is not possible without the passage of time, and the passage of time always brings about loss. The longer we live the more things pass by, pass away. Our memories are full of things we shall never experience again because the experience cannot be separated from the moment it was experienced, and that moment is gone forever. That is actually what being past means: being irretrievably lost. And sometimes, and more often as we grow older, we look back and long to be there again; and knowing that this can never be saddens us. As another poet, A. E. Housman (1896), puts it in "The Land of Lost Content":

That is the land of lost content,
I see it shining plain,
The happy highways where I went
And cannot come again.

The underlying sentiment is also expressed nicely in Kris Kristofferson's song "Me and Bobby McGee", where the singer, echoing Carroll, declares his willingness to sacrifice all of his tomorrows for just one single yesterday. The willingness to swap *all* of one's tomorrows for one single yesterday must be a complete mystery to the immortalist. But the truth of the matter is that even if we were granted an indefinite number of tomorrows, this would not bring back to us any of our yesterdays or make up for their loss. This does not, of course, mean that the past is generally preferable to the present or the future. We may, in fact, look back to our past with nothing but relief, happy that certain events lie behind us. Indeed, we may be very happy with our present and be looking forward to what still lies ahead of us. But even if we by far prefer our present to our past, this very present will soon be past as well, and the better the present is, the more we shall feel its loss when it is gone. Hence even if our lives lasted forever we might still suffer from, and gradually be wearied by, the sheer passage of time, which, by its very nature, incurs loss after loss. That may well be part of what makes growing old so hard: not so much the gradual weakening of the body, but the sheer accretion of past in our minds. It seems to me that what makes us young is less the possibility of a long future lying ahead of us, than the fact that there is not much past behind us yet. Accordingly, if the desire for everlasting youth that today's life extensionists expect to be able to satisfy very soon is not merely, and perhaps not even principally, a desire for *bodies* that do not age, but also for *minds* that do not, then they may have a problem.

Bernard Williams, in his well-known paper on the tedium of immortality, discusses the fictional case of Karel Čapek's Elina Makropulos, who gets tired of life after 342 years and chooses to die because her "unending life has come to a state of boredom, indifference and coldness" (1973: 82). Williams argued that, should we ever manage to extend our lives indefinitely, we would all sooner or later experience the same boredom, so that death would no longer be an evil to us. Thus, according to Williams, the insufferable state Elina Makropulos finds herself in has nothing to do with who she is. It is not her personal inability to do something worthwhile with her long life that makes her want to end it; rather, the eventual boredom is generic and inevitable.

Naturally, those who believe in the desirability of radical life extension are quick to dismiss Williams's claims as unfounded. As Harris declares, in his typically curt manner, "only the terminally boring are in danger of being terminally bored, and perhaps they do not deserve indefinite life" (2007: 64). Thus Elina Makropulos and Bernard Williams himself belong to a particular type of person who simply cannot deal with immortality because they suffer from what Harris calls a "terminal failure of the imagination" (*ibid.*).[9] In truth, the world is so rich that there will always be something to occupy an inquisitive mind. Moreover, science and technology progress at such a fast (exponentially increasing[10]) rate that we shall never be short of new developments that give us plenty to do and think about and make sure that life will forever remain an exciting adventure, at least for those whose minds are sufficiently alive and alert.

However, it is doubtful whether the world will really change enough to sustain our interest in the long run. In many respects, of course, the world has changed considerably during, say, the past 2,000 years, and it will most likely continue to change during the next 2,000 years. Yet, in other respects, it has remained remarkably unchanged. What engages people's minds is essentially the same as it has always been. Basic human needs and desires have not changed. Our lives still revolve around love and hate, playing and

fighting, the search for pleasure and understanding, and the struggle to survive in an occasionally hostile world. Arguably, there may
never be a shortage of new things in the world: new discoveries to be
made, new achievements to be proud of or new worlds to explore.
But to the extent that these novelties engage our interest they are
merely variations of the same old themes. What they provide is yet
another source of pleasure, occasion to prove oneself, or affirma-
tion of power. Even though our interest in these things is undeni-
ably strong, it is hardly inexhaustible. It is entirely conceivable that
we can get tired of all of this: of hating, and loving and caring for
anything at all. Even the thirst for knowledge is not insatiable. And
it does not really matter whether things stay essentially the same,
or we, being who we are, look at things in essentially the same way,
so that even though things may always be sufficiently different to
capture *someone's* interest, we ourselves may eventually find ourselves incapable of realizing this potential and failing to discover
anything interesting about them. According to Williams, the reason
why, given eternal life, I shall eventually reach a state where I shall
no longer wish to be alive, is not so much that I shall then have had
enough of the world, but rather that I shall "have had altogether too
much of *myself*" (1973: 100, emphasis added). The reason for this is
not, as Harris suspects, that I am such a terminally boring person,[11]
but rather that for all the changes I might go through during my life,
I cannot avoid relating these changes to myself as *my* changes and
thus adding them to the story of my life – a process by which, as it
were, the weight of being me steadily increases. Kass has pointed
out – rightly, I think, that after a while:

> no matter how healthy we are, no matter how respected
> and well placed we are socially, most of us cease to look
> upon the world with fresh eyes. Little surprises us, nothing
> shocks us, righteous indignation at injustice dies out. We
> have seen it all already, seen it all. … Many of us become
> small-souled, having been humbled not by bodily decline
> or the loss of loved ones but by life itself.   (2004: 318)

Kass introduces these reflections as part of an argument against the
desirability of radical life extension. More than half a century earlier,
H. G. Wells and Julian Huxley proposed a similar argument:

The bad habits he has acquired, the ineradicable memories, the mutilations and distortions that have been his lot,
the poison and prejudice and decay in him – all surely are
better erased at last and forgotten. A time will come when
he will be weary and ready to sleep.

(Wells *et al.* 1934: 1434)

So according to these writers, it is actually good that each one of us
is being replaced after a while by somebody who still has the fresh-
ness and innocence that we have irretrievably lost. Although I tend
to agree with this assessment, to argue this point is difficult and I
shall not try it here.[12] My own point is rather different. What I want
to suggest is that the process Kass and his predecessors describe is
in fact *inevitable* (although in some cases it may take longer than
our usual eighty years or so until it becomes noticeable) and that,
owing to this inevitability, the goal of radical life extension, namely
the preservation of eternal youth, is impossible to attain. We simply
cannot endlessly continue looking upon the world with fresh eyes.

That the process described above is inevitable can, of course,
be contested. Lisa Bortolotti and Yujin Nagasawa have pointed out
that Elina Makropulos in Čapek's play *The Makropulos Affair*, on
which Williams based his interpretation, is an immortal living in a
world of mortals, and that this fact may be "partly responsible for
her solitude and sense of detachment" (Bortolotti & Nagasawa 2009:
264), which would suggest that if everybody else were also immortal, Elina Makropulos would feel differently about her life. This is a
good point, which is supported by the sociological literature on the
subject. The fact is that many people who are biologically old do
not always *feel* old, just as there are people who do feel old without
actually *being* old (Baum 1983; Karp 1988; Cremin 1992; Thompson
1992; Barak 1999; Nilsson *et al.* 2000). According to Paul Thompson, you can "feel old at any point in adulthood. ... Feeling old is
feeling exhausted in spirit, lacking the energy to find new responses
as life changes. It is giving up" (1992: 43). Remarkably, whether one
feels old or young seems to be not *directly* dependent on the state of
one's body. Old people may suffer the effects of their ageing bodies,
such as declined bodily function, difficulty in moving around or
dizziness, without actually feeling old. Margareta Nilsson and colleagues (2000) found that there are three aspects that contribute to

one's *feeling* old: (a) when one feels helpless and a burden to others; (b) when one no longer recognizes one's former self (one's present self being fatigued, listless and indifferent and generally having different mental qualities than one's previous self); and (c) when one feels separated from others owing to a difference in life experience and the loss of siblings and friends and generally people of one's own generation who share one's experiential background. This last aspect is obviously relevant to the Makropulos case. Following Bortolotti and Nagasawa, it seems likely that Elina Makropulos's separateness is at least part of the reason why she decides that she has had enough of life. If that is so, then she might see things differently if there were enough other immortals around who shared her condition, to whom she could relate and who would be able to understand her. Since a physically fit and healthy immortal would have no reason to see themselves as a burden to others (Nilsson's first aspect of feeling old), nor (if we assume that the often-described listlessness of old age is directly dependent on the bodily decline) to think of themselves as different from what, or who, they used to be, then indefinite life extension may, after all, be possible without compromising the ability to feel young.

However, the truth is that we cannot be sure how we shall feel when we live indefinitely extended lives for the simple reason that nobody has done it yet. We may still find our lives meaningful; we may not become bored by the world or our continuing selves; we may still be happy to be alive. On the other hand, even though eighty-year-olds even today, with their bodies in decline, may still "feel young", that does not tell us anything about how they would feel when they lived to 160, even with their bodies in good shape. Sociological evidence suggests that feelings of loss are an important factor in the constitution of mental age, that is, how old one feels. And, as I have argued above, loss is inevitable owing to the nature of time and will necessarily accumulate the longer one lives. It is possible that there is a threshold for each one of us, which may well differ from individual to individual, beyond which we fall victim to Kass's small-souledness, when little surprises us any more and nothing shocks us. After all, if one can be physically old and still feel young – in other words, if there is no necessary connection between the ageing of the body and the ageing of the mind – then one can also stay physically young while becoming old mentally.

However, even if the above reflections are thought plausible, one may want to object that it is still better to continue living with an aged mind in a youthful body than not to live at all. Perhaps life will feel rather dull after a while, or at least not as exciting as it used to be, but so what? Even if it is true that, as Yann Martel writes in *Life of Pi*, "first wonder goes deepest; wonder after that fits in the impression made by the first" (2002: 50), that does not mean that second and third wonders are not desirable at all and death is the better option. True, it does not. It all depends on how little wonder is left in the end (which we will not know until we get there) and how much value we attach to our mere existence. If we believe that (almost) any existence is preferable to non-existence, then no argument will persuade us that radical life extension is not worth pursuing. However, few people seem to feel that way. We could after all, and with equal justification, argue that if the only way to live forever was to live forever in a state of physical decline, then we should embrace it, because living in such a state would still be better than not living at all. Yet many people would regard permanent old age as a curse rather than a blessing. Hardly anyone seriously wants to be old forever. A fate such as the one the mythological Tithonus had to suffer until he was somewhat released by being turned into a cricket is to be deplored and not envied. Yet if not only the body ages, but also the mind, and if only the ageing of the body, but not of the mind, can possibly be arrested through scientific and technological advances, then the indeterminate prolongation of life will eventually lead, one way or the other, to a situation that may turn out to be just as unbearable as Tithonus'. We may be forever mentally old.[13] Why should this be more desirable than to be forever physically old?

We could, of course, always kill ourselves if it turned out that life became unbearable after a while. Therefore, it has been argued, life extension is a win–win situation. We cannot lose. If we find that a life without physical ageing, one that is not naturally ebbing away, does not suit us, we can just leave. In other words, we would not lose the *option* of dying, just the *necessity* of it. As Harris remarks: "Those, who are bored can, thanks to their vulnerability, opt out at any time" (2007, 64). But is it good to have the choice? Given our fear of death, or rather of being dead or no longer being alive, we would almost certainly find it very hard to choose nothingness. It is much easier to accept a death that comes naturally and with certainty than a death that has to be deliberately chosen. I person-ally would rather not be forced to decide between taking my own life and going on with a pointless life. But that is ultimately a deci-sion that everyone has to make for themselves.

However, if we think it likely that our minds will indeed age in the way described above, then there is another reason to wish that our lives end before we reach a stage in which we find ourselves in the predicament of, as Williams says, having had altogether enough of ourselves. Aristotle has argued that a person's life can be considered happy or unhappy only when it is over. Happiness requires:

> not only complete virtue, but also a complete life, since many changes occur in life, and all manner of chances and the most prosperous may fall into great misfortunes in old age, as is told of Priam in the Trojan Cycle; and one who has experienced such chances and has ended wretchedly no one calls happy. (*Nicomachean Ethics* I.9)

Thus a disaster that strikes us shortly before our death (and, for Aristotle, even one that strikes us *after* our death) is not only something that must be weighed against all the happiness we have experienced during our lives, but rather something that may com-pletely obliterate all this happiness and make our life *as a whole* an unhappy one. In this way, the suggested incrustation of the mind, which would take the wonder out of life and would make us experi-ence everything new as a mere replication of the old, may in retro-spect devalue the original experience and shed suspicion on the first wonder, thus making our whole life a miserable one. The more often you repeat the experience of loving someone, the less precious the first time you loved seems to be. If you come to despise, or be bored by, all things beautiful, if you are no longer capable of seeing the beauty (and wonder surely forms a great part of the experience of beauty), then it may seem to you that there never was beauty in the first place: that it was at best a pleasant illusion. Do we really want to look back at our lives one day, telling ourselves that nothing really mattered and nothing was really worth it?

Another reason to shy away from the prospect of indefinitely extending our lives at the price of an aged mind is that we may consider it better for there *to be* first wonder rather than second wonder. That is, we may adopt an objective point of view and, out of the conviction that the ability to discover the world anew is intrinsically valuable, forego the opportunity to extend our own lives in order to make room for others who can still do what we have long ceased to do: to look at the world with fresh eyes.

There is another idea that is often evoked when people seek to highlight the attractiveness of indefinite life extension, which strikes me as just as incoherent as the idea of eternal youth, and for similar reasons. It is the idea that immortality will allow us to pursue alternative life paths that we are now prevented from pursuing by our all-too-short lifespans. Thus Alan Harrington boldly states that in "eternity – always excepting the possibility of accident – men and women will have the chance to live out all the unlived lives and travel the untraveled paths that they wish they had explored" (1969: 182). Thus, according to James Stacey Taylor (2009: 109), ageing and death function as "biological constraints" that compromise the instrumental value of our autonomy by preventing us from pursuing all the options we might wish to pursue:

> A person cannot, for example, be both an internationally renowned mathematician and an Olympic-standard tennis player even if she were capable of excelling in both fields, for each of these goals requires a degree of dedication during the same period of a person's life that would preclude the pursuit of the other. (*Ibid.*)

Now it is, of course, true that we sometimes wish we had chosen some other path of life and that we often, even when we are entirely happy with the choices we have in fact made, wonder what would have happened if we had chosen differently and wish it had been possible to avoid the choice altogether: to both do what we did *and* do what we did not simply because we did the other thing. In other words, we wish that we had more than one life to live. It may seem, then, that radical life extension will help us fulfil this hitherto impossible dream by providing ample opportunity to live one life first, and then another, and then yet another. We shall, in short, be able to live all the lives we have ever dreamt of.

However, the trouble is that *one* single person cannot live *two* or more lives. Once you have made a choice you cannot go back to make a different one, because every action has consequences, every path you take leads you somewhere else, and builds on the narrative that makes up your life. "Way leads on to way", as Robert Frost writes in his poem "The Road Not Taken". It is not the *lack* of time that prevents us from leading more than one life. On the contrary, it is time that does: time and the fact that my actions must spring from what I am, or else they would not be *my* actions at all. I need to be committed to what I do, need to be serious about it. Perhaps I can now resolve to learn to play the piano and become a professional musician after I have done philosophy for, say, a century. But if what I am doing now is important to me, why should I suddenly stop doing it after a fixed time, and if making music is important to me, how can I possibly wait for a century before I devote myself to it? Taylor's example of the brilliant mathematician who could also be a brilliant tennis player and who, through life extension, will be given the chance to be both, is far-fetched for several reasons. First, while it is probably true that I cannot be a world-class tennis player and *at the same time* a great mathematician, I don't see why I shouldn't play tennis first, say from fifteen to twenty-five, and then pursue a career in mathematics, all within the lifespan that is currently allowed to us. Second, since I have yet to hear of a world-class tennis player who after their retirement (usually in their early thirties, but occasionally even earlier – Björn Borg retired at the age of 26) became a world-class academic, it is probably safe to assume that there are not too many people around that are so exceptionally talented in two very different fields. Third, it seems unlikely (or at least far from certain) that those who are indeed exceptionally gifted in two different fields and who feel that they cannot possibly spend less than a lifetime on either of them, while being patient enough to wait for sixty years or so until fully exploring the second of their talents, will, after all those decades that they have spent on their first career, be as interested in pursuing their second career as they were at the beginning. Fourth, even if they are, the fact that they can then leave their first career choice behind them for good, now dedicating themselves fully to the other one, suggests that one can indeed become tired of doing even those things that one loves most. And if that is the case, then there will surely come a day when one also gets tired of pursuing that other career.

Of course, I might someday lose my interest in philosophy (or mathematics) and discover my interest in music (or tennis) instead, but that is something that may or may not happen to me, and not something that can be planned in advance.[14] Similarly, you can truly love someone and be with them and at the same time wish you could also have been with someone else, because you realize that that would have been a good life too, but you cannot truly love someone and at the same time already look forward to the day you can replace them with somebody new. You may, of course, lose a love and then find another (or indeed love two people), but you can never find a love in the first place if you regard them as merely one in a long, hopefully never-ending series of lovers and loved ones. Likewise, you cannot be a saint for a century and then be a rogue for the next. You may, of course, *turn* from a saint into a rogue (or, possibly, from a rogue into a saint), but you cannot *choose* to be first the one and then the other. To live a particular life means to be committed to certain values (or the lack thereof). You cannot just try it out, wear it and eventually shed it like a garment that you no longer like or that has fallen out of fashion. Decisions need to be made, and occasionally require sacrifices. Someone who really was talented in many ways was Albert Schweitzer. He gave up various promising careers – as a philosopher, a theologian, a musical scholar and an organist – to work at his own expense as a medical doctor in Africa, looking after the native population. Would Schweitzer have acted differently if he had known that his life would span, say, two or three centuries instead of the ninety years that he in fact had? Would a longer lifespan have freed him to pursue those other careers as well as his career as a "jungle doctor"? No, it would not, because he was who he was because of the decisions he had to make. What he chose *not* to do defined his life just as much as what he chose to do. And this is the case with all of us. There are no unlived lives to be lived in a never-ending future. All we shall ever be able to do is continue the one life we have, with all the missed opportunities, all the roads we have not chosen to take. We cannot start again from scratch, unless, that is, we are willing to completely cancel out the accumulated past. But as I am going to argue in the next section, even then it is doubtful whether it is really *we* who start this new life.

How do we cancel out the accumulated past? The only way I can think of to do that and thus avoid the ageing of the mind is by erasing one's memory of the past: forgetting everything we have ever learned and witnessed. In other words, there is only one possible Fountain of Youth, and that fountain is the River Lethe. However, even complete memory erasure might not entirely free us from the accumulated past, which sediments not only as a set of memories, but also as a clearly defined character that structures and confines the way we perceive and process the world. Yet even if we managed to somehow overcome this additional problem, complete memory erasure seems to be a strange way of achieving eternal youth. After all, one of the great perils of old age is memory loss, which we tend to identify with the progressive disintegration of the person (cf. Katz & Peters 2008). Following John Locke (1894), personal identity is commonly regarded to depend on the ability to connect one's present experiences with one's past experiences, that is, to form a mental image of the past and appropriate it as an image of one's *own* past. It is quite ironic that the only possible way to retain (or periodically regain) our (mental) youth over time seems to be the deliberate engineering of the very thing that to many people is the clearest symptom of old age and its detrimental effects and that accounts for much of the fear that accompanies the prospect and the experience of ageing. And what would such a life, or such a series of consecutive lives, be like? It would resemble most the life of Peter Pan who, in J. M. Barrie's play, is the boy who stubbornly refuses to grow up and thereby retains an at first sight very appealing youthfulness. Yet what is often overlooked is that Peter Pan, the archetypal *puer aeternus*, pays a high price for his eternal youth: he has a remarkably short memory. He very quickly forgets his enemies (Hook) and his friends (Tinkerbell and Wendy), and every next day he starts all over again. There is no real commitment in his life: no deep personal relations, no development, no story. His is the shallow, unchanging life of the animal that lives entirely in the present moment, and not a human life at all (cf. Lundquist 1996; Yeoman 1998). Such a repetitive existence is attractive only if you do not look at it too closely. For all practical purposes, Peter Pan dies each night and is reborn the next morning, without any memory of his former life, so that we cannot even say whether the boy who goes to sleep and the one who wakes up are the *same* person or not. Is it the same Peter Pan, or a different Peter Pan? It is impossible to tell, and that is the reason why Peter Pan is not even a person, or at least not *one* person. If a lack of memory is a *necessary* requirement of eternal youth, so that we need to erase our memories periodically in order to regain our youth, we not only will have to pay the same price as Peter Pan, but will also disconnect our consecutive lives in a such a way that it is doubtful that it will in any meaningful sense be *we* who lead the fresh life after the complete erasure of our memories. Although there will then be *somebody* who is young and has a brand new start in life, it will not be us.[15]

I have argued that the project of radically extending our lifespans, although perhaps technologically feasible in the near future, may well fail with regard to its main objective. Assuming that the purpose of life extension is not the prolongation of old age, but the preservation or recovery of youth, our efforts are less likely to be successful if youth is not merely a condition of the body, but also, and even more so, a condition of the mind. Although we may be able to arrest the ageing of the body, we may not be able to arrest the ageing of the mind that comes with experience. Even by periodically erasing our memories we cannot achieve our goal because memory erasure would imply the annihilation of the person that we are. And that is, I think, the reason why some people, although they do not wish to die, very wisely do not want to live forever either.

7
GOING CYBER

"Help us to get rid of our bodies altogether," said Winterslow. – "It's quite time man began to improve on his own nature, especially the physical side of it."   (D. H. Lawrence, *Lady Chatterley's Lover*)

We have always remodelled the external world according to our needs and desires. That is, of course, not very unusual. Most animals take active part in rebuilding their environment to construct a suitable niche for themselves (Odling-Smee *et al.* 2003). Yet no animal does it so thoroughly and extensively as we do. We have never really stopped being busy making our environment fit for us, have never tired of constantly rebuilding the world in such a way that it assists us in our will to live and to live well. That is part of what makes us human. However, when it comes to our survival and well-being, a potentially hostile environment is only part of the problem. The world we live in may, if unchecked, thwart our aspirations and even kill us, but it is our own human body that allows this to happen in the first place. So in order to be safe, it seems that controlling our environment is not enough; we also need to gain complete control over our bodies to compensate for their natural frailty. But just as controlling the external world largely means replacing a natural environment with an artificial, human-produced one (retaining only those aspects of the former that are found useful or harmless), controlling the human body also means replacing those parts of it that can no longer perform their function, that foreseeably will one day fail in performing it or that do not perform their function as well as we may wish. This replacement is as much therapy as it is enhancement. Given that the human body, as it is naturally constituted, is *itself* a danger to our continued well-being, any improvement on the body's natural constitution is a remediation of a defect and thus therapeutic.

The replacement of human body parts by devices that simulate their function is, of course, not new. Artificial limbs have been used for thousands of years. Today the technology is so advanced that limbs can be controlled directly through conscious thought, which initiates muscle contractions that are converted into electronic signals, which in turn move the limb. It appears that users of such advanced devices are still not entirely happy with the results. This suggests that as yet prosthetic limbs cannot adequately replace biological limbs (Biddiss & Chau 2007), although they may soon be able to.

Artificial cardiac pacemakers implanted in the body have been successfully used for fifty years now, and artificial hearts and lungs are already being tested on live patients. Cochlear implants can replace ears and compensate for loss of hearing by stimulating nerve fibres directly in the brain. Similar devices are being developed for the restoration of sight. By connecting a blind person's brain to a video camera that sends signals directly into their visual cortex, William Dobelle and his teams managed to restore their ability to see the outlines of objects and thus to use their sight to navigate their bodies (Dobelle 2000). Another device, called Eyeborg, invented by Adam Montandon in collaboration with the colour-blind artist Neil Harbisson, translates visual data into sound waves, which are then interpreted (although not directly *seen*) as colours (Wade 2005).

All these developments indicate that, in principle, our sense organs are dispensable since we can create their effects or, more precisely, what they allow us to know and do, by other means. We do not even seem to need a body, at least not a functioning one, to interact with the world. BrainGate, a brain implant developed by the American company Cyberkinetics in 2004 (now BrainGate Co.), allows patients who have suffered a total sensory and motor loss of their limbs and torso owing to a spinal cord injury to control external devices connected to a computer through muscle contractions initiated by their thoughts (Hochberg *et al.* 2006). Even the brain itself might be replaceable. Alzheimer's patients and others suffering from the effects of brain damage located in the hippocampus may soon be helped by having the damaged parts replaced with an artificial brain prosthesis: a microchip hippocampus (Berger *et al.* 2005; Berger & Glanzman 2005).

What we witness here is what is often described as an increasing cyborgization of the human, where "cyborg" can be defined as a human being some of whose parts are artificial. In light of these developments it may appear reasonable to expect that this is only the beginning and that we shall progress further until we have achieved the goal that is implicitly pursued in all those innovations that couple human beings with fast-paced hypertechnology: complete independence from nature; unrestricted autonomy. For as long as we are hooked to this organic body, we shall never be entirely free and safe. The organic body is a limitation that is resented by many who hope that we shall be able to overcome it not too far in the future. "Soon we could be meshing our brains to computers, living, for all practical purposes, on an 'immortal' substrate, perhaps eventually discarding our messy, aging, flesh-and-bones body altogether" (B. Klein 2003). The human body is not only regarded as dispensable: it is an obstacle, an enemy to be fought and to get rid of. It ages and makes us age with it, eventually annihilating us. It is "messy", disorderly and dirty; it brings chaos and decay into our lives. "Flesh-and-bones" is a material that is deemed unsuitable for an advanced, dignified, enlightened and happy existence. So let us abandon it if we can. Good riddance to bad rubbish! "If humans can merge their minds with computers, why would they not discard the human form and become an immortal being?" (Paul & Cox 1996: 21).

Yet in order to become truly immortal, our goal should be to become a "cyberbeing": a being that is more than just interlinked with machines, more than just partly a machine itself, and even more than a machine in its entirety. Gradually replacing human biology and the messy organic body with a more durable and more controllable substrate is certainly a considerable improvement, but is by no means sufficient. Why not go a step further and, if at all possible, discard the physical body altogether? That is, any *particular* body, any body that is *essentially* and not merely accidentally ours, not only something we use and can discard when proved not useful enough or no longer useful, but rather something that defines our very existence and has, as it were, pretensions of *being* us. In other words, why not relocate and transform our existence in such a way that we are no longer bound to any particular material substrate, be it organic or non-organic, because all we need, if anything at all, is the occasional body-to-go as a communication facilitator, hardware on which to run the program that we shall then be (Moravec 1989).

> Imagine yourself a virtual living being with senses, emotions, and a consciousness that makes our current human form seem a dim state of antiquated existence. Of being free, always free, of physical pain, able to repair any damage and with a downloaded mind that never dies.
>
> (Paul & Cox 1996: xv)

The *telos*, the logical end point, of the ongoing cyborgization of the human is thus the attainment of "digital immortality", which is more than just "a radical new form of human enhancement" (Sandberg & Bostrom 2008: 5). Rather, the desire to conquer death, that "greatest evil" (More 1996), is its secret heart: that which gives the demands for radical human enhancement their moral urgency. And the best chance to attain what we desire is through the as-yet-still-theoretical possibility of mind-uploading.

"Uploading is the transfer of the brain's mindpattern onto a different substrate (such as an advanced computer) which better facilitates said entity's ends" (Kadmon 2003).[1] To upload our minds to a computer would allow us not only to transfer our existence to a more durable substrate, but also to roam the world of cyberspace without any clearly marked physical constraints or time limits. We could be anywhere and everywhere, all in a blink of an eye and for all time, until the world itself ends. How is this supposed to work? Theoretically, we will first scan the structure of a particular brain and then "construct a software model of it that ..., when run on appropriate hardware, will behave in essentially the same way as the original brain", that is "produce the phenomenological effects of a mind" or, more precisely, of a particular mind (Sandberg & Bostrom 2008: 7). At least that's the idea. Whether or not that will really one day be possible nobody really knows, despite occasional protestations to the contrary. The scanning of a whole human brain is no doubt conceivable. So is the construction of a sufficiently accurate functional model of it. All we need is the right technology, and the exponentially growing speed with which technology has developed in the recent past certainly suggests that it will not be long before

we have that technology available. It might, however, still prove too
difficult a task to emulate a whole brain. Moore's Law or Kurzweil's
Law of Accelerating Returns (Kurzweil 1999: 30–33), according to
which the time period between salient events (both in natural and
in technological evolution) grows shorter the further we progress,
might prove not to be laws at all but merely generalizations that
describe fairly accurately what has happened in the past, but not
necessarily what is going to happen in the future. Yet even if we
manage to emulate a whole brain, we may still find that the hoped-
for effect, namely that the model actually gives rise to subjective
awareness, will fail to appear.

Whether or not "the phenomenological effects of a mind" will
indeed appear obviously depends on what the mind is and in what
way it is dependent in its existence on the body. We would have to
assume that some form of functionalism is true: that, in the words
of artificial intelligence pioneer Marvin Minsky, minds are what
brains *do* (Minksy 1986: 287). This generally means that the mind
supervenes on the physical and is not dependent on the specific
material constitution of what it supervenes on. We are to assume
that the mind is based on the functional relations between physical
elements and not on those elements themselves. Most versions of
functionalism allow for multiple realizability, which means that they
are open to the possibility that mind, although not necessarily the
same mind, can be implemented by different physical properties.
Hence we should be able to recreate a particular mind, say mine, by
any means that permit the recreation of my mind's (or more precisely, my brain's) functional relations. So, as Ned Block has pointed
out, if we were able to assign binary values to each member of the
Chinese population and then persuade them to simulate those relations by following strict instructions of input–output regulation (i.e.
of what to do in response to what they perceive is happening), then,
if functionalism is true, that should result in the emergence of a
mind such as mine (Block 1978).

While this looks like an absurd consequence because we find it
hard to imagine that people could be used to create such a thing as
a mind, it is not exactly a convincing refutation of functionalism.
Since nobody has yet, for obvious reasons, attempted to organize
a large population of people to simulate a neural network and thus
create a mind, we cannot completely rule out the possibility that it

may actually work. Whether the mind really can be disconnected from its current biological substrate or whether it is dependent on the special causal powers of the organic brain, as John Searle (1990) has argued, is a matter of mere speculation, as long as we have not had the chance to put the theory to the test by actually producing an accurate whole-brain emulation and then seeing what happens. In other words, it is an empirical question, which we cannot decide on purely philosophical grounds.

However, the artificial creation of *a* mind is one thing, the recreation or transplantation of a *particular* mind that actually belongs to someone as *their* mind quite another. If what we want to achieve is not merely the creation of an intelligent – that is, actually conscious and self-conscious – *machine* or the creation of a *model* of the human mind in order to improve our understanding of how it works, but rather some form of personal *immortality*, then we shall have to make sure that the mind that does appear when we simulate the functional relations of a particular brain is not only qualitatively identical to the mind it is modelled on, but also numerically identical to it. Yet even qualitative identity is far from certain when a particular brain has been successfully emulated. It is entirely conceivable (although perhaps unlikely) that an artificial brain or brain substitute A* that mirrors accurately all functional relations of a particular organic brain A, although indeed producing certain phenomenological effects, does not produce the *same* effects as the original, organic brain. This is just assumed. But as first Jorge Luis Borges (1964) and then Arthur C. Danto (1981) have shown with their thought experiments, identical syntax does not guarantee identical semantics. Two artworks can be absolutely indistinguishable as objects and still be entirely different as artworks, not because they are interpreted in a different way, but because they are simply not *about* the same thing. The *form* is identical, but the objective(!) *meaning* is different. Similarly, we may find that the actual phenomenological constitution of the mind is not as thoroughly causally determined by the structure of the brain as we like to assume.

But even if the mind resulting from a particular brain emulation will indeed be qualitatively identical to the mind it is supposed to copy, the two minds also need to be *numerically* identical, which is an *additional* requirement. This means that for the successfully instantiated mind to be mine, it would *not* be sufficient if it were in every respect indistinguishable from my mind. Rather, it would have to be literally the same. There seems to be a conceptual difference between a mind that actually is mine, and a mind that merely thinks, feels and remembers exactly as I do, and hence is *like* me in all respects except that it happens not to *be* me. Think of two copies of the same book that, despite their having exactly the same design and content, are still *two* copies and not identical to each other.

But hang on, isn't that exactly the point of the functionalist theory of mind that the *same* mind can be instantiated by two or more material substrates that may differ considerably from each other in their make-up and appearance, as long as they are functionally equivalent? Let us have another look at the book analogy. It is true that two copies of the same book are still *two* copies. But it seems also to be true that these two copies are copies of the *same* book, that is to say, the same literary (fictional or non-fictional) entity that is represented by the symbols we find in both of them. Say you have two different editions of James Joyce's *Ulysses*. Both editions are very different in appearance. The covers are different, as is the paper used, the page size, the size and typeface of the letters and so on. In fact, there is hardly anything that is the same in both editions, except, that is, the story itself. The *Ulysses* as a particular literary creation seems to be equally present in both, so that if one of the two copies were destroyed, the *Ulysses* itself would easily survive the destruction. And we can imagine an indefinite number of editions of the *Ulysses*, all different from each other, but all containing, or instantiating, exactly the same story. For that story to exist and to continue to exist, it does not even have to be actually printed. It might only be available in electronic form as an e-book to be read at a computer screen, or as an audio-book to be listened to rather than read. Or it might only exist in the mind of a single person, as in Ray Bradbury's novel *Fahrenheit 451*, where various books, that is, specific literary entities, are saved from oblivion by having book-keepers assigned to them whose task it is to memorize and thus preserve them for future generations.

Can we not understand the mind in a similar fashion, as a distinct (although evolving) mental entity that can be indefinitely replicated in various forms without thereby changing its identity? If the mind is rather like a book and the brain like the specific material representation of that book (i.e. the book as a concrete material object), then there seems to be no question that a mind that is syntactically and semantically identical to mine really *is* mine, just as the *Ulysses* is literally the *same Ulysses* (and not a *further Ulysses*) in each of its various representations.

However, there is one element that is forgotten in this analogy. This element is the reader. Without the reader (or listener, or thinker), the *Ulysses* does not exist. It is instantiated primarily not in a material object, but in a mind that interprets a certain series of symbols in a certain way and thereby creates or recreates the specific entity known as the *Ulysses*.

Now let us suppose that you are reading a copy of that particular book and I am reading, at the very same time and at the same pace, a copy of the same book. Let us further suppose that we are both utterly immersed in it and do not think of anything else but what we are reading. One might then say that our minds, while we are reading, are qualitatively identical with each other. However, it seems that you would still be you and I would still be me, and not simply because we happen to inhabit different bodies. If our minds are distinct entities in the first place then there is no reason they should not remain distinct even when their contents happen to become identical. It seems strange to assume that as long as you and I have different thoughts (and I am using the word "thought" here in the wide sense of Descartes' "*cogito*") we are distinct entities, but as soon as we think alike we become one and the same. Just as a book, in order to exist, needs a reader, the mind needs a *self*. And just as the reader is not the book, the self is not the mind. Rather, it is a particular *appropriation* of the mind. The same book can be read by different readers. Similarly, the same mind might be "read" or had by different selves. Note that I am not claiming that this is actually possible; I am just saying that it is *conceivable*.

However, it has been argued that the notion of different selves makes no sense, because "self" is just a particular quality of the mind, which is the same quality in all minds: "An experience must be a universal across times as well as across brains. This experience of being you, here *now*, would be numerically the same *whenever*, as well as wherever, it was realized" (Zuboff 1990: 53). We can call this quality "immediacy". If this view is accepted then my above argument fails. Identical minds could not be had by different selves. So if I managed to recreate my mind by uploading its entire content to a computer, I would also have succeeded in recreating my self. However, if there is in fact only one self, then there is also only one self when the minds are *different* from each other, as is commonly the case. In other words, you are me and I am you even if our minds are not at all alike. But if that is so then mind-uploading becomes needless, because I am already immortal. For when I die, that is, this particular instantiation of the self, then I continue to live in you, as in fact I have been doing all along.

So how likely is it that a software model of my mind, uploaded to a computer, will really be *my* mind in the sense that it is really *I* that will exist in this new material form? Kurzweil has brought forward an argument that seems to show that this is most likely indeed (Kurzweil 1999: 52–5). He asks us to imagine a person ("Jack") who starts out as a normal human being and then gradually has parts of his body replaced by better, artificial ones. He begins with cochlear implants and then adds, step by step, other devices – advanced imaging processing implants, memory implants, and so on – until, eventually, he takes the final step of replacing his whole brain and neural system with electronic circuits. In other words, he has his brain scanned and the information then stored in a computer. Is he, after the completion of that final stage, still the same person, still the same old Jack? Well, we probably would want to say that he is still the same person after he has had his cochlear implant. And also with enhanced vision and enhanced memory we would hesitate to call him a different person. "Clearly", writes Kurzweil, "he has changed in some ways and his friends are impressed with his improved faculties. But he has the same self-deprecating humor, the same silly grin – yes, it's still the same guy." So where exactly do we draw the line? When does Jack cease to be Jack? It seems that if Jack remains the same person after each replacement, there is no reason why he should suddenly become a different person (in the sense of ceasing to exist and being replaced by someone else) after the last and final replacement. Let us call this the *argument from graduality*. According to Kurzweil, it should not make any difference if Jack's body is replaced gradually or in one go. Even if the transition from an entirely organic body to a machine takes place in one quick step, Jack will still be Jack. But will he really?

Well, he may still have his "self-deprecating humor", but his "silly grin" surely has been lost in the transition. Does that matter? To

Jack's friends it might, but it is irrelevant to the question we are trying to answer, as is, by the way, Jack's sense of humour. Because even if Jack changes completely and loses all the little peculiarities by which his friends used to recognize him, so that they might say that he has become a different person altogether, it might still be him in the sense of being the same self. Over the course of a lifetime I may change considerably, but as long as *I* undergo this change I am the same self, although not necessarily the same person, depending on how we want to define the word "person". If we take "person" to mean, for example, with John Locke, "a thinking intelligent Being, that has reason and reflection, and can consider it self as it self, the same thinking thing in different times and places" (Locke II.Xxvii.9), then it is not entirely clear that I am still the same person I used to be when I was a child of two. But the same self I surely am, because *what* I am is one thing, *that* I am quite another. However, although I remain the same self – that is, the same subject of experience, despite many changes in my character – the converse is also true, and for the same reasons: I might not seem to change at all (same "self-deprecating humor" and all), but still cease to be, while a different self takes my place that has all the properties I, or my mind, used to have, without *being* me at all. So again, will Jack still be Jack after he has given up his organic body for a life as a program installed in a computer? That is what the argument from graduality suggests, but on what grounds exactly?

Kurzweil's argument is clearly a variation of the ancient paradox known as the ship of Theseus, in which we are asked to imagine a ship that is being maintained by having those of its parts replaced that are no longer functional, until eventually all of its original parts are gone and everything is new. The question then arises whether the ship is still the same ship or rather a different one. Some will argue that since there is no step along the way of gradual material change where we can say that *now* the ship is a different one, it remains the same all the way through, whereas others will argue that it cannot be the same since the material constituents that together formed the ship no longer exist (or if they do exist, perhaps used to build a new ship, then this ship would be identical to the original one rather than the one with the replaced parts). Who is right? Well, neither. It is a paradox precisely because there is no obvious answer to the question. And that is because a ship might have a name but it does not have an identity, not in and by itself. And because it does not have one, it cannot change it suddenly. *We* preside over its identity, and it makes no difference whatsoever to the *ship* whether or not we call it the same after it has all its parts replaced. In certain contexts and for certain purposes it might be appropriate to call it the same ship, and in other contexts and for other purposes it might be more appropriate to call it a different ship. Unfortunately, we do not have that option with people. A person either is the same self or they are not, and whether we *regard* them as the same or as different has nothing to do with it.

The argument from graduality is, in fact, *always* fallacious because it denies the reality of change. It seems reasonable to assume that a heap of sand from which one single grain is removed will still be a heap, but even though we are not able to pinpoint the exact moment when, after the removal of yet another grain, the heap ceases to be a heap (because there is no such moment), we will at some point all agree that it is no longer one (Sorites paradox). At some stage (and it might not always be the same), we shall begin to doubt whether "that thing there" is still a heap. From then on, our reluctance to still call it so will grow until it has sufficiently diverged from our idea of a heap that it will no longer seem appropriate to call it that. Similarly, when a person gradually changes, so that their character eventually is very different from what it used to be, we shall at some stage begin to doubt whether it is still the same person, until eventually we shall accept that the person we used to know, in a manner of speaking, no longer exists. But there is no definite threshold here: no point in time where one becomes another person or, rather, character. However, there are distinctive and radical changes that really *are* sudden. If you applied the argument from graduality to, say, the states of matter by reasoning that since water at a temperature of 20°C is liquid, it will still be liquid if we lower its temperature by one degree, you will obviously be proved wrong, provided you repeat the procedure often enough, because we all know that the water will start turning to solid ice at some clearly defined point. That is no gradual change and it has nothing to do with the vagueness of our concepts. Rather, the change is comparatively sudden and very real. And it might well be that when it comes to the individual self we are dealing with a similar situation. The self may survive the gradual cyborgization of the human body through various changes, but only up to a certain critical point. When that point is reached the self might disappear (either to be replaced by a different self or to vanish entirely without being replaced at all).

It is worth pointing out, though, that while, for all we know, the identity of the *self* may change abruptly, our identity as *human beings* is not likely to do so because it is not confined by sharply demarcated boundaries. This means that my self is not necessarily a human self. Although we may find ourselves reluctant to call a being human that exists as a software program in a replaceable robotic body, this does not imply that the no-longer-human is not the same individual it used to be when it was still human. Just as I can remain myself even when my character changes so considerably that my friends are no longer able to recognize me, it seems that I can still be me after I have shed my humanity. One does not lose one's humanity in the way one loses one's virginity, or one's job, or one's self: in one decisive step. Taken by itself, losing one's humanity is not a real change at all. The predicate "human" is itself a human classification, just as the word "heap" is, so that my continuing humanity depends on the elasticity of the currently prevalent image (or images) of the human (Hauskeller 2009). Only after what I have become can no longer be aligned with the vague and changing ideas that people have about themselves as humans, I am human no longer. Bostrom's "Albert", the fictional retriever whose mind has been uploaded and cognitively enhanced so that he can now tell his story to a television audience on the Larry King show can hardly be taken seriously as a dog (Bostrom 2004). He has become almost human, or something that is neither human nor dog. But he may still be the same individual he was before the upload: or maybe not, if it turns out that one's self is *in fact* inseparable from the organic substrate in which it has developed.

The possibility of replacing one's brain and body presupposes an ontological distinction between body and mind, a particular kind of Cartesian substance dualism. The mind is supposed to be not the brain, but "structure" and "pattern", which contains "information" that can in principle always be separated from its organic basis, replicated and reinstantiated in an indefinite number of different material forms. The brain is the (replaceable) hardware and the mind the software: the ghost in the machine (Potts 1996). However, this is not thought to be a peculiarity of the brain–mind relationship, but rather a particular case of a general feature of reality. Not only is the mind said to be nothing but information, but also the quality of being alive: "from the perspective of many contemporary biologists, life is just an interesting configuration of information" (Doyle 2003: 20); "All living organisms are no more than walking algorithms" (Kadmon 2003). Yet non-living things are also algorithms, except that they do not walk. They, too, are configurations of information, only less interesting ones: "Whatever is happening in the universe ... is all information" (Paul & Cox 1996: 34). Thus the whole of reality is understood as being *essentially* information. Whatever else exists or seems to exist are just ways this information is conveyed and processed. It is the form of its appearance, but not the thing-in-itself. It is not the "really real". Just as Richard Dawkins once described living organisms as vehicles for the replication of "selfish genes" (Dawkins 1976), they are now being understood as vehicles for the preservation and transmission of information. As Katherine Hayles has pointed out correctly:

> Underlying the idea of cyberspace is a fundamental shift in the premises of what constitutes reality. Reality is considered to be formed not primarily from matter or energy but from information. Although information can be carried by matter or energy, it remains distinct from them. Properly speaking, it is a pattern rather than a presence. (1996: 112)

However, the truth of this *information idealism* is far from obvious. Rather, it is a substantial metaphysical claim, which ought to be treated as such. We need to ask whether the assumption is at all justified. Are we really no more than bits of information? Are we just "walking algorithms"?

It seems to me that not even the mind, let alone a particular person, can be adequately described as information if what we mean by the word "mind" is more than just content. And we usually do. Our own minds at least are conscious, and it is this consciousness that seems to make them minds in the first place. It is doubtful whether there can be minds that are not conscious (without stretching the meaning of the term beyond recognition). Having a mind generally means being to some extent *aware* of the world and oneself, and this awareness is not itself information. Rather, it is a particular way in which information is processed (which is different from the way in which, say, information in an electronic circuit is processed), but this way does not add anything to the already existing information. It is not simply information about how to process other bits of information. That is why, theoretically, your mind can contain the same information as mine and still not *be* mine (or, as in split-brain patients, different information and be mine nonetheless). Even though we do not understand how it is possible for there to be such a separation, your mind will always stay yours, and mine, mine. For the mind is always *somebody's* mind, which means that there can be a mind only when there is a *self*. A mind without a self is inconceivable. What is conceivable is a mind that is qualitatively identical to mine and yet somebody else's.

However, that there is no mind without a self does not imply that a particular self is nothing but a particular mind. This, too, is an unwarranted Cartesian assumption. Although my mind is part of what I am, I am not my mind. I am there even when I am completely unconscious. I breathe and the blood is pumping through my veins (assisted perhaps by an artificial heart). I am, although my mind may be blank. My body harbours my self while my mind is absent. So I am not my mind. Neither am I my brain, although it is no doubt also a part of me. We tend to exaggerate the importance of the brain to the extent that we confuse our own actions with the actions of the brain. We find plenty of statements such as: "The human brain is one that loves, feels empathy, projects into the future, and contemplates a lifetime of memories. It is subject to pleasure and joy, and a good laugh" (Paul & Cox 1996: 273). Of course, the brain does none of these things. It does not laugh, and neither does it love, feel empathy and so on. *We* do. The brain certainly helps but it is still we who act and relate to our environment. The brain is only one of our organs (albeit a very important one), that is, an instrument that we use in order to accomplish certain tasks in accordance with our general desire to survive in this world. My brain is situated in a body, as is my mind, which is one of my modes of existence, no more and no less. Although, let's face it, we don't have the slightest clue how conscious experience comes about and how there can be such things as selves in the first place, it is rather unlikely that mind and self are directly produced by the brain, as is commonly assumed. There is no direct evidence for that. The brain develops and changes with the experience we accumulate during our lives, and it does so because it has a particular job to do within the system that we call a living, conscious being. It rises to the occasion. The fact that we can manipulate the mind by manipulating the brain, and that damages to our brains tend to inhibit the normal functioning of our minds, does not show that the mind is a product of what the brain does. The brain could be just a facilitator. When we look through a window and the window is then painted black, our vision is destroyed or prevented, but we cannot infer from this that the window produces our ability to see. The brain might be like a window to the mind. Surely the mind is not in any clear sense localized in the brain. Alva Noë is right when he declares the locus of consciousness to be "the dynamic life of the whole, environmentally plugged-in person or animal" (2009: xiii). We are not our brains, we are "out of our heads", as Noë puts it, reaching out to the world as "distributed, dynamically spread-out, world-involving beings" (*ibid.*: 82).

The only selves we have ever encountered are situated, embodied selves: agents that interact with the world and each other through and in their bodies and minds. We have never known even ourselves in any other way. And when we relate to other selves, we always relate to them as complex wholes that do not merely exist as minds (and whose apparent location in a particular body is purely accidental). When we love someone we love them for what they are, and what they are is not hidden away. Rather, what they are is manifest in their bodies, in the "way you hold your knife", the "way you sip your tea", and, yes, in Jack's "self-deprecatory smile" too. People are there for us "body and soul". It would be hard, if not downright impossible, to love (or, for that matter, to hate, or care in any way for) a software program, even if it were conscious. Perhaps we could not even care for ourselves then. So if we really managed to upload our minds to a computer one day, the best we could achieve thereby would be the continuation of a stripped-down, rudimentary self. And that is probably not the kind of immortality most of us would regard as desirable.

We have seen that the hope of attaining "digital immortality" through a completion of the ongoing cyborgization process, that is, through mind-uploading, rests on several questionable assumptions. We have no evidence whatsoever to support the idea that (a) even a perfectly accurate software emulation of a human brain will actually result in conscious experience. This will only happen if the formalist theory of mind is true, which we have no way of knowing and which we have no reason to believe until we encounter a mind instantiated in something that is not a living, organic body. But if it does result in conscious experience, then we (b) still have no guarantee that it will be anything like the experience of the mind we intended to duplicate, or recreate. Should this be the case, though, then we may (c) still see our hopes disappointed by the fact that the newly created mind, although qualitatively identical to the mind whose continued existence we intended to ensure through the emulation, is not numerically identical to it. In other words, it may be a different mind or, more precisely, a different self. Although the self may be preserved through various stages of increasing cyborgization, the final step may prove one step too far and end the existence of the self. This is not only possible, but indeed very likely, since the final step is different from the previous ones in so far as it relies on the possibility of _copying the_ self (instead of merely preserving it through a series of changes). Yet the only thing that _can_ be copied is information, and the self, _qua_ self, is not information. But even if we managed to not lose the self during the copying process and to somehow connect it to the new non-organic substrate, we would (d) have trouble recognizing ourselves. For what we think of as ourselves is very much tied to our bodily existence and as such far more comprehensive and richer than a mere mind can ever be.

* * *

Recently, while having breakfast and at the same time preparing Bostrom's paper "Golden" for a seminar on transhumanism that I teach, my eleven-year-old daughter Hedi came in and asked me what I was reading. When I told her about mind-uploading, what it was and how it was supposed to work, she became very agitated and insisted that such a thing was impossible. When I asked her for a reason she declared that humans had a soul and computers did not. So I gave her the usual philosophy teacher's spiel about what she thought the soul consisted in, where it was located, how we could know that a human had one and a computer did not and so on, but all to no avail: she remained adamant that it was impossible.

But I kept going at her. Finally, exasperated by my verbal attacks, she ended the discussion with the following remark, which, although I would never have put it that way myself, struck me as capturing the very essence of the kind of objection that I intended to raise with the above argument: "Look, Dad," she said, "nobody can catch a soul in a box and then stuff it into a computer." That's exactly it, isn't it?

8

LOOKING GOOD

Beauty in the flesh will continue to rule the world.
(Florenz Ziegfeld)

Since we live in and through our bodies, very much *being* this particular body rather than merely having it, we find it difficult to pretend that the internal and external constitution of our body has little or nothing to do with our identity: with what makes us us. The health of our bodies is our health, and when our body is in pain, we are. Moreover, for others we are merely present through our physical manifestations, the way we sound, smell and, more than anything else, look. Yet by being present for others we also become present for ourselves. We assure ourselves of our own reality by being the object of other people's perceptions. We are there (or conscious of our being there, which amounts to the same thing) because we are there for others. And as *what* we are there also depends on how others perceive us. That is why bodily appearance is so important to us. Our looks are like an advertising board: they announce to the world both that we are and what we are. And because we know that only too well, we want to give the right impression and look our best. Unfortunately, many of us are conscious of some flaws in our appearance, and even the most beautiful woman and the most handsome man get older and gradually lose their shine. We never really look good enough, or only for a short while. We don't because our faces and bodies never fully communicate how special we really are, or feel we are.

When I google the term "enhancement", the first hit I get is a general definition of enhancement by the free online dictionary, according to which to "enhance" means to "make greater, as in value, beauty, or effectiveness". The second hit is a Wikipedia entry on "human enhancement", which is defined as "any attempt to temporarily or permanently overcome the current limitations of the human body through natural or artificial means". The third, fourth and fifth hits are websites on, respectively, cosmetic surgery, photographic breast enhancement and "male" enhancement. Let's have a closer look at the first two (reserving the third one for the next chapter).

The first of those three websites, the one on cosmetic surgery, has the internet address www.enhancement.co.uk, which already indicates how the term enhancement is likely to be understood by most people, namely not as cognitive enhancement, mood enhancement or moral enhancement, but simply as an improvement of bodily appearance. Outside academia, to enhance oneself primarily means one thing and one thing only: to make oneself look better. The website promises to provide independent guidance and advice about cosmetic procedures but its primary goal is clearly not to inform but to convince. It targets people who are not entirely happy with their lives and who believe this may have something to do with the way they look, and then attempts to persuade them that cosmetic surgery is going to solve their problems and is therefore what they need and want. "Are you ready to take the first step towards becoming the brand new you?" is the question with which the site welcomes its visitors, thus suggesting both the achievability and the desirability of a complete transformation of the self, a wholesome identity switch (despite a few risks that no doubt are worth taking), that is going to take place through the transformation of one's appearance. The old, tiresome and disappointing you will be replaced by a much more satisfactory and fulfilling "new you" – if you are "ready" for it, that is, bold enough to try (starting with the first step of seeking information about the available procedures). "If you want to look as good as you feel and are willing to invest in improving your quality of life, why not do so in 2013?", that is, right now. An apparently common discrepancy is alluded to between the way we perceive ourselves (i.e. the way we think we truly are) and the way others perceive us. We feel good, but do not look as (good as) we feel. We are actually very nice and loveable, but others fail to perceive us that way. We are great in bed, but the length of our penis suggests otherwise.

We are actually quite young "in our hearts", but others cannot see that because they are being deceived by our wrinkles and sagging breasts. This discrepancy, it is suggested, compromises our quality of life: we are worse off than we would be if we actually looked as good as we felt. And in the unlikely case that we do not feel that good at all and that our appearance matches exactly the way we feel (namely bad), then presumably cosmetic surgery can also help us feel better by helping us appear better to others. In any case, the new you is the true you. That is why the envisaged change is never meant to be merely a change of the way we look. By changing our appearance we hope to change ourselves or at least the way we are being perceived by others, which may amount to the same thing. It is a change of our *persona*, a word that originally meant the mask an actor wears, or the character that he represents, but not accidentally has come to mean the actual self: that which lies *beneath* the mask. The mask represents the real thing, both by those who wear it and by those who look at it. Fortunately, the right mask, the one that reflects what we feel we truly are, or should be, is only a credit card away. To get hold of it we should, as the website suggests, be willing to spend a lot of money. It's our life, after all. Our well-being depends on it, and it would be foolish to be stingy. The new, true you is worth every penny. And there is so much we can do. There is virtually no part of the body whose appearance cannot be, in some way or other, enhanced. The website www.enhancement.co.uk lists fifty-two different cosmetic enhancement procedures, the most popular being breast augmentation (£3,500–£7,000), eyelid lift (£2,500–£5,000), neck lift (£4,500–£5,500), facelift (£5,000–£8,500), tummy tuck (£4,500–£7,500) and liposuction (£4,000–£8,000). The costs are not exactly small change, but for most people, if they really set their minds to it, they are at least affordable, and millions of people every year decide to treat themselves with a cosmetic makeover.

A considerably cheaper alternative, however, is suggested by the fourth of my hits. It leads to one of those YouTube do-it-yourself videos in which somebody demonstrates how to do certain things that you might be interested in doing without being exactly sure how. In this one you learn how you can make your breasts appear larger in photographs of yourself by using the *Adobe Photoshop* graphics editing program. According to the site statistics, this video has been watched by more than six million(!) viewers since it was uploaded three years ago. In comparison, YouTube videos that demonstrate how to install a kitchen sink attract an average of 15,000 viewers per year, and those explaining how to write a good philosophy paper a meagre 350. The amount of interest in photographic breast enhancement is remarkable because the body part in question is not actually changed in any way: it just looks good for those who cannot actually see it, but only an image of it. This image, however, is sufficient for presenting oneself in the virtual world that many of us spend an increasing amount of time in. When social networking sites such as Facebook or Twitter supersede the need to actually meet each other in person, that is as physical, embodied entities, for the purpose of discovering and shaping one's identity in mutual awareness, the photographic image of the body comes to fulfil the same function that the actual body used to: it tells others that we are and who we are. Suddenly in possession of hundreds of "friends" whom we may never have actually met, and dozens of "followers" for whom our virtual presence is the only presence that is ever going to matter to them, the need to change our actual physical body no longer arises. It is sufficient to change our image. This is as little a lie, an attempt to deceive others, as the transformation of the physical body is. It is simply a reversed Platonism. The shadows on the wall are not falsely seen as the real thing: they *are* the real thing. The mask is the character is the actor. The forms have descended into the cave and have dressed themselves up as shadows. It is an act of deliberate self-creation. The new, true you is the you that can be seen by others. It is truer than the old you because it better reflects the way you feel about yourself. The truth lies in the inside, but the inside demands to become the outside. You may not even be a woman, and yet you may still truthfully claim to be a big-breasted one, which is what the manipulated image conveys. It thus tells a truth about you that your body (small-breasted or possibly even male) effectively conceals. The enhanced image is truer (to the real self) than the unenhanced body.

For those, however, who still go out and meet real people instead of merely their cyberspace representations, it is still the body itself that needs to be enhanced to match and express the inner you. This might require something as drastic as a sex change or, on the contrary, a more pronounced expression of your (physical) sex, or might simply be achieved by making yourself more beautiful (be it

136

according to your own idiosyncratic standards or those predominant in the age and society you happen to live in). Numerous firms promise exactly that if you buy and use the beauty products they have on offer, and it is fascinating to see how the rhetoric that is being employed to sell those products mirrors the arguments routinely used by proponents of human enhancement. One that, in this respect, can be seen as representative of many similar others promotes "permanent makeup" procedures that will give you perfectly shaped and coloured lips, eyes and brows for a couple of thousand pounds. Its website welcomes us with a professed commitment to liberalism. Everybody, we are informed, "should have the right to enhance their own natural beauty" (Natural Beauty Enhancement 2012). So, far from being a frivolous undertaking expressive of one's deplorable vanity, engaging in cosmetic enhancement is to be seen as the exercise of a basic *right*. To be aided in the attempt to become as beautiful as we can possibly be is something that we are encouraged to regard as being *owed* to us. And why exactly is that? Because in seeking cosmetic enhancement, all we really do is affirm our very own being. We just want to be ourselves, and who could deny us that? The clue is the word "natural" and how it is employed. It is our *natural* beauty that we have a right to enhance. How is that to be understood? Obviously, not in the sense that we are already naturally beautiful, because if we were we would not need any enhancement, at least not in this area. Neither does it mean that the way we look by nature is in need of improvement, that natural beauty is judged to be deficient compared to (post-intervention) artificial beauty. Instead, rather paradoxically, it is the *outcome* of the cosmetic intervention that is claimed to be natural. The enhancement consists in bringing out the beauty that we naturally possess but that hitherto has remained largely invisible.

The idea of an inner beauty that just has to be made visible by a process of cosmetic sculpting echoes Michelangelo's famous assertion that every block of stone has a statue inside and it is the sculptor's job to find it. Today's sculptors are cosmetic surgeons and, to a lesser degree, beauty advisors, and their blocks of marble are actual human bodies, whose inner beauty they attempt to release and bring out. We then have a right to become as beautiful as we can be because we have a right to be as beautiful as we truly *are*. We have a right to be seen as who and what we are. What the promised treatment thus does is "help you bring more of 'your' star quality to the surface". We are beautiful, we are special, and we have every right to modulate our body so that it reflects this truth. Once this is achieved and our body no longer conceals what we are (the statue inside the block of marble), but rather is the perfect expression of our being (the block of marble shaped to the form of the statue), we shall finally feel, as we should, at home in our body, and no longer imprisoned in it (cf. Davis 1998: 287). Accordingly, cosmetic enhancement promises to be "one of the most liberating experiences of life", and as such a "life changing treatment": it will boost our confidence, allow us to be socially at ease, and generally "revitalize" our life. Television shows such as *Extreme Makeover*, which ran for five years successfully in the USA, have found their way to Britain to convince British viewers, too, that by using all available means, including cosmetic surgery, to give yourself a better appearance you can become a new person (that is to say, the person you have always known you were) and thereby really turn your life around. Women who have managed to get accepted for the televised radical transformation of their appearance from nondescript or even decidedly plain to dazzling give us the usual spiel about how the procedure has been the greatest thing that has ever happened to them and that from now on their life will be very, very different from what it used to be and, without doubt, much more wonderful, sounding like a transhumanist raving about the glorious posthuman future to come.

And perhaps it will. Beauty, after all, not only sells, but also pays (Hamermesh 2011). People who look good, in accordance with the predominant standards of beauty, are on average more successful in their careers, partly because people who are happy with the way they look tend to be more confident (and confidence is an advantage in many professions), and partly because most of us prefer to work with people who are pleasant to look at rather than with people who are not. It also makes it easier to find a desirable partner: one who is good-looking, too, or wealthy, intelligent or successful in some other way. All this is, of course, not very surprising, and we do not really need a professor of economics to tell us this. There are all sorts of reasons why we should expect a certain correlation between good looks and well-being. What is actually surprising is that the correlation is not greater than it is:

Fifty-five percent of the people in the top one-third of looks
stated that they were satisfied or very satisfied with their
lives; 53 percent of people in the middle half of looks said
the same thing; but only 45 percent of the worst-looking
one-sixth of the population said they were satisfied. Bad
looks and unhappiness with life go together.   (*Ibid.*: 174)

Well, yes, but apparently not as much as one would have thought: of
the best-looking, a staggering 45 per cent still feel unsatisfied with
their lives, and not less than 45 per cent of the worst-looking *do* feel
satisfied. This suggests that while good looks may have *some* impact
on well-being, the impact is not that significant after all. Yet in a
competitive society, even a small advantage may well seem worth
striving for. Bringing one's appearance in line with one's perceived
inner worth is then not only a matter of self-affirmation, but a precondition of social and professional success. Again, this insight is
anything but new. In fact, the rise of cosmetic surgery after the First
World War was almost entirely owed to the widespread preconcep-
tion that to be successful one has to look the part. A 1927 beauty
guide for young women with the promising title *Any Girl Can Be
Good Looking* urged its readers to take the whole thing very seriously indeed:

Competition is so keen and ... the world moves so fast that
we simply can't afford not to sell ourselves on sight. What
if we are kind? And quick-witted? ... People who pass us on
the street can't know that we're clever and charming unless
we look it.   (Haiken 1997: 91)

Plastic surgeons of the 1920s and 1930s, eager to expand their
market after the surge of patients requiring reconstructive surgery
in the aftermath of the First World War lost its steam, were only too
willing to spread the same message (*ibid.*: 104–5), and this has not
changed one bit in the meantime. Cosmetic enhancement is still
being advertised as a matter of social survival: the survival of the
fittest-looking. Those fittest-looking, however, may, in a competitive society, really be the fittest. This situation has brought about
a change in the way the very notion of self-improvement is understood. The distinction between what one is and what one appears

to be has all but disappeared, and to improve oneself now primarily means to change one's looks. A striking example of this new understanding is the following New Year's resolution of an American teenager from the 1980s: "I will try to make myself better in any way I possibly can with the help of my budget and baby-sitting money. I will lose weight, get new lenses, already got new haircut, good makeup, new clothes and accessories" (Brumberg 1998: xxi).

Yet seeking thus to improve oneself is not merely an option: something that we may or may not choose to do. Nor is it simply a moral right. Rather, it is regarded very much as a moral duty. Society certainly owes you its help and support, but you also owe it to yourself and to others to be the best you can. There is no excuse for letting yourself and others down: for accepting the worse when you could have the better. For in the face of alternatives, bodily features that have previously been regarded as normal have come to be seen as defects. As early as the 1930s, any divergence from the norm that might possibly spark a feeling of inferiority was reconceptualized as a "deformity" or "disfigurement" (Haiken 1997: 122) and as such in need of treatment. Since objective criteria for what constitutes a deformity were lacking, the patient's own view came to be decisive, and if one felt inferior because others seemed to be better looking than oneself, that was enough. As soon as there was a real possibility to change one's appearance for the presumed better, a substandard appearance was no longer acceptable, be it natural features such as a nose that was deemed too long or too short or too "Jewish", or acquired ones such as the traces of ageing in bodies and faces, which accumulate in the course of any person's life. Not to use available technologies to enhance one's appearance would amount to deliberately harming oneself and frivolously, and indeed culpably, remaining in a state of disabledness, which is exactly the point that Harris keeps making today with respect to human enhancement in general.

According to Harris, the use of enhancement technologies is morally obligatory because enhancement is always the prevention of harm. What counts as a harmful state or, in short, a disability depends entirely on the context, and more precisely on the available alternatives. I am disabled when I am less able than I would have to be. I am harmed when I do not enjoy the advantages that I might enjoy. "A disability", claims Harris, is simply "a physical or mental condition we have a strong rational preference not to be in" (1993:

180), and we have such a rational preference when things could be better than they are. Consequently, disease must be defined "relative, not to normal species functioning or species-typical functioning, but relative to possible functioning" (Harris 2009: 150). Seen this way, in a world in which cosmetic surgery can achieve almost any change in appearance that happens to be desired by a person, not looking good is a disease and expressive of a moral failure, showing at best a lack of courage and determination and a certain disregard of others and at worst a sinful squandering of one's inherent potential for self-perfection.

However, what it means to look good may vary depending on historical and social context as well as on the values endorsed by the individual who decides to undergo one of the many available enhancement procedures. Obviously, standards of beauty change. While small breasts might have been regarded as beautiful, and hence desirable, in the 1920s, big breasts were the must-have in the 1950s. And today you can choose, and some women opt for bigger breasts and others for smaller ones. Perhaps one day a beautiful woman will be required to have no breasts at all, or to have more than two. But it is not all about standards of beauty. To look good does not always mean to look beautiful (according to those standards), and even where it does mean that, it is seldom an end in itself. Often it is a means to an end, and not always the same end. Some want to look better (i.e. be more beautiful than they are) in order to better blend in (Davis 1998: 287): to no longer be made fun of, socially ostracized or simply undervalued because of one's perceived ugliness or substandard looks. "Did you know that plastic surgery improves lives? It's true! Have you ever felt ashamed or embarrassed about a particular body part or facial feature you possess?" (Brixey 2012). The objective of the intervention is, then, to change one's appearance in such a way that it no longer is a source of embarrassment. The objective is *not* to stick out, not to be seen as different. And for a long time having bodily features that marked one out as belonging to a particular group of people that was, for one reason or other, widely perceived as inferior has been a major source of embarrassment. Thus cosmetic surgery has often been used to get rid of both visible signs of race, be it "Jewish" or "Negroid" noses, dark skin or "Asian" eyes and features that seemed to indicate some kind of disease or deficiencies of character or intelligence (cf. Haiken

1997: 179–86). It is a fact that our bodies are constantly being read by others, and that their various features are interpreted, rightly or wrongly, as indicators of inner qualities. That is why it seems so important to take control of our appearance and make sure that others see us the way we want to be seen. That is what, in practice, looking good really means.

Yet while some wish to cosmetically enhance themselves in order to not stick out and to appear normal and just like everybody else, others are hoping for the exact opposite: they seek cosmetic enhancement because they desire nothing more than to stick out and to be seen as special, as *not* like everybody else. This can be achieved by becoming more beautiful than others, but also, and perhaps even more easily, by making one's appearance markedly different from that of other people. Anything may do as long as it is not in danger of appearing normal. This goal might even be attained by a seemingly wholehearted endorsement of the current standards of beauty. The late Michael Jackson is an interesting case. While it is not known exactly why he underwent the gradual transformation of his face, it is likely, based on the direction and the nature of the changes, that originally he simply intended to look more white. However, what he achieved was a unique countenance that made him instantly recognizable all over the world. Another interesting case is the Brazilian-born housewife Sheyla Hershey, who has achieved a certain fame for the simple reason that she keeps having breast enlargement surgeries, which have over the years increased the size of her breasts to a level that has earned her a place in the Brazilian edition of the Guinness World Records book as the woman with the largest augmented breasts in Brazil. Needless to say, after having had a dozen or so operations, she now looks more frightening than sexy, and finds it impossible to do certain things such as tying her shoelaces, her breasts being too much in the way for that. And yet, she does not seem to feel any regrets, and indeed, by following a certain standard of beauty to the point of absurdity, she has at least acquired a unique appearance. She sticks out. It is worth pointing out that the logic that seems to have guided her in her transformation is not unlike the logic often used by advocates of human enhancement to convince us of the intrinsic desirability of certain kinds of enhancement, such as cognitive enhancement or lifespan extension: namely, that more of a good thing is likely to be even better. To be intelligent is thought to be good and desirable; hence becoming even more intelligent must also be a good thing. Being alive is valued by all of us; hence being alive for even longer must be good, too. Big breasts are beautiful; hence even bigger breasts must be even more beautiful. As this last case makes very clear, this kind of logic is fallacious. However, it may well be that the real purpose of the transformation was never to become more beautiful in the first place. Maybe the real purpose has been all along to become different, to stick out. And maybe that is also the goal that we secretly pursue when we endorse those other suggested enhancements. They are attractive not so much because they promise to increase our well-being or make our lives better or richer in other ways, but above all because they promise to make us different.

While Hershey still pays lip service to current standards of human beauty, there are others who seek to transform themselves in ways that seem to openly defy those standards. Some try to acquire an animal-like appearance, such as Erik Sprague, also known as the Lizardman, who has had various body modifications, including sharpened teeth, a full-body tattoo of green scales, and a bifurcated tongue, or Jocelyn Wildenstein who has ruined her (conventionally) good looks by subjecting herself to a number of facial surgeries that were meant to give her a more catlike appearance. Others, such as Lucky Diamond Rich, the "world's most tattooed person", simply seek to transform their bodies into works of art. In their own perception and in that of their fans, many of those body artists certainly look good and perhaps beautiful in their own weird way, although the more sophisticated ones, such as the French artist Orlan, have used cosmetic surgery to question the very notion of looking good by mimicking traditional standards of beauty and their endorsement by male artists and the art world that they are seen to represent.

All this shows, though, that what it means, concretely, to look good depends largely on what we want and how we want to be perceived. Accordingly, to enhance the way we look can mean all sorts of things, depending on our personal interests and goals. It can mean to look more normal: to become acceptable. It can mean a celebration of beauty, or a celebration of idiosyncrasy and uniqueness. It can even consist in turning the body into an instrument with which to push forward an artistic agenda, or a political agenda, or both. Thus Kathryn Morgan proposed that women attack the reigning ageist ideology and the oppressive beauty imperative by deliberately uglifying themselves: "women might constitute themselves as culturally liberated subjects through public participation in Ms. Ugly Canada/America/Universe/Cosmos pageants *and use the technology of cosmetic surgery to do so*" (1998: 278–9). Morgan encouraged feminists to actively participate "in the fleshly mutations needed to produce what the culture constitutes as 'ugly' so as to destabilize the 'beautiful' and expose its technologically and culturally constitutive origin and its political consequences" (*ibid.*: 279), suggesting that they bleach their hair white, use wrinkle-inducing creams and have their face and breasts surgically pulled down. This way, Morgan hoped perhaps a bit too optimistically, we might learn to revalorize ugliness and old age, which, in the general perception, largely go together. Clearly, though, it is this revalorization itself that we would have to think of as the intended enhancement. That is to say, what is suggested is not so much an attempt to instantiate a new standard of beauty (with its complementary standard of ugliness), but rather an attempt to render considerations of beauty irrelevant. So the goal is no longer to enhance our beauty or make us better looking, but rather to enhance our perception in such a way that beauty and ugliness cease to matter. The goal is to make us insensitive to beauty and thus eliminate differences in looks as a source of unfair treatment.

However, this might be easier said than done, precisely because beauty is, for most of us, far more than just a surface feature. As long as beauty signifies other things – such as belonging to the right group, specialness, health, power and, perhaps more than anything else, life and youth – we shall continue to attach weight to it, unless we also become indifferent to those other things, which is rather unlikely. Although we certainly can decouple the concepts of ugliness and old age and easily imagine a young ugly person and (although somewhat less easily) a beautiful old person, it is hard to deny that our obsession with beauty links back to our obsession with youth. Being beautiful, or looking good, has almost become synonymous with having a youthful appearance. For someone past a certain age, to look good simply means to look younger than one actually is, so perhaps by trying so hard to look good and to keep looking good we once again try to hold on to our youth and, ultimately, our life. In 2012, Yves Saint Laurent launched a range of skin products called by a name that neatly captures the ideology that feeds the cosmetic industry: "Forever Young Liberator". By looking as young as possible, in defiance of our real age, we stave off the very suggestion of mortality. We are telling ourselves and others that death is still far away, if it is real at all. Beauty thus functions as a surrogate for youth. As long as we cannot have the real thing we make do with its simulacrum, pretending that it is the real thing, which we can do precisely because the measure of truth that we apply is not the actual age of the physical body, but the felt age of the inner you. Holding on to a youthful appearance cannot make you younger, but it can more truthfully reflect how young you actually still feel and thus, where it counts, are. It is an attempt to control our destinies: an act of self-creation that foreshadows other such acts. It is like a dress rehearsal for immortality.

This may also be the reason why our obsession with our looks is so often linked to the desire to appear sexually attractive as much and as long as possible. Sexual desirability is the hallmark of youth, signalling to others and to oneself that one is still an active player in the game, still in the business of giving life (at least potentially, but it is the potential – the power – that counts), and that consequently death is still far, far away. Yet since our idea of human beauty is so strongly linked to our sexuality and to what we regard as sexually desirable, today more than ever, it is no longer sufficient to look good with one's clothes on. One should also strive to "look good naked", and more than anything in those areas of the body that are usually not shown in public and that are most closely associated with the sexual act, that is, genitalia. Thus for men, increasing the length and size of their penis (in reality or in appearance, through "penis enlargement pills", surgery or mechanical devices) is often the first choice when it comes to the cosmetic enhancement of their bodies, and numerous websites cater to their needs and wants. Women, on the other hand, are strongly encouraged not to put up with a substandard vagina, and again various enhancement methods, reaching from the application of creams to cosmetic surgery, are suggested to remedy the situation. A website advertising an online publication on labia enhancement ("Looks do matter down there!": Labiaenhancement 2006) deftly employs the language of autonomy and self-creation to sell its product:

145

Just say no! To an unattractive vagina that makes you frown. No woman on earth wants to be "ugly" down there … It's every girl's dream to have perfect and pretty vaginal lips. Women who are not blessed with pretty vaginas feel inadequate and deformed in their most intimate body part.

(*Ibid.*)

Moreover, it is suggested that you cannot really be a good woman, that is, good *as* a woman, if you do not have a pretty vagina: "Feel pretty and feminine by improving the aesthetics and beauty of your genitalia. To be a feminine woman, you need to be feminine down there. And the only way to be feminine is to have a pretty vagina!" (*ibid.*). In other words, if you really want to *be* a woman, that is, a *true* (= feminine) woman, instead of being a woman by name only (that is a non-feminine woman and hence not a true woman), then you must have a vagina that looks the part: a pretty, feminine one. Without it you cannot be counted as a good-looking woman, and for a woman to be good-looking is the same as being a good woman, one that is good as a woman (Little 1998: 166).

The idea of the good woman is clearly an ideological construct that is being evoked to sell a certain range of so-called female enhancement products. The idea of the good human that lurks in the background of the academic enhancement debate may well have a similar function. However, beauty is an area that is usually not mentioned by those who advocate human enhancement, that is, the making of "better humans". The reason is probably that it seems more superficial and not really a core capacity of the human as such, but also that it is somewhat less tangible or concrete. It is already hard to define female beauty and male beauty, that is, to find a standard for each sex with which to measure improvement. Two women can look very different and still both be beautiful. If we ignore the distinction between the sexes, the notion of beauty becomes even more abstract. Human beauty is harder to determine than female beauty or male beauty. Yet, still, at least we are in familiar terrain. We do not have to go beyond our experience. We usually recognize human beauty when we see it. It is hard to understand, though, how one should become superhumanly beautiful, that is more beautiful than any human that currently lives or has ever lived in the past. We can imagine that we all are as beautiful as the most beautiful among us, but we cannot really imagine being even more beautiful than that. To create even more beautiful humans seems impossible, because our standards of beauty are so much tied to the human form. But isn't that also true, *mutatis mutandis*, for our understanding of morality, emotions and intelligence? Aren't they all, in one way or another, tied to the human form or human condition, in such a way that we find it hard to imagine a being that is not just different, but *better* in those areas than any mere human could ever be?

9

GETTING STRONGER

Guardian: What would your super power be?
Margaret Atwood: The flying-around thing. With a cape.
("Q&A: Margaret Atwood", *Guardian*, 28 October 2011)

My son Arthur is four years old. He loves superheroes. His current favourite is Spiderman. A while ago it was Batman. He is the proud owner of various action figures representing those heroes, some important helpers (such as Robin), and their eternal enemies, commonly known under their generic name as "baddies". He can play with them for hours on end, enacting stories that he has made up. He also enjoys wearing a superhero costume (with bulging muscles, which is very important for him) and pretending to be one himself and thus to be able to climb walls, make giant leaps from one tall building to the next (usually represented by different corners of the sofa), run with superhuman speed so that nobody can catch him, and beat up baddies (mostly me) with his superstrong fists. When he thinks of having superhuman powers, he does not think of being supersmart, supergood, super-controlled or immortal. He thinks of being a lot stronger than he currently is, and a lot stronger than anyone else he knows. His daydreams are about having physical powers that would allow him to overcome every obstacle put in his way, to do everything he wills, and to no longer feel small and dependent. I suspect he hates being permanently told what to do and what not, and it is not only we, his parents and guardians, and other grown-ups who tell him that, but also mostly the world itself that does it. It tells him, in so many ways, "You can't do this!" and "You can't do that!", and although he may hope that some of the stuff he cannot do he will be able to do in the future, when he is bigger (which might, for all he knows, take millions of years), there are many things that there is no hope he will ever be able to do even as an adult, unless, of course, he somehow acquires superhuman powers and abilities. If I could have a rational discussion with my son about human enhancement and what it would consist in, then I am pretty sure what he would say. For him, the radically enhanced human or posthuman would certainly not be an uploaded mind or some other intellectualized form of existence. Instead, the "better" human would be a superhero, one in complete control of his (physical) environment: a master of the universe.

Physical strength is the most obvious, the most visible, sign of superiority. There are superheroes with enhanced mental capacities, for instance the ability to read other people's minds, but in themselves such powers have little attraction. They become of interest only when they have some impact on the visible, material world, when they translate into control over the physical. This is what ultimately matters most to us, as long as we are ourselves physical and thus vulnerable beings, which can be violated, enslaved and destroyed. Just as we attach so much importance to the beauty of our bodies because such beauty bears the promise of eternal youth, we long for physical strength (or, again, at least the appearance of physical strength) because it suggests the power to protect oneself from alien (that is, natural) forces and to implement one's will on the external world. This is probably the reason why books on the philosophy of human enhancement occasionally have cover illustrations that would seem more appropriate for a bodybuilding exercise guide than for an academic discussion of the topic. Thus Harris's *Enhancing Evolution* (2007) bears the striking image of Superman's strong arm with its bulging biceps on the cover, and there does not seem to be any irony intended here. Similarly, the cover of Savulescu and Bostrom's edited collection on *Human Enhancement* (2009) shows the silhouettes of various hyper-muscled male figures. Clearly, the visual signs that we normally associate with physical power in humans (i.e. well-built muscles) are meant to represent human enhancement in general, which might give us some indication of what human enhancement ultimately is all about, namely physical power: to be in a position where nobody and nothing can touch us any more; where the world around us has, as it were, finally been tricked or beaten into submission. We are no longer content (if we ever were) with being a thinking reed, as Blaise Pascal had it: a being that, despite its feebleness and the very real possibility of finding itself crushed by the universe, is still, by virtue of its understanding, infinitely superior to it. While Pascal (just as Kant and numerous other enlightenment thinkers after him) urged us to elevate ourselves by thinking well, "and not by space and time which we cannot fill" (*Pensées* 347, my translation), we now endeavour to do exactly that: fill space and time and thus make it impossible for the universe, let alone a drop of water, to destroy us. We have decided that there is no dignity in knowing that one has to die. A life that must end in death, this allegedly most terrible of all evils, is always undignified. So we have to protect ourselves; have to get stronger, a lot stronger; have to be durable, indestructible, ineliminable, *unkaputtable*. Big muscles function as a metonomy for this wished-for all-round protection.

In October 2011 I attended a conference on "Transforming Human Nature" held at Dublin City University. Taking place at the same time and in the same venue was a bodybuilding competition. So while we were in our conference room upstairs talking about radical human enhancement and the differences between posthumanism and transhumanism, in the rooms below us there was a gathering of hundreds of men who had actually enhanced themselves to a posthuman level, or at least to one that made them look decidedly different from all the humans that most of us had ever encountered in person; it was a rare occasion to view human enhancement in action. And they really did look different: hardly human any more, with their grotesquely swollen bodies, which contrasted sharply with the now disproportionately small (that is unchanged and hence human) size of their heads. During coffee breaks we mingled, which I am sure must have been quite a spectacle: a bunch of pale, bookish and not especially athletic academics amid all those tanned bulky "man-mountains", who made each of us feel like Gulliver in Brobdingnag. It was certainly intimidating, and I would not have dared to mess with any of them, but the funny thing about bodybuilding is that its purpose is not so much to increase a person's actual strength and physical ability (with a view to the performance of certain tasks that require such strength) but, rather, once again, to make people *look* strong. Bodybuilding, just like cosmetic surgery, is all about looking good, although looking good is here defined as looking strong. But it is still the looks that count and that are assessed and evaluated in competitions. The right look can be, and is, achieved by working out, but also by the use of certain chemicals such as anabolic steroids or somatrophin (synthetic human growth hormone), both of which stimulate muscle growth and endurance, oxygen enhancers, which allow longer exercise, and other enhancement drugs that aid, in one way or another, the development of muscle tissue. Yet since it is the looks that are important and not actual strength, bodybuilders often use substances that merely blow up the muscle without actually making it stronger. Through injection of Synthol, or other site-enhancement oils, in the right places, muscles can be made to look far more impressive than they are.

Yet, of course, there are also many people who are genuinely interested in enhancing their physical strength and abilities and who do not bother too much whether they also look the part. In contrast to bodybuilders, competitive athletes actually have to *be* strong, and not merely appear strong, to succeed. If a runner looks faster than another, but is actually slower, then she is very likely to lose, and if she does not, it is not because she looked fast. If an Olympic weightlifter looks as if he could snatch 220 kg, but cannot, then looking as if he could does not help him one bit. In sport we can no longer pretend. We have to be what we aspire to be. And for some, to be successful in their chosen sport is enormously important and in fact more important than anything else. Thirty years ago, the practising physician Gabe Mirkin asked more than a hundred competitive runners whether they would take a "magic pill" that guaranteed them an Olympic gold medal, but would also kill them within a year; more than half of them declared they would take the pill (Todd 1987: 88). It seems that for those athletes winning the competition is of the utmost importance. It does not really matter how they get there as long as they do get there. Whether it is natural talent or hard training or a combination of both that eventually earns them a medal, or a "magic pill" that guarantees success no matter what, does not seem to make any difference. It is the outcome that counts, in this case being able to run faster, or jump higher, or lift more weight than anyone else. And that desired outcome is so important that apparently some are willing to give even their very lives if that is what it takes to ensure it. Yet why exactly is that so important?

When Savulescu and colleagues (2004) argued for the legalization of performance-enhancing drugs, they defended the taking of such drugs as being entirely in accordance with the spirit of sport and in fact with that of humanity. Ironically, the authors made a point of distinguishing the "old naturalistic Athenian vision of sport", which had as its goal to "find the strongest, fastest, or most skilled man", from a more modern idea of sport, which treats humans as humans. Since the former sees humans basically (but wrongly) as a particular kind of animal (the goal in a horse race being also to find the fastest horse), we should develop and support an understanding of sport that does justice to the difference between humans and animals: "Humans are not horses or dogs. We make choices and exercise our judgment. We choose what kind of training to use and how to run our race" (*ibid.*: 666). It is this (self-)creative aspect that makes human sport allegedly so different from animal sport. "To choose to be better is to be human" (*ibid.*: 670). That is why, the authors claim, taking performance-enhancing drugs should be permitted: they make sport even more human by allowing athletes to exercise even more choice. However, what they do not seem to realize is that the whole thing is not that different from animal sport after all, since what ultimately counts is still who is the fastest, strongest and so on. The difference is merely that now it is no longer about *finding* "the strongest, fastest and most skilled man" (*ibid.*: 666), but instead about *becoming* it. Is that really such a big difference? It is still unclear why it is important to be the strongest, fastest and so on. And although, of course, the athlete now gets a choice about whether they want to use drugs and, moreover, which drugs to use (to be selected from a whole battery of substances with different effects), in all likelihood it will not be the athlete who deliberates about the best chemical strategy to guarantee success. Rather, there will be some kind of chemical adviser who will choose the best combination for them, so that, as far as they are concerned, it could just as well be a magic pill that is being handed to them. Savulescu and Bennett Foddy suggest that we adopt what they think is the (only) rational approach by allowing safe performance enhancers to support "the display of human physical excellence" (Savulescu & Foddy 2011: 305). "These drugs", they claim, "do not subvert the nature of the sport; indeed, they encourage athletes to become paragons of the sporting ideal: supermen" (*ibid.*: 309).

I am sure my son would agree that the creation of supermen is a goal worth-pursuing. Yet if that really is the ultimate goal, which we are not supposed to question because our desire to become such a superman is somehow proof of our humanity, why then should we restrict the athlete's choice by insisting that drugs be safe? Isn't that also an infringement of their autonomy and their right to self-creation? And indeed, as Savulescu and Foddy are quick to remind us, safety is far from being the highest priority. Instead, safety requirements should be reasonable because many sports are inherently risky, and what we need to do is *not* make them as risk free as possible, but rather determine which risks are acceptable. If there were no risks at all, then there would be nothing much to admire and to sustain our interest:

> today we demonize the men who courageously push themselves to the human limit and beyond. We should admire them, rather than denigrate them. They give us the spectacle we want, and we complain when they push themselves to the limits we expect. *(Ibid.*: 311)

It takes courage to face the risks necessary to push oneself "to the limits we expect", and the more risk someone is willing to take the more courageous and hence admirable they are. It should not surprise us, then, that apparently a great many athletes would gladly take the above-mentioned magic pill that would guarantee them success, even though it would also cost them their lives. They are not being stupid, but are simply heroes: superheroes, in fact, at least potentially. And although not all heroes are bound to be superheroes, all superheroes are heroes; they take risks to help create a better world. If drugs increase the risk, even better! Thus it has seriously been argued that the more risks one is willing to take, the more one deserves to win.

> It is a well-established principle of professional ethics that benefits and rewards should be distributed according to efforts and risks undertaken. Athletes should not be treated differently. If an athlete risks her health to attain victory, while others are more prudent, it is only fair that the victory goes to the former. (Tamburrini & Tännsjö 2011: 277)

Suddenly what makes one deserving of victory is not that one is prudent, but, on the contrary, that one risks everything for victory, as if ignoring all consequences and the willingness to sacrifice everything for being, say, the fastest runner was praiseworthy in itself. Armed with this logic we could argue that all rules in sport that are designed to protect the athlete from serious injury should be abolished. After all, all they do is diminish the spectacle value and make the athletes less admirable. So by all means let them risk all and give us blood, give us heroes, give us *panem et circenses*. For that is the true spirit of sport: the essence of what sport is, and should be, all about. Or is it?

It is often argued that we need to allow performance-enhancing drugs in sport to "level the playing field" and to give everyone a chance to win: "the winning odds of the competitors might be leveled out by intentional and goal-oriented efforts to achieve a higher sports performance level" (*ibid.*: 283). The taking of drugs is such a goal-oriented effort. It makes things fairer. This is probably an effective argumentative strategy, for we tend to disapprove of people getting treated unfairly. Unfairness is bad; fairness is good. The unequal distribution of natural talents is decried as a "genetic lottery", which is claimed to be inherently unfair, as all lotteries are, so it becomes morally imperative to employ countermeasures, such as drugs. Thus performance enhancers are essentially fairness drugs. However, the whole argument relies on the plausibility of the claim that nature can be unfair. Can it? Is it really *unfair*, as opposed to, say, merely unfortunate, that not all of us are world-class sprinters, or swimmers, or footballers, or some other sort of modern superhero? Does it even make sense to say that? It seems to me that it does not, unless one assumes that nature is a rational agent who gives out talents and can choose what and how much to give to whom, and who has deliberately withheld from me the football talents of, say, Wayne Rooney. Or we need to assume that there is a God behind it who is responsible for what I am and what I am not. For a distribution to be unfair, someone must be responsible for it. And if we do not assume that there is such a one, then I may well resent the fact that I am not as good as Rooney, but I can hardly see it as unfair. Neither, by the way, is it unfair when someone else wins the lottery and I do not. It would only be unfair if the results had been rigged. To complain about the alleged unfairness of the fact that one does not win the lottery while others do is plain silly, and it is just as silly to complain about the alleged unfairness of the "genetic lottery". It is like complaining bitterly about the unfairness of it all when we were planning to have a picnic and now it is raining. "This is so unfair!" No, it is not: just unfortunate.

It makes more sense to claim, as Claudio Tamburrini and Torbjörn Tänssjö also do, that it is not fair that people who are naturally more talented than others should be allowed to win in competitions rather than those who are willing to risk their lives by taking performance-enhancing drugs. There is, after all, a decision to be made here whether performance-enhancing drugs should be allowed or not. And someone has to make that decision and then be responsible for the consequences. Yet whether or not we are inclined to regard this particular outcome (that the naturally talented have an advantage over the talentless, or less talented, risk-takers) as unfair depends largely on what we think should be the focus of athletic competitions, and I very much doubt that many people think that those who are willing to take the greatest risks should be rewarded by allowing them to win. It is far from obvious that a daredevil mentality should always be allowed to trump natural talent, and there is nothing inherently unfair about attaching greater importance to the latter rather than to the former.

However, most athletes would probably welcome the opportunity to physically enhance themselves any way they like without any legal restrictions, as long as that would allow them to become a better athlete. But what exactly does "better" mean in this context? In most cases it will simply mean to have a better "chance of winning in athletic competitions" (Holm & McNamee 2011: 292). Let us be quite clear about what *that* means. It does not mean that those who are "better" win those competitions, just as the doctrine of the survival of the fittest does not really imply that the fittest survive. Rather, those who survive are, for precisely that reason, to be regarded as the fittest. Their fitness is *defined* by their ability to survive. So they do not survive because they are the fittest, but they are (being declared) the fittest because they survive. Similarly, athletes do not win competitions because they are the best, but they are to be seen as the best (i.e. better than others) because they win competitions. This is how their being better is *defined*. And, of course, it is not just any athletic competition we are talking about, but always a particular one, the particular demands of which are like evolutionary pressures to which the athlete adapts with his training. His sport is his niche. And the more he adapts to the specific circumstances of his chosen discipline, the less he is capable of succeeding in others, unless they are very similar (*ibid.*). So whatever he does to enhance himself, he never really becomes a "better athlete" as such. He might become a better runner (meaning one that has a better chance of winning in running competitions), and perhaps not even that. Maybe he will only become a better 100m and 200m sprinter, but not better at all at 5,000m. But what the point of *that* is remains entirely unclear. Perhaps some will be happier when they have received an Olympic gold medal, but surely it is possible to live just as happily without one. There does not seem to be any real point in winning athletic competitions, or at least not more point than there would be, say, in a hamster's decision to become the fastest wheel-runner, or in someone's aspiration to win a pancake-eating competition. "The winner of a pancake-eating contest has dropped dead while accepting his prize for gorging on 43 of the banana and cream stuffed desserts" (*Sky News*, 10 March 2009); but that is presumably okay because winning this thing was surely worth it. And highly deserved, as his death proves! A true pancake superhero! Essentially, athletic competitions are just a different form of pancake-eating contest.

It is this utter pointlessness that makes competitive sport such an interesting test case for the enhancement debate. It does not seem to fulfil any purpose apart from that of showing that one can do the deed, that one can be better than others and that it is possible to break the record, to be even faster, or stronger, or whatever. However, it being possible is not good for anything else. It is an end in itself. Yet nobody seems to be disturbed by that, least of all the most vocal proponents of physical enhancement:

> The rationale has to do with a notion of elite sport as a way of exploring the limits of human nature. We arrange the competition in order to find out where the limit is for what is possible for a human being to achieve. We want to explore, not only where the limit is, but also who is, in the relevant aspect, the most perfect human being. Once we find this out, we make this human being the subject of our admiration. At last we have found the Übermensch. (Tännsjö 2009b: 324)

But what do we do once we have found him? Why would we want to find him in the first place? The answer is that we don't or, at least, finding the *Übermensch* does not seem to be enough. We are not really interested in finding out about limits; we are interested in *overcoming* them. The *Übermensch* (here representing the best that humans currently can hope to be) is thus only the starting-point. The most perfect human being is, after all, only perfect in comparison to other humans who have not yet reached the same heights of what is humanly possible. The use of modern technology, however, will allow us to go beyond that: to transcend current limitations, to "boldly go where no man has gone before". Sport is seen as an important part of that exploration:

> In elite sport we can test out the results of such enhancements and see, not where the limits are of the (given) human nature, but how far we can push them. We can enjoy what we see at the competition, and we can feel admiration for all the scientific achievements that have rendered possible the performances. And we can thank the athletes for taking the inconvenience to test them out before us.
>
> (*Ibid.*: 326)

So the admiration remains, but it is no longer the athlete that is its object, but the science and technology that they are allowed to showcase (and of course also those who have created it). Just as we use animals to, among other things, study biological functions and certain diseases and to test for possible cures (after which we may or may not thank them for their services to humanity; usually we just kill them), we should soon be able to use athletes for the study of methods of human enhancement. They will help us to see how far we can go and thus do a great service to humanity. But again, what exactly does the service consist in? Well, presumably it consists in showing us what is possible. Or rather, *that* it is possible. Their continuing success in breaking records strongly suggests that all human limits are merely temporary: that, no matter how unchangeable they seem to be, we shall eventually overcome them; and the ones after them; and the ones after *them, ad infinitum*.

That this endless pushing forward, for the mere sake of it, is the be all and end all of human existence has first been argued, once again, by More (1996) in his seminal paper on transhumanism. Much of the widespread fascination with the possibilities of radical human enhancement seems nourished by an endorsement of the same values that More advocates with his extropian philosophy: boundless expansion, self-transformation, dynamic optimism.

> This is the core of the Extropian approach to meaningfulness: Life and intelligence must never stagnate; it must re-order, transform, and transcend its limits in an unlimited progressive process. Our goal is the exuberant and dynamic continuation of this unlimited process, not the attainment of some final supposedly unlimited condition. ... The Extropian goal is our own expansion and progress without end. (*Ibid.*)

Professional competitive sport, glorified by Savulescu and others, exemplifies this kind of endless striving. The problem with this is not so much that there is ultimately no purpose to it, but rather that all efforts are focused almost entirely on getting a competitive advantage. It is all about showing that one can beat other competitors and, perhaps more than anything else, nature itself. Everything, including one's own body, and indeed one's very existence, becomes a means to that end, which not only remains for ever external, beyond reach, because there is always more to compete with, new enemies to be fought, new triumphs to be sought, but which is also completely disconnected from the means in the sense that it does not matter at all which means we use to pursue it. We are to transcend boundaries, but it makes no difference which boundaries and no difference how we go about it. All boundaries are equally bad. The athlete needs to break records, but it does not matter in which discipline and in which manner. All disciplines are equal with respect to the goal that unites them all: the pushing of human limits. Whether you run, or jump, or swim to be able to do this – the nature of the activity itself – is of no importance. Thus the runner ceases to be a runner and the swimmer to be a swimmer, while both become just another proof of humanity's extraordinary abilities, or just another experiment in human enhancement. When the runner no longer primarily wants to run, and the swimmer to swim, and instead both primarily want to *win*, then something has been lost: something that is a precondition for having a good life, or a life at all. It is what Aristotle called *praxis*, an activity that is valued for what it is, in contrast to *poiesis*, which is an activity that is valued for what it produces. Both *praxis* and *poiesis* have their place in our lives, but if all our activities were merely poietic, always directed towards a future (especially one that will always remain future), and never constitutive of the lived presence that we find in *praxis*-activities, then our whole existence would appear meaningless. Kass rightly reminds us that:

> most of life's activities are non-competitive; most of the best of them – loving and working and savoring and learning – are self-fulfilling beyond the need for praise and blame or any other external reward. In these activities, there is at best no goal beyond the activity itself.   (2003: 24)

Sport can, of course, be this, too. Yet the problem is that for many it no longer is, and demanding that athletes be allowed to take (safe) performance-enhancing drugs to assist them in their desire to "become better" only fortifies this shift in focus from the present to the future, leading to an indefinite postponement of life itself.

There is perhaps no other area in which what Kass calls the "attitude of mastery" is so widely and unabashedly celebrated as an end in itself, although echoes of this obsession with transcending boundaries and the attainment of superpowers can be found in other places, for instance in a certain heavily promoted understanding of human and especially male sexuality, which finally brings me to the fifth search hit on "enhancement" mentioned in the previous chapter. It leads to the Sinrex website advertising "male enhancement pills for real male enhancement" (Sinrex 2013). This "most complete male enhancement pill" promises "stronger, longer, and harder erections", an increase in sexual stamina, an enormous (420%) increase in semen volume and, last but not least, explosive orgasms. Thus, by taking this pill, you can really expect to get, as Pauly Morgan once put it, the "penis you were always meant to have" (1998: 279) and, presumably, thereby also become the man you always wanted to be. The pill virtually guarantees an all-round enhancement: power on various levels and happiness. It is a wet dream of omnipotence that is not accidentally being marketed as "male enhancement", that is, enhancement of the male as a male. So it seems that while women become better women through beautification, an important part of which is the improvement of their vagina's looks, men become better men by getting stronger and more powerful, and it is in their penis and what they can do with it that this power and strength manifests itself most. The underlying imperative is the same as in competitive sport: improve yourself; become better; get stronger; go longer, wider, faster; become the best.

10

BEING AT HOME IN THE WORLD

Gratitude is the sign of noble souls.
(Aesop, *Androcles and the Lion*)

As we have seen, an increasing number of philosophers and scientists argue that we should use (or should at least not be prevented from using) biotechnology to enhance human nature in various ways. However, some obstinately believe that we should not. To justify their scepticism, those "bio-conservatives", as they are derisively dubbed by their melioristic opponents, have brought forward various arguments, none of which has been found compelling by those who advocate human enhancement. In this chapter, I want to look at one particular argument and the notion that forms its backbone. The argument was proposed by Michael Sandel (2007). The notion at the core of the argument is that of "giftedness".

Sandel discusses the case of an athlete who excels in his chosen sport not as a result of extensive training and effort, but because of drugs and genetic amendments. Sandel claims that such an athlete's success would not be *his* success at all. If there is achievement here it belongs to those who invented the drugs or the relevant enhancement technology. The athlete ceases to be an agent and becomes a mere machine programmed by others. Sandel believes that this is a problem, but he also believes that it is not the main one. Besides effort, there is an at least equally (if not more) important second aspect to the athletic ideal, namely (the display and cultivation of) *gift*. And this is an aspect that, according to Sandel, ought to be preserved, not only in competitive sport but generally as an object of experience and appreciation. Here is Sandel's argument in his own words:

> The deeper danger is that they [i.e. enhancement and genetic engineering] represent a kind of hyperagency, a Promethean aspiration to remake nature, including human nature, to serve our purposes and satisfy our desires. The problem is not the drift to mechanism but the drive to mastery. And what the drive to mastery misses, and may even destroy, is an appreciation of the gifted character of human powers and achievements.
>
> To acknowledge the giftedness of life is to recognize that our talents and powers are not wholly our own doing, nor even fully ours, despite the efforts we expend to develop and to exercise them. It is also to recognize that not everything in the world is open to any use we may desire or devise. An appreciation of the giftedness of life constrains the Promethean project and conduces to a certain humility. (2007: 26–7)

Now what exactly is Sandel saying here? Admittedly, his argument is not entirely clear, but I take him to mean roughly the following: human enhancement (particularly, but not exclusively, genetic enhancement) should be avoided because it is dangerous, and it is dangerous because, or in so far as, it represents *hyperagency*, that is the aspiration to remake nature in such a way that it serves our purposes and satisfies our desires (even more than it already does) or, in short, the *drive to mastery*. The use of the term "represent" is perhaps slightly misleading in this context because although it might be plausibly argued that genetic enhancement is a paradigmatic case of hyperagency or of acting out the drive to mastery, and therefore is particularly suitable to represent, or stand for, hyperagency in general, it is obviously not this representational aspect that makes it dangerous. The danger must lie somewhere else, namely in the fact that the attempt to enhance humankind as a whole is an *expression* or *embodiment* of the drive to mastery. This is what I take Sandel to mean here. When we are trying to remake nature we are following this drive (whether or not this is what *motivates* our actions), and thus affirm and very likely reinforce it. The drive to mastery lies no longer dormant or within, comparatively restrained by natural boundaries, but has found a powerful vehicle that supports and accelerates its spread. If this interpretation of Sandel's argument is correct, then the reason for not pursuing human enhancement is that we should not give in to and thereby encourage and assist the drive to mastery. But why shouldn't we? What is wrong with the drive to mastery? Sandel gives an answer that leads the argument to its apparent conclusion. We should not follow this drive, he says, because by doing so we lose "an appreciation of the gifted character of human powers and achievements." Instead of aspiring to remake nature we should rather recognize that "our talents and powers are not wholly our own doing" and that "not everything in the world is open to any use we may desire or devise." This is what acknowledging the "giftedness of life" means. If we do acknowledge it, the drive to mastery gives way to a "certain humility". And that, we may add, is good, whereas not having this humility is bad. But is it really?

Frankly, this whole train of reasoning does not sound like a conclusive argument at all. Of course, it can hardly be contested that, as Sandel says, "our talents and powers are not wholly our own doing". Even though we may choose to develop certain natural talents and let others lie idle so that the powers we gain through practice owe their existence to a large degree to our choices and efforts, there must be something *given* on which to build. I cannot *choose* to become a great musician or novelist, no matter how much I am prepared to work for it, although there probably are people who might have become great musicians or novelists if only they had properly nurtured their talents. Normally, at least, our talents (if not our powers) are beyond our control. However, genetic engineering might help us change this and induce talents that we would not have had otherwise. Even though our talents and powers are not wholly our own doing *now*, they may well be in the future when enhancement techniques are universally available and routinely used. After all, as we have seen earlier, that seems to be the whole point of human enhancement: to become able to choose what we are.[1] Yet even then, Sandel could point out, something must always remain given. If nothing were given there would be no ground from which to make a choice. If I want to give myself a certain talent, I have to employ certain capacities. I must be able to want this talent, to correctly judge the desirability of it and, finally, to bring it about.

In other words, it requires talent to create talent. So our talents and powers really are never *wholly* our own doing and never will be. But what follows from that? Why should this be a reason not to undertake the deliberate creation of talents and powers? Sandel says that acknowledging the giftedness of life *also* means recognizing that "not everything in the world is open to any use we may desire or devise". Is this meant to be a descriptive or a prescriptive statement? Taken as a *descriptive* statement it does not tell us anything about whether or not we should pursue human enhancement. Perhaps there are things that we shall never be able to use at our will. But if that is so we need not be concerned about these things. What cannot be done cannot be done, and the question whether we *ought* to do it simply does not arise. If, on the other hand, the statement is prescriptive and means that there are some things in the world that we *ought* not to subject to any use we may desire or devise, then it is unclear on what grounds this claim rests. Presumably those things that we ought not to use any way we please are our talents and powers, the reason being apparently that they are not "wholly our own doing". But clearly the fact that our talents and powers are not wholly our own doing does not warrant the conclusion that we should abstain from manipulating and changing them. So again, what exactly is Sandel's argument?

Well, for one thing we can safely say that he is trying to introduce a new perspective to the discussion of human enhancement. Usually the discussion focuses on the question whether what is initially thought to be an improvement of human nature might not turn out to have severely damaged it. As it is commonly framed, the question is whether a particular kind of enhancement, for example memory enhancement or the extension of human lifespan, will really benefit those who are subjected to it. Would they really be better off than we are now? Perhaps they would lose more than they would gain. Sandel, however, is concerned not so much with the harm that we might inflict on the supposedly enhanced, as with the harm that we might inflict on *ourselves*. This is not always recognized.[2] Enhancement, for Sandel, is not primarily wrong because it harms the enhanced but rather because it harms the enhancers. When A enhances B, B might not be harmed at all, but A *always* is, and that is why it is always wrong to attempt to enhance someone (even ourselves). And why are the enhancers harmed even when the enhanced are not? Because they allow their inherent drive to mastery to reign and all humility to disappear. For Sandel, humility is a virtue, and virtue is what the whole argument seems to be about.

If we all agreed that humility was a virtue and that the attempt to make better people was detrimental to humility, then we would have at least a *prima facie* reason to oppose human enhancement. It is only a *prima facie* reason because we might decide that although humility is a good thing, there are other things that are even better, so that if we can gain the latter by sacrificing the former we should do it. But, of course, humility is far from being generally accepted as a virtue today. It is reputed to be a decidedly Christian virtue, which has no place in a modern, enlightened society. Being humble traditionally means to know that one's power is very limited, that there are others who are far cleverer and more talented than we, and finally, and most importantly, that all human power is negligible compared to the power of God.[3] An attitude such as this does not exactly encourage the transgression of boundaries. Consequently, those who advocate human enhancement tend to echo Nietzsche and deny that there is any special worth in humility. "I personally do not regard humility as a virtue", writes Harris curtly (2007: 113), and More goes even further by denouncing humility as a false virtue invented by the Church to keep humanity at bay and to prevent any progress:

> Apart from the sheer falsity and irrationality of religion it has had the unfortunate consequence ... of debasing humanity. By inventing a God or gods and elevating them above us, by making external divinity the source of meaning and value, and by abasing ourselves before these higher powers, we have stifled our own emerging sense of personal value. We can look up while on our knees, but we cannot walk forward. (1996)

So is that what Sandel wants us to do: fall back on our knees and thus dispense with standing upright and walking forwards? Sandel does not talk about God, though. Instead, he talks about the giftedness of life: about powers and talents that are not wholly our own doing. We are asked (or advised) to be humble not in the face of God's absolute power, but rather in the face of that dark ground of our own being, by virtue of which we are what we are, which then in turn allows us to aspire for something better. And being humble means to appreciate this and not try to interfere with it. But is there any reason why we should be humble in the absence of religious belief? It seems that for there to be such a reason some good must result from it, but so far it is unclear what this good might consist in.

Even Kass (2003), who shares Sandel's scepticism with regard to human enhancement, thinks that the notion of giftedness is not very helpful. The giftedness of nature, he points out, "also includes smallpox and malaria, cancer and Alzheimer's disease, decline and decay":

> Modesty born of gratitude for the world's "givenness" may enable us to recognize that not everything in the world is open to any use we may desire or devise, but it will not by itself teach us which things can be fiddled with and which should be left inviolate. The mere "giftedness" of things cannot tell us which gifts are to be accepted as is, which are to be improved through use or training, which are to be housebroken through self-command or medication, and which opposed like the plague.   (*Ibid.*: 19)

According to Kass, the fact that something is "given" does not tell us anything; what we have to ask ourselves is rather whether there is something precious in what has been given to us (2003: 20). Harris (2007: 112–13) makes the same point and agrees (for once) with Kass that what we have been given is not necessarily good, and only what is good should be taken into account, morally speaking. So it seems that Sandel's argument from humility and the giftedness of life is very weak indeed.

However, neither Harris nor Kass properly distinguish between the "given" and the "gifted" and they both overlook the special connotations of the latter. Being gifted means that one has received (natural) gifts. A gift is not merely something given. Anything can be given, but not anything can be a gift. There are various features that distinguish the gift from the merely given. First, a gift is something that has been given to us as a *good*. If *someone* has given it to us, then it must at least have been *intended* to benefit us. Otherwise it would be no gift at all. If you give me a load of rubbish, I will hardly consider it a gift, even if I get it for my birthday (unless, of course, I like rubbish, but then it is no longer rubbish to me). I may, however, be the receiver of something that has not been given to me by anyone in particular. I can then still regard it as a gift, but only if it really is good or at least appears good to me. For this reason, disease or the proneness to disease may be given (although usually not given by someone), but would not normally be considered a gift (although it could be under certain circumstances, namely if the bearer of the disease benefits from it, for instance by reminding them what is really important in life).[4] A healthy body, on the other hand, *can* be considered a gift, because for one thing it has been given to us (in the sense that there is only so much we can do ourselves to make and keep it healthy) and for another because it is a good thing to have.

Second, a gift cannot be demanded, acquired or earned. There is no *right* to be given a gift. A gift is something that could just as well not have been given. A gift can be something unexpected, and it is always undeserved, or non-deserved. Thus understood, we do not always appreciate health, or even life itself, as a gift. Often enough we feel, on the contrary and with no good reason, that we deserve all the good things in life: those we have and those we do not have. If we fail to gain enough good things or if they are denied to us, we tend to feel that life is treating us unfairly. We protest that we deserve better. This very common, but actually deeply metaphysical, notion is expressed quite well by the transhumanist Nick Bostrom. Bostrom thinks it quite likely that we shall "in this century master technologies that will enable us to overcome many of our current biological limitations" and thus "get the opportunity to truly grow up and experience life as it should have been all along".[5] That life should have been much better than it has hitherto been for anybody at any time is an odd claim that makes sense only within a normative framework that provides for some kind of natural right to happiness. But, of course, there is no such right, or at least it is very difficult to see whereupon such a right should be based. The truth is that we are neither here to be happy nor, as Arthur Schopenhauer believed, to be unhappy (thus deserving all the suffering we have to endure during our lives). If, on the other hand, we do not believe in such a right, if we do not believe that we have deserved everything good that we've got (but not the bad!), and more, then everything good that actually does happen to us is experienced as a gift.

Third, a gift is not a loan. A loan has to be returned to the lender. A gift, on the other hand, has to be accepted and kept.[6] It must not be returned to the giver, and can only be returned at the risk of insulting them. That does not mean that a gift is entirely free in the sense that it does not put the recipient of the gift under any obligation. One has to take good care of the gifts one has received, cherish them, even if one does not like them very much. If a gift is given to you and you toss it in the bin, arguing that it is yours and you can do with what is yours whatever you like, then you have misunderstood the nature of the gift. Also, in many societies each gift requires a corresponding gift in return (Mauss 1990). Every gift creates an obligation, but it is a curious, informal kind of obligation, because just as you had no right to the gift in the first place, the giver has no right to receive something in return, not even gratitude.[7] To demand that the gift be reciprocated devalues the gift and in fact negates it by turning it into a business transaction.

Because the gift is given freely, it is (or should be) received with gratitude (despite there being no *right* to gratitude). In contrast, when we receive only what we deserve, or think we deserve, we do not feel any gratitude at all. If the gift is reciprocated (usually not immediately,[8] but after a considerable lapse of time, because immediate reciprocation would amount to a refusal of the gift) it again appears not as the fulfilment of an obligation, as something that had to be done, but as a free act of goodwill, so it may again elicit gratitude. So in this peculiar relation, when I give something to you and you give something to me, we can both be grateful to each other, which of course is not the case in a commercial transaction. When I enter a shop, hand over a certain amount of money to the shop attendant and receive some commodity from him in return, we may verbally thank each other, but in fact neither of us will feel particularly grateful to the other,[9] and because we don't, the transaction has created no particular social bond between us. Exchanging gifts, however, by inducing mutual gratitude, does create such a bond (Godbout 1998: 7).

The most remarkable aspect of the gift-specific obligation, which lifts it clearly above any commercial transaction, is that although the gift ought to be reciprocated, it need not necessarily be returned to the one who gave it. We do, for instance, spend lots of love, care, energy, time and money on our children, and on the whole give them much more than they will ever be willing or able to return. But if they do appreciate the gift, they may well try to give some of it back to their own children. Similarly, blood and organ donors, or people who give to charities, usually do not give because they have received anything from those (in most cases anonymous people) they are giving to. But in spite of this, they are frequently motivated by a sense of gratitude, a feeling that they have received plenty of good, without particularly deserving it (Titmuss 1970; Simmons *et al.* 1977). As a result, they want to give back some of what they have received. The psychoanalyst and child psychologist Melanie Klein, who believed that for the development of a healthy mind it was crucial to provide the infant with opportunities for enjoyment and thus constitute a sense of gratitude as early as possible, once remarked that gratitude "is closely bound up with generosity. Inner wealth derives from having assimilated the good object so that the individual becomes able to share its gifts with others. This makes it possible to introject a more friendly world" (Klein 1957: 19). Charity springs from gratitude, and not a gratitude that is directed to a particular person, but rather an unspecific gratitude that is directed towards the world in general. If, on the other hand, someone believes that everything they have is wholly their own doing, they will not have any reason to feel gratitude and, without gratitude, no reason to help others. Thus a lively appreciation of the giftedness of life and the ensuing sense of gratitude appear to be prerequisites to the kind of human bonding that transcends the casual relationships of mere economic exchange.[10] And if that appreciation is what humility means, then the latter is a virtue precisely because it is at the heart of all human solidarity. This is also recognized by Sandel himself:

> Here, then, is the connection between solidarity and gift-edness: A lively sense of the contingency of our gifts – an awareness that none of us is wholly responsible for his or her success – saves a meritocratic society from sliding into the smug assumption that success is the crown of virtue, that the rich are rich because they are more deserving than the poor.　　　　　　　　　　　　(Sandel 2007: 91)

Now it might be objected that the whole notion of the many good things in life that "are not wholly our own doing", and indeed of life itself,[11] as gifts tacitly presumes the existence of some kind of God. According to Arthur Caplan, the "metaphor of the gift makes no sense in the secular context such as Sandel proposes. Gifts require a giver but nature offers no likely suspects to occupy this role" (2009: 208). It stands to reason, or so it seems, that there can be no gift without a giver, that is, an agent to whose deliberate action one owes the good one has received. So who is it that has given us life, health, talents and powers? It is not really our parents because they merely initiated a process over which they had little, if any, control. Neither can it be nature, unless we think of it as a purposeful, quasi-divine agent. If we do not believe in some kind of God and hence in the existence of a divine giver, then it does not seem to make sense to speak of the goods we receive from no one in particular as gifts, except in a loose metaphorical sense, so as to express our feeling of appreciation for what we have received without our own doing. Perhaps we can, without making illicit assumptions, appreciate the natural goods as goods, but we cannot reasonably feel *grateful* for them without presupposing the existence of God. So is Sandel's conception of giftedness too religious to be taken seriously as an essential part of a secular philosophical argument? Sandel (2007: 93) himself denies this, and I think with good reason. Gratitude is *not* primarily an emotion that is directed towards a particular person. We can feel gratitude in various situations and for various things. We can be grateful for the love we have found, for being healthy, for our children and their being healthy, and for having a job we like to do (or, at times like this, having a job at all). We can be grateful for having a body with organs that allow us to see and hear, smell and taste, feel and be generally aware of the world around us. We can be grateful that we are still able to walk and that we have been able to walk in the first place. And if we are not, there are still innumerable other things for which we can be grateful, not the least of which is our being alive. In none of these cases are we grateful to anybody in particular, not even to God. In fact, we do not even have to believe there is a God. We may still be grateful. We may even be grateful for not believing in God. The popular (particularly in the USA) bumper-sticker slogan "Thank God I'm an atheist!", which is sometimes attributed to the eminent evolutionary biologist J. B. S.

Haldane, is on the surface a performative contradiction, but in truth only the paradoxical expression of a widespread sentiment of non-personal gratitude (as well as, of course, a political provocation). God functions here merely as a placeholder: a concession to the grammar, but not the essence, of gratitude. We are grateful without religious beliefs, simply because we know we have not *earned* any of this, and none of it was *due* to us. Instead, we know we have simply been lucky (and some of us feel lucky and hence grateful that we have not fallen for what Richard Dawkins (2006) recently called the "God delusion"). On the other hand, G. K. Chesterton may have had a point when he, citing Rossetti, remarked that "the worst moment for the atheist is when he is really thankful and has nobody to thank" (1923: 88). But even this is an acknowledgement that one *can* be thankful in the absence of anyone in particular to thank.[12]

In this vein, Robert Solomon (2002) argues for what he calls a naturalistic conception of gratitude. Solomon believes that the non-personal kind of gratitude that I have just described:

> is an extension of our more usual, interpersonal emotion. In this case it is the emotion and not the specificity of its object that ultimately determines its meaning. Whether or not there is sufficient personification of fate to warrant personal thanks, the recognition of fate in any sense implies that we are the beneficiaries of good fortune in a cruel universe. This should dictate gratitude, even if there is no one or nothing in particular to whom that gratitude is directed. (*Ibid.*: 104)

And he continues:

> It is also odd and unfortunate that we take the blessings of life for granted – or insist that we deserve them – then take special offense at the bad things in life, as if we could not possibly deserve those. ... Whether or not there is a God or there are gods to be thanked, however, seems not the issue to me. It is the importance and the significance of being thankful, to whomever or whatever, for life itself. ... We might say that one is grateful not only *for* one's life but *to* one's life – or rather to life – as well. (*Ibid.*: 105)

I agree mostly with Solomon's account. However, it seems to me that, by describing non-personal gratitude as an *extension* of inter-personal gratitude, he grants too much to those who insist that only the latter is gratitude *proper*. In fact, non-personal gratitude is much more common, and much more *basic*, than interpersonal gratitude. Of course, sometimes we are grateful to particular people, for what they have done for us. But that is rather the exception. And it certainly does not define our sense of gratitude. That is to say that this kind of situation is not where we have learned to feel grateful or how to feel grateful, nor what gratitude really means. We do not first experience gratitude in these interpersonal cases and then later transfer this feeling to situations where there is no one in particular to be grateful to. If we had never experienced the feeling of gratitude in relation to the gifts of life, we would not be able to feel it with respect to another person because we would not be able to appreciate what they have given us. It has been objected to me that children acquire the concept of gratitude by being taught to say "thank you". This may well be, but the *concept* of gratitude is not the issue; the feeling is, or the attitude that accompanies it. We do, of course, teach our children to say "thank you", but that is obviously not the same as teaching them actually to *be* grateful. Surely we can learn to say "thank you" when it is expected or appropriate without really meaning it. In order to *mean* it, that is to actually *feel* gratitude, we need to appreciate what is being given to us as an undeserved good. So how do we learn that what we get is not ours by right, that we could just as well have not received it, that, in other words, it is a gift? I am not sure if something like that can be taught at all. I suspect that either we have it in us to appreciate life and the good things in life as gifts or we do not. If we do, we shall feel grateful for what we have and what we receive no matter whether someone gives it to us or not. However, only if we do shall we be able to feel gratitude when someone does something for us that they did not have to do. There is no reason to believe that children first need to learn to say "thank you", that is, to participate in a social ritual, before they can acquire a sense of gratitude. As far as I can see, there is no causal or logical connection between the social act and the feeling. Of course, it is hard to imagine a community of humans who are grateful to the universe but not to their fellow humans when they receive a gift from them. I would not say it is logically impossible, but it is probably psychologically impossible. But this impossibility does not prove that interpersonal gratitude is more basic than what we may call cosmic gratitude. Only if a community were possible whose members felt truly grateful to each other, but never for being alive, or for being able to see the beauty of the world, or for anything else that was not given to them by someone, could the derivative nature of non-personal gratitude be shown. But although one may imagine such a community, I do not think that it is in reality possible.

Our gratitude for being alive is not merely a derivative or metaphorical kind of gratitude. It is perfectly real and, moreover, perfectly adequate. "Gratitude recognizes the fact that we are not, in fact, the authors of our own destiny, that we owe our good fortune to others and, perhaps, to luck" (*ibid.*: 105–6). In other words, gratitude recognizes the giftedness of life.

In "La Begueule", a little-known poem from 1772, Voltaire approvingly cites one "Italian sage" who claimed that "the better is the enemy of the good". Ironically, this quote is surprisingly often taken out of context and misunderstood as a call for constant improvement. It is taken to mean that nothing is so good that it cannot be improved upon. The good is only just good enough and, in the face of the better, not good at all: not worth preserving. The better is the enemy of the good in the same sense as the good is the enemy of the bad. However, this is not at all what Voltaire intended to say. Although he acknowledges that there is room for improvement with respect to the goodness of our hearts, our talents and our knowledge, he advises caution: let us not pursue pipe dreams, he says, for happy is he "who stays at his place and guards what he has got" (*vivre à sa place, et garder ce qu'il a*), thereby echoing his anti-Leibnizian hero Candide's final insight that we *must take care of our garden* (Voltaire [1759] 2007: ch. 30). To guard what one has is the practical appreciation of giftedness. (Also to cultivate it, of course, but to cultivate something is not the same as overcoming it and leaving it behind.) The worth of what has been given to us is here acknowledged as an absolute value in the Kantian sense, that is, a value that allows for no comparison. It is not good merely in the absence of something better or in comparison with what is worse. Rather, it is good in itself, absolutely. The better is the enemy of the good in the sense that by confronting the good with the "better", the good changes its appearance and re-emerges as the "worse". When we focus on the better that we might achieve, we tend to forget what is good about what we already have. It is, in other words, an act of conceptual devaluation, which in turn justifies the demand for improvement. Optimism regarding the future has as its flipside pessimism regarding the present. This pessimism may or may not be justified. It all depends on whether we set our hopes on the future because the present actually is found deficient, or we judge it deficient merely because we envisage a (largely imaginary) future that is (in some unspecified sense) better. The way calls for human enhancement are framed often suggests the latter. Bostrom precedes his article "Why I Want to be a Posthuman when I Grow Up" (2008) with a quote from Bishop Berkeley:

> I am apt to think, if we knew what it was to be an angel for one hour, we should return to this world, though it were to sit on the brightest throne in it, with vastly more loathing and reluctance than we would now descend into a loathsome dungeon or sepulchre.
>
> (Berkeley, quoted in Bostrom 2008: 107)

This is to say that this world, no matter how rich and beautiful it may appear to us, lacks all beauty for the angels and is regarded by them only with loathing, and if we could only see what they see we would feel about it exactly as they do. But we do not even have to have angel eyes ourselves to have our view of the world changed. The mere belief that an angelic perspective on the world is possible already has the effect of diminishing our appreciation of the goods that this world has to offer. Bostrom goes on to utilize this effect in the course of his argument for radical enhancement when he imagines what our posthuman future will be like:

> You have just celebrated your 170th birthday and you feel stronger than ever. Each day is a joy. You have invented entirely new art forms, which exploit the new kinds of cognitive capacities and sensibilities you have developed. You still listen to music – music that is to Mozart what Mozart is to bad Muzak. (2008: 112)

So that is what we can look forward to once we have sufficiently enhanced ourselves: that we will no longer be able to appreciate great art as we know it. Of course, what we consider great art today will be recognized as not being great at all. In the face of the art we are going to create, Mozart's music will appear dull, and so will, say, da Vinci's paintings and Shakespeare's plays. In fact, everything that excites, fascinates and enraptures us today will no longer be of any interest to us whatsoever. But can we really believe that what makes Mozart great is entirely comparative, that there is nothing of intrinsic value in his music? Is the only reason we find greatness in some artworks that at present we have nothing better? Not only do I find this highly implausible, but it also, by rendering all values relative, contravenes the rationale of the whole human-enhancement project. For if the things that we regard as good today are only good so long as there is nothing better, if there is nothing of absolute value, then the same holds true for what we shall regard good in our posthuman future, and then there is actually no good reason why we should swap our present condition for a posthuman one, unless, of course, we shall, as Bostrom suggests, feel vastly more joy at living our lives than we do now. But shall we really? Why should we if we cannot seem to find enough joy in our present state of being? Why should we be satisfied then if we are not satisfied now? There will, after all, always be the possibility of something being even better than what we have. The u

An appreciation of the giftedness of life includes an appreciation of what is good in what we have, and good not in a relative but in an absolute sense. As good in this sense we may regard our own existence, talents and abilities, but also what we find in our natural and human environment: the beauty of nature, the music and books we can enjoy, and much more. Without an appreciation of all this, we cannot be truly happy,[13] because happiness needs to be grounded in some sense of objective good, of doing things that are truly worth our while. What Sandel calls the drive to mastery, whose ultimate end is nothing less than complete control over nature, is an attitude that denies absolute value to all things including all human achievements. Whatever we may want to point out as good and hence worth preserving, the proponent of radical human enhancement will always feel inclined to reply that it is not nearly good enough: "That's nothing, we can do better than that" seems to be his general attitude to life. But can we really? And even if we can, is it good for us to look at the world with this kind of disparaging attitude, that is, to regard all Mozart as potential muzak?

According to Jacques Godbout, the "transformation of a stranger into a familiar is what the gift is all about" (1998: 30). This is true not only with respect to social relations, but also, I dare say, with respect to our relation to the world as such, to the universe as a whole. Seeing the good in what we have, that is, appreciating the giftedness of life, helps us feel at home in the world. It creates a bond and connects us to the rest of the world, which then no longer appears hostile and forbidding: an alien place that may perhaps be best described as enemy territory.[14] The drive to mastery and the denial of giftedness affirm this enmity. They reinforce an almost Manichaean point of view, according to which it is either "us" (the Promethean, nature-defying, boundary-transgressing, star-reaching human) or "them" (nature as the evil power that prevents us from rising to the stars where we belong). Taking a stance against nature becomes a matter of survival and of self-affirmation. It is a matter of life and death: of who is going to win and who is going to lose. From that perspective, the physical world is out there to be subjugated and vanquished or else be allowed to subjugate and vanquish us. We are not part of it, and it will eventually destroy us, unless we rebel against nature's tyranny, whose foremost expression is the inevitability of death (vividly portrayed in Bostrom's "Fable of the Dragon Tyrant" [2005b]). However, as Bryan Appleyard has rightly pointed out, it "is the fact of loneliness, not death, that is most shocking about our time on earth. By loneliness I mean here the feeling of being disconnected, of having no home" (2007: 123). Cultivating a feeling of giftedness and not giving in to the drive to mastery is a remedy to that kind of cosmic loneliness. It reconciles us even to our own mortality by allowing us to identify with the course of nature and thus, as it were, enlarging the self. It creates the same "feeling of unity" that Mill (1998: ch. 3, §10) hoped would one day make it as natural for us to care for our fellow beings as it is now natural to us to care for ourselves. To regard one's life as a gift means to regard it as something precious and at the same time something that, precisely because it is so precious, we have a duty to pass on. "We owe God a death", says the brave soldier Feeble in Shakespeare's *Henry IV* (part 2, act 3, scene 2), thereby emphasizing not the worthlessness of human life, but rather the obligation that comes with the reception of a life. And part of that obligation is that we do not cling too fiercely to it: that we give up our lives when we consider this necessary in order to secure a greater good in the conviction that our own existence is not all that matters. If we regard life as a gift, we find ourselves desiring to give something in return. We feel that we have an obligation to fulfil, which we do best by eventually making room for new people to whom we pass on the gift of life. Dying, thus understood, is an act of sharing – of sharing the good that is being alive, or, as Bill McKibben puts it, "simply one more transaction in an endless gift economy" (2003: 165). By striving for immortality (which takes the drive to mastery to its logical conclusion), we, on the other hand, conspire to keep the world for ourselves. We deny the gift and hence do not feel any obligation to reciprocate. All deals are off. The only thing that ultimately matters is our own existence. As Appleyard observes, to "the immortalists, a future in which they do not exist has become a personal affront" (2007: 30). The difference between those who wish to eradicate death, or at least get rid of ageing and the inevitability of death (such as Kurzweil [2005], de Grey [2007] or Harris [2007]) and those who have serious doubts about the wisdom of that specific kind of enhancement (such as Kass [2003, 2004]), Fukuyama [2002: 57–71] or Sandel himself) is mainly that the former regard life as such a good thing that they want to keep it for themselves for as long as possible, whereas the latter regard it as such a good thing that they want others to be able to enjoy it too. In other words, what separates them is mainly a different outlook on life and the role we play in it.

However, it may be objected that the indefinite extension of human lifespan through biomedical advances is only one of many different forms of enhancement that are currently actively pursued or envisaged. And most of them do not seem to be sought for selfish reasons at all. Advocates of radical human enhancement often emphasize that we have a moral obligation to develop and use enhancement technologies in order to increase the happiness or the flourishing of future generations (Savulescu 2001; Harris 2007). In other words, it is other (in many cases not even yet existing) people who are most likely to benefit from the proposed scientific endeavours. So selfishness does not seem to be the issue. Accordingly, Kamm (2009) has argued that the "desire for mastery", contrary to what Sandel seems to believe, does not normally motivate those promoting human enhancement. And even in those few cases where a researcher really was motivated by such a drive to mastery, this would not render the enhancement itself morally impermissible. The motive a person has for their action may be taken into account when it comes to assessing their character but it cannot make the action itself wrong. By seeking mastery, we may perhaps justly be regarded as a "bad type of people" (*ibid.*: 97), but what we *do* may still be considered proper and good. However, it seems to me that Kamm misunderstands the point of Sandel's argument. Similar to Habermas in his *The Future of Human Nature*, Sandel is in fact not trying to answer the question whether or not it is morally *permissible* to pursue human enhancement. Rather, he questions whether it really is a *good idea* to do so, whether it will do us any good, and whether we will not lose far more than we would gain. He is not saying that it is *immoral* to seek enhancement, but rather that it is *unwise*. Neither is he claiming that by giving in to the "drive to mastery" we become a "bad type of people". Again, it is not so much a question of being good or bad in the moral sense, but rather of what makes a good human life. By losing the sense of giftedness we do not become bad: we become impoverished;[15] we lose something that is important, perhaps even essential for a good human life.[16] For that, the actual motives people have for promoting and seeking human enhancement are largely irrelevant. I need not be motivated by a drive to mastery in order to fall victim to it. A particular kind of action can be an expression of the drive to mastery without being motivated by it. When Sandel talks about the drive to mastery he is not concerned with a particular vice that befalls individuals, but rather a "habit of mind and way of being" that pervades the beliefs and practices of a community, society or culture (Sandel 2007: 96). Evidently, Kamm does not sufficiently appreciate the difference. Responding to Sandel's claim that without a vivid sense of giftedness human solidarity would all but break down, she comes up with a very practical and seemingly sensible solution: "if having the option to enhance leads many people to improve themselves or others, there will be fewer instances of people who are badly off, hence fewer who require the assistance of others" (2009: 125–6) In other words, there will no longer be any need for solidarity, and hence for an appreciation of giftedness. But for Sandel, solidarity is not a means but an end. It is part of what makes human life worth living.[17] Without solidarity we would glide into a monadic existence: independent perhaps, completely autonomous perhaps, but also very lonely. The "feeling of unity" that Mill valued so highly would be gone.

However, Buchanan has argued that even in a "world replete with biomedical enhancements" (2008: 25) there would still be plenty of opportunities for sensing giftedness. A lack of control, he believes, is an ineradicable part of the human condition, which not "even the most extreme biomedical enhancements" are likely to conquer. Thus, contrary to what Sandel seems to think, there is no danger that we will ever have to face a "giftedness shortage" (*ibid.*: 26). Yet first of all, it is by no means certain that a lack of control is ineradicable. Many proponents of human enhancement explicitly seek to expand the extent of human control (with the ultimate goal of gaining complete control over nature) and seem to be convinced that this is really possible. If they are wrong, then one of the major reasons for seeking human enhancement has disappeared. And second, the question is not really whether there will still be opportunities to experience giftedness, but rather whether our sense of giftedness will suffer or is already suffering by our trust in the happiness-maximizing or control-maximizing powers of enhancement technologies. The question is whether the application of such technologies will make us less *inclined* to appreciate giftedness.

In his latest book, Anthony Appiah remarks that "what we *are* matters for human flourishing as well as what we *do*" (2008: 64). Sandel's emphasis on giftedness is an attempt to remind us that what we do shapes what we are, and vice versa, and that philosophical ethics, instead of seeking solutions to moral or practical conundrums, should pay more attention to questions of existence (*ibid.*: 198). Virtue, I said earlier, is what Sandel's whole argument seems to be about: but virtue understood in an Aristotelian sense as a precondition of the good life. A lively appreciation of giftedness may well be such a precondition.

11

CONCLUDING REMARKS

What do we want in man, asked Franz Boas a hundred years ago: physical excellence, mental ability, creative power or artistic genius? We need to make a decision here, thought Boas, if we want to create better humans, because we cannot have it all. And right he was. There are so many different ideals between which we would have to choose if we wanted to enhance the human, so many different conceptions of what it means to be human, and what it means to be a good human and a better human, so many different goals to pursue, so many different lives to live, none of which is in itself better than any of the others, more humanlike, more desirable, more worth pursuing. It all depends on what we want, and we do not all want the same. Even if we did, what we wanted might not be consistent, for instance not to die *and* not to live forever. Each step we take in the project of human enhancement, we take in a certain direction. There is more than one path to follow, and if we follow one we cannot follow another. Each step, unless it is entirely haphazard (which it never really is), embodies and reinforces particular value decisions, even though we may not always be conscious of them.

That does not necessarily mean that we should not take any such step. We are not perfect, after all. It does mean, however, that we need to think very carefully where we want to go and what exactly we want to achieve, and if we do that we might, just might, come to the conclusion that things are not so bad right now as they may seem. It is all well and good to want to make the world a better place, even if the means chosen to accomplish that goal is the creation of better humans, but this is easier said than done. First we need to figure out, and agree on, what makes this world, or *a* world, a good place, and a human a good human. The notion of the "good", and *ipso facto* the "better", is meaningless and cannot give direction to our striving if we are unable to connect it with something concrete, for instance a world in which everyone is incredibly happy (or at least more people than now, or for longer periods of time, or simply happier than people currently tend to be), or a world in which people have finally understood everything that is to be understood, in which they have solved the mysteries of the universe (or at least substantially more of those mysteries), or a world in which people live in peace and harmony with each other (or are at least considerably less inclined to hurt and kill each other).

Yet such a connection, as G. E. Moore pointed out a long time ago, is never analytical and thus always precarious; that is, the good and the better can in principle always be understood as something different entirely. In other words, it is never *obvious* and never uncontentious what the better is. You can, of course, always *define* the better with respect to a particular situation: simply start with the premise that such and such *is* the better. If we assume that a longer life is, all other things being equal, a better life, so that the longer we live the better it is, we can easily and correctly infer that any intervention that increases average human lifespan is an improvement and as such desirable. But it immediately becomes difficult when we ask ourselves *why* we should make that assumption. We cannot simply infer from the fact that life is usually perceived as good that having more of it (in terms of its duration) is also good (or would be perceived as such). So we need to ask in what way a longer life would be a better life. And for that it is certainly useful to think about what makes *this* life, the life that we know, with its 80-plus years, good.

Also, in actual fact things are never equal. Instead, if you change one thing you will also change other things, and you might not always like those other things. I am not saying that we should never try to change anything. My point is merely that what is better in one respect may not be better in other respects and, more generally, that in order to meaningfully say that it *is* better you need to specify the respect in *which* it is better. If you do that, that is, if you define the context of the evaluation, then "making something better", even if that something is a human person, can without doubt have a fairly clear meaning. If we believe that, say, soldiers who were able to stay awake and alert for forty-eight hours at a stretch would be better soldiers, then we have a clearly specified context, in which the word "better" has acquired a specific meaning, so that we can truthfully say that a cognitive enhancement drug that enables them to accomplish that feat has made them better. But by calling this an enhancement, and especially a human enhancement, we strongly suggest that this is somehow a good thing in itself, without further qualification, as opposed to being merely instrumentally good, that is, in relation to a certain goal, which in itself, within the boundaries of that context, is neutral, neither good nor bad, although it can then be seen as either good *or* bad in relation to *other* purposes. In the case of the super-alert soldier, knowing that super-alertness is (in the usual public understanding of the word, namely as some kind of *improvement*) an enhancement with respect to the goal of super-alertness, does not tell us anything about the desirability of super-alertness in soldiers beyond the context that is being defined by that goal. We do not even know whether super-alertness makes better soldiers, because in order to do so we would first have to reflect on the role and purpose of soldiers and which skills and capacities we think a good soldier should ideally have. And even if we do that and come to the conclusion that super-alertness is a good quality in soldiers, so that the more super-alert they are the better soldiers they are, or the better they are as soldiers, we still have not asked, let alone answered, the much more important question whether we want soldiers to be better in that way; whether having better soldiers is good for us; or for whom it is good, and when and where, and to what purpose; and finally whether someone who has become a good soldier, or a super-alert one, has also, for this reason, become a better human.

The problem with human enhancement is not so much that it is morally wrong or bad. It is neither, although particular interventions designed to enhance certain human capacities may well be morally wrong or morally dubious, while others may be morally permissible, or perhaps even morally obligatory. The main problem with the project is not that human enhancement is morally wrong, but rather that we lack any clear idea of what it would actually consist in without being aware of that lack. There is no such thing as human enhancement, understood as the enhancement of the human as a human. People often speak as if they knew exactly what better humans would be like, and they seldom hesitate to file certain changes in the human constitution as instances of human enhancement. But in a logical sense, human enhancement does not exist. All we ever get is particular roles and purposes, in respect to which certain things, actions and developments are good, while others are bad. Thus there can certainly be cognitive enhancements of various kinds, all of which might be found useful for the execution of some task or other. In the real world this usually means that the enhancement of those capacities boosts performance and thus enhances production, but surely in order to judge this a good thing on the whole, we would need to know what exactly is being produced and to what purpose. And while it might be beneficial for the individual to be more "competitive" in a competitive society, it does not follow that competition as such (i.e. the fact that we find ourselves living in a competitive society, which forces us to be competitive too) is beneficial for us, either as individuals or as a society, or as a human community.

I do not think that intelligence or, more generally, the ability (or more precisely, abilities) to solve certain cognitive tasks (better than others) is in itself intrinsically valuable. Its value seems rather instrumental. It is good for certain purposes, but not for all. Thus I do not really believe that there really are (cognitive) general or all-purpose means. There is nothing that is good for *all* purposes. In general, the value of instrumental rationality is highly overrated, because ultimately it does not contribute much to personal happiness. Perhaps certain styles of thinking do, but so far not even the existence of such different styles of thinking (which cannot all be enhanced at the same time) has been properly acknowledged in the debate. There is a tendency to assume that ultimately there is only one way to make things better, which is independent of our beliefs, needs, desires, ends and values. Thus it is assumed that there is such a thing as *the* moral human. Yet there are in fact different, mutually incompatible aspects to morality, different, incompatible moral frameworks, and an endless variety of situations that demand a tailored response, a response that cannot be predicted. Judgement is

always needed, and there is no way to determine once and for all, ⟨
and in advance, what the right judgement, say for all rational beings,
is going to be. We cannot even say that morality itself is *always*
good. Was Gauguin wrong to leave his family behind to pursue his
artistic ideals? From a moral point of view (or *some* moral point of
view) he probably was, but there might be other points of view that
are also to be considered and that might take precedence here. We
simply do not know. Worse, we *cannot* know because there is no
clear general answer, one that is independent of the situation and
the persons involved.

For similar reasons we cannot, or should not, think of the better
human as the (in a subjective sense of the word) *happy* human. It is
not very likely that our lives will ever be "wonderful beyond imagination", whatever that means, but again, even if they will be one day,
in the sense that all worries and all suffering will have vanished from
human experience, it is not obvious that this would be good for us.
For one thing, what is wonderful for you might not be wonderful for
me, and for another, not all suffering is bad, perhaps not even intrinsically, but certainly not in the context of a full human life. Some
degree of suffering, or at least the possibility of suffering, is certainly
necessary in order to preserve certain things that are essential to
what we commonly regard as a good life, such as human love and
care for things and people. Also, sometimes happiness would simply
not be appropriate, such as when the situation requires or invites
other emotional responses. As there is often no general answer to
the question what we should do in a certain situation, neither is
there a general answer to the question how we should feel: or, for
that matter, how long we should live. Death, as we have seen, is not
necessarily an evil, certainly not for society or the human community as a whole, and the desire for perpetual youth might ultimately
be inconsistent. We may still relish the prospect of living a little
longer, or of not visibly ageing any more, or at any rate not so fast,
but there is always a price to be paid. The long-living human is not
necessarily a better human, and a world in which humans generally
live longer is not necessarily a better place. Ultimately it all depends
on what we want and value most, and that is also dependent on
what it means to be human. But what it means to be human is what
it means for *us*. *We* decide what it means to be human or, rather,
since this is not really a conscious decision, we find ourselves having

certain intuitions about it, which then in turn guides our decision-making about, among other things, so-called human-enhancement techniques. Human nature in a relevant sense, that is, in a sense that we can find normatively significant, is a mythological construct (Hauskeller 2009), nothing more, designed to help us make sense of the world and our place in it. Our answer to the question who we want to be (or what "we want in man") largely depends on how we answer the question who we are (or what man is), that is, how we think of ourselves. Do we think of ourselves more as an individual, in our essence disconnected from all other individuals, or more as part of a community, which, functioning as a larger self, joins us to the other parts? Only if we believe the former can we conceive of the death of the individual (or rather, for me, *my* death, and for you, *your* death) as the "greatest evil". Do we think of ourselves as essentially minds that are only accidentally connected to a body, or rather as fully embodied beings whose existence cannot be separated from the living, breathing and very human body that we are all intimately familiar with? Only if we believe that the organic body made of flesh and blood is at best unnecessary, and at worst a serious obstacle to human emancipation, can we be convinced that human salvation lies in the complete disembodiment and "digital immortality" that is promised by utopian technologies such as mind-uploading. Do we think of ourselves as being blessed simply because we are alive and can enjoy so many good things, without having done anything special to deserve them or, rather, as grossly neglected and awfully mistreated by a hostile and unforgiving nature that could have done so much better? Only if we feel that we have been treated unfairly by the world (and possibly its creator) can we believe that we are *entitled* to posthuman bliss.

There is, in fact, a lot of faith being expressed in the enhancement debate, on both sides. Perhaps too much faith. Sure enough, there is the bioconservative faith in the essential goodness and rightness of the present human condition (not perfect perhaps, but the best of all possible worlds), but there is also the corresponding faith shared by those who urge us to follow the route of human enhancement, namely faith in the power of science and technology to heal, to make good what nature has messed up, and to finally take us where we have always meant to be. It is basically the faith that it will all be fine in the end if we just do the right thing now. The world will be a better place and we shall be truly human. Me, I am sceptical about such claims and hopes. Always the pessimist, I guess. Or perhaps rather the optimist, I don't know. Eventually we shall see how it all turns out, this giant project of being, becoming and staying human. In the meantime, let us live our lives, and live them now and as best as we can.

NOTES

1. INTRODUCTION

1. Gregory Stock approvingly quotes these words by Watson in his book *Redesigning Humans* (2002: 12). According to Stock, Watson said this at the Engineering the Human Germline symposium, UCLA, 20 March 1998.

2. The term "enhancement" can, of course, be understood in a more neutral way that would allow us to call a particular change, through which something is added to an entity or a capacity, an *enhancement* without thereby implying that it necessarily constitutes an *improvement*. That we conceptually distinguish enhancement and improvement was strongly suggested by, for instance, Ruth Chadwick, who argued that by conflating those two concepts we would "prejudge the issue of acceptability and desirability" (2008: 31). This is true, of course, but there are two reasons why I choose not to follow Chadwick's suggestion and to adopt her "additionality view" of enhancement. First, it does not make much difference whether we ask ourselves whether a proposed change that is discussed as an enhancement really *is* an enhancement or whether that enhancement is really desirable. In both cases we still have to answer the difficult and crucial question of how and on what grounds we should decide whether the change is or is not good or desirable. My second reason for not following Chadwick is simply that most people, when they call something an enhancement, *do* in fact imply that it constitutes an improvement. It is what most people mean when they speak about enhancement, and particularly *human* enhancement.

3. MAKING BETTER HUMANS BETTER

1. Cf. "We do not deny that cognitive enhancement is indispensable for moral enhancement. It could assist us in finding out what the moral truth is and which moral beliefs are justified" (Persson & Savulescu 2008: 173).
2. Cf. "Would those made or engineered to be born smart be within their rights to deprive the rest of us of our rights, presumably with humanitarian intent? In a word: yes" (Wikler 2009: 354).
3. Cf. "There's likely to be an enduring and substantial barrier between people whose intellects have been radically enhanced and people with unenhanced intellects. It's unlikely to be as temporary or as permeable as the barriers racism and religion occasionally create. I suspect that, should they be positively disposed toward us, beings whose intellects radically exceed our own will be more disposed to view us as pets than as potential mates" (Agar 2010: 31). However, Nicholas Agar believes that posthumans are in fact more likely to be not so disposed: "There's a good chance that the dominant moral code of human–posthuman societies will be human-unfriendly" (*ibid.*).
4. Allen Buchanan (2009) has argued that radically enhanced posthumans could not have a higher moral status than humans since moral status is a threshold concept that does not allow for grades. Since human basic rights are person rights and humans will always be persons just like posthumans, they will have the same moral status and the same basic rights. However, posthumans may still be justified to grant themselves more participation rights than humans, and they may also *mistakenly* believe that they have a higher moral status.
5. This is what Savulescu suggests: "But if the non-human life forms are greatly superior in the characteristics which define human persons, like the difference between us and Neanderthal man, it may be that we should care more for them than we do for humans. We might have reason to save or create such vastly superior lives, rather than continue the human line" (2009: 244).
6. So even if posthumans did not feel any solidarity with each other and in that sense were less moral than ordinary humans tend to be, this might be considered unproblematic since solidarity would no longer be needed. This is the position that Frances Kamm seems to take when she criticizes Michael Sandel for claiming that a sense of giftedness is needed to sustain human solidarity: "if having the option to enhance leads many people to improve themselves or others, there will be fewer instances of people who are badly off, hence fewer who require the assistance of others" (Kamm 2009: 125). However, it is not clear at all whether human solidarity really is a good thing simply because, being vulnerable, we need it, or, rather, that solidarity is *intrinsically* good in the sense that it is better for humans to be both vulnerable and feel solidarity with each other, rather than suffer the absence of both.
7. Other, more indirect methods of moral enhancement relying on modern (and in many cases not yet available) technology have been envisaged, such as the use of artificial agents with a "global conscience" to control the

behaviour of individuals (Bibel 2004: 71) or the use of an enhanced ability to predict behaviour, which would allow us (whom?) to interdict undesirable behaviour before it occurs (Roco & Bainbridge 2003: 160).

8. The ultimatum game is played with two players, one of whom has to divide a sum of money or an amount of other things of value or interest to the players, while the other can accept or reject the proposal. If the second player rejects the first player's proposal, both end up with nothing, so the first player has to decide how much (or how little) he has to offer the second player to make them accept the offer.

9. In their most recent writings on the topic, Persson and Savulescu (2011c) seem to be inclined to accept the utilitarian view, largely because they have shifted their attention away from the threat of terrorism to climate change and world poverty and the reluctance or inability of people to agree on effective measures to fight them.

10. According to Sunstein (2007: 46), the average American values the life of an American at 2,000 times more than that of a non-American. If that is true, is the average American then prosocial at the personal level or at the group level?

11. The first law of robotics: "A robot may not injure a human being or, through inaction, allow a human being to come to harm".

12. Or from a lack of judgement and sheer stupidity, in which case cognitive enhancement might be just as urgent, and perhaps more, than moral enhancement. Cf. Fenton (2010); Harris (2010).

4. FEELING BETTER

1. "Wer die Schönheit angeschaut mit Augen/Ist dem Tode schon anheimgegeben" (August von Platen, "Tristan").

5. BECOMING TRULY HUMAN

1. This is not to say that everything that restricts our *individual* autonomy is referred to as nature. Other people are not normally perceived as agents of nature, even though they obviously do restrict our autonomy. So when we speak of nature as a threat to autonomy we tend to regard humanity as a unified whole whose agency is limited by non-human (or perhaps non-rational) forces.

2. I don't mean to say that we are all born with a fully developed self. The self certainly does develop over time, and how it develops may very well be influenced by the decisions we make. However, we do not normally consciously decide to become a certain person and, when we do, we do so because we already *are* a certain person (in this case one that has a strong desire to develop into a different person).

3. From Nick Bostrom's home page, www.nickbostrom.com.

4. The declared transhumanist Nick Bostrom professes the same sentiment:

"I want to make the world a better place" (http://www.nickbostrom.com/ papers/2index.html).

5. This list of human activities is, of course, not exhaustive. There are many others more, and perhaps some of those mentioned will not be considered human *propria* at all. It is also clear that we can imagine a human being that never laughs and cries, or one that never has sex and never desires to. But we may still want to claim that it is typical for humans to laugh and cry and have sex, and a human life from which these things are missing is deficient in that respect and not a fully human life. In this sense these activities *define* our human existence. They give a particular shape to it.

6. Analogous to Kant's "self-caused immaturity", which Bostrom (2005c) cites.

7. It may well be that Pico had mainly the moral progress of mankind in mind. However, his myth of origin still constructs an anthropology that lends itself to the transhumanist agenda of unlimited self-creation.

6. LIVING LONGER

1. It has, for instance, been shown that the ageing process, and particularly the *rate* at which an organism ages, is regulated by specific genes, which can then be manipulated in order to increase average lifespan (see Guarente & Kenyon 2000; Hekimi & Guarente 2003). For a comprehensive summary of all scientific developments that raise hopes for eliminating ageing, see de Grey & Rae (2007).

2. Nick Bostrom and Toby Ord (2006) suggested an alternative psychological explanation, the "status quo bias", which is the irrational preference that things stay as they are despite the fact that we cannot give a good reason why the present state of affairs should be regarded as optimal. According to Bostrom and Ord, this bias is the main reason why some people oppose radical human enhancement (including radical life extension).

3. This claim has been ably defended by Burley (2006).

4. It has been argued that it is not the dead that are being harmed through death but the living. Geoffrey Scarre makes the point that it is the shortness of human life that is bad, not death itself: "shorter-lived people really are worse off than longer-lived people *while they are still alive*" (1997: 273). But Scarre is mistaken when he claims that "short lives ... have actual, living subjects" (*ibid.*: 279), because a life cannot be short before it ends. It is death that makes it short, so only once I am dead can I be said to have had a short life. Hence the shortness of life cannot be an evil for the living.

5. That is why arguments that focus on the value that life and continuing to live has for the living do nothing to invalidate the Epicurean conclusion that death is no evil for us. Kai Draper (1999), for instance, argues that we have good reason to be sad and disappointed to see our lives end when we could reasonably have expected to live longer and reap the benefits that would have come. Yet the disappointment is merely an expression of what we knew all along, namely that normally life is a good for us and we do not want to die.

6. Although it may be a *contingent* fact that there is limited space for people to live in, it is a fact nonetheless. So I have *in fact* benefited from the death of others, just as others will *in fact* benefit from my death. And even if that were to change, so that the existence of others would no longer depend on my death, and my existence would no longer depend on the death of others, that would still not make the death of others bad for us. It would simply be not good (i.e. positively beneficial).

7. This point is also emphasized by Kass (2004: 310–11).

8. The premature death of the young can be seen as tragic, not because death is an evil for them, but because in a young person life is still conspicuously present as the great good that it no doubt is. And when the young die we deplore the loss of this good. Thomas Nagel (1970) has argued that it is that loss, rather than the state of being dead, that makes death an evil. But his argument is not convincing because a thing can be good without its absence being bad. When I, for instance, enjoy a trip to the seaside and appreciate it as a good, it cannot be inferred that it would have been bad for me if I had decided to stay at home and catch up with my reading instead. From the fact that a particular condition (like that of being alive) is good for us, nothing follows regarding the goodness or badness of alternative conditions (such as being dead). Moreover, it is not clear why the *loss* of something good should be *in itself* (that is, in the absence of any distress that this loss may cause) worse than not having it in the first place. In other words, why should *losing* one's life be worse than not having been born at all? See on this point Brueckner & Fischer (1986: 226–7).

9. The objection is expressly directed to Williams (and Walter Glannon) in Harris (2002: 289).

10. As Ray Kurzweil (1999) argues with reference to Moore's Law.

11. While it may be true that, as Larry S. Temkin remarks, "Some people bore easily, and others do not" (2008: 203), it is not very likely that this would make much difference *sub specie aeternitate*.

12. For one such attempt see Jonas (1992): "The ever-renewed beginning, which can only be had at the price of ever-repeated ending, is mankind's safeguard against lapsing into boredom and routine, its chance of retaining the spontaneity of life" (*ibid.*: 39).

13. A similar point was made by David Gems (2003: 36).

14. Note that it is of course possible for me to divide my time and pursue both philosophy and music (if they are both equally important to me), but if I can do that then I will not need an extra life to do so.

15. Glannon has argued that "a substantial increase in longevity would be undesirable because it would undermine the psychological grounds for identity and prudential concern about the distant future" (2002: 268). I agree with Glannon's general assumption that our interest in the future depends on the extent to which we can expect to persist "through time *as the same person*" (*ibid.*: 277). However, whether a life *without* occasional memory erasures would really destroy personal identity over time, we can only know once we have tried it. Surely the question whether or not personal identity in the form of "psychological connectedness", which Glannon believes to consist

in the holding of "particular direct links between mental states, such as the persistence of beliefs and desires, the connection between an intention and the later act in which it is carried out, and the connection between the experience of an event and one's memory of it" (*ibid.*: 270), will be compromised, is an empirical and not a philosophical one.

7. GOING CYBER

1. Interestingly, the author of this web article calls himself "Adam Kadmon", which is a term used in the Kabbalah for the "primal man".

10. BEING AT HOME IN THE WORLD

1. This is, of course, an idealization of what genetic engineering really allows us to do: when I say that *we* shall be able to choose what *we* are, I deliberately ignore, in unison with many proponents of human enhancement, the differences between individuals, and treat humanity as if it were a single subject that enhances *itself*. In fact, in most cases it will be *some* of us who shall choose what *others* are going to be, which, due to the ensuing inequality between those who make the decisions and those who have to bear the consequences, poses ethical problems of a different kind, which I am not going to discuss here. Cf. Habermas (2003).
2. See for instance A. David Kline (2007), which argues that an appreciation of giftedness is morally only relevant with respect to specific-purpose enhancements because these are "more likely to have unintended consequences that are unwelcomed by the child" (*ibid.*: 21). The consequences for the child, however, are not what Sandel is worried about.
3. Norvin Richards (1988) discusses yet another common understanding of what it means to be humble, namely "to have a low estimate of oneself". Since it is not clear how this can be a virtue, Richards proposes that humility instead be understood as the ability to resist pressures and temptations "to think too much of onself". This revised understanding is roughly in line with Sandel's own understanding, but less specific with respect to the *reason* why the humble does not think too much of himself.
4. Precisely for this reason, the Canadian actor Michael J. Fox, who suffers from Parkinson's disease, describes his apparent misfortune as a "gift" in his memoir *Lucky Man*. "Despite appearances," he writes, "this disease has unquestionably directed me toward what is right and good" (Fox 2002: 5). Similarly, the American writer Flannery O'Connor came to see the early death of her beloved father as an expression of God's grace, "like a bullet in the side" (Gooch 2009).
5. Nick Bostrom's homepage (www.nickbostrom.com), accessed October 2007, but since then changed.
6. Admittedly, there is the increasingly popular practice of "regifting", which involves giving away as gifts to third parties things that one has received as

a gift oneself. The reason why this appears acceptable, however, is that the regifting usually takes place in a charity context, where the real or alleged purpose is to benefit those who are in more need (of the gift) than oneself.

7. Cf. Lyons (1969). Jacques Derrida (1991), in a deliberately common-sense-defying analysis of the notion of the gift, criticizes Mauss for linking the gift to exchange and thus subjecting it to economic reason. According to Derrida, any obligation, and any reciprocation, destroys or "annuls" the gift. In fact, the gift as a gift is already annulled when it is perceived *as* a gift by either the giver or the receiver. While this requirement, which is meant to preserve the absolute freedom of the gift, neglects both the fact that there is neither a right to the gift, nor to any kind of counter-gift, and that the ultimate end of the gift is the creation of a community, it has the advantage of cutting off the gift from the agent and thus allowing for gifts that have not been given by anyone (as, in Derrida's strongly Heideggerian reading, being and time).

8. The exchange of gifts at Christmas is a remarkable exception.

9. There are exceptions, of course. The owner of a small local shop may feel grateful to his customers for continuing to buy at his shop and not at the new superstore nearby, and the customers may feel grateful to the shop owner for providing a valuable service to the community despite the meagre income it generates. In both cases, however, gratitude is appropriate precisely because what is received in exchange for what is given is appreciated as being more valuable than what one has given and hence as a gift that could just as well be withheld.

10. Cf.: "the practices associated with gratitude are a manifestation of, and serve to strengthen, the bonds of moral community – the sharing of a common moral life based on respect for each person as having value in himself" (Berger 1975: 305).

11. Jacques Godbout describes birth as "a definitive giving of the self, the gift of life, the original gift, which inscribes the gift relationship and its concomitant state of indebtedness in every individual ... The chain of gifts begins here for everyone, in a debt that can only be discharged by giving life in one's turn, establishing the fundamentally non-dyadic, asymmetrical character of the gift itself" (1998: 39–40).

12. Perhaps God can be reinstated as a regulatory idea in Kant's sense, never to be known, but subjectively necessary to make sense of our gratitude.

13. This is why Bill McKibben is absolutely right when he urges us to "do an unlikely thing. We need to survey the world we now inhabit and proclaim it good" (2003: 112).

14. This is not to say that the universe is quite the opposite: a friendly, welcoming place. The universe is neither good nor bad. It just is. But we can still feel at home in it when we recognize ourselves as part of the whole.

15. Cf. Parens (1995). Erik Parens argues that some attempts to enhance humans will impoverish them by reducing their subjection to change and chance and thereby reducing their "fragility". For Parens, human fragility is a good-making property, just as giftedness and its appreciation are for Sandel.

16. Cf. "We need, both here and elsewhere, to get beyond seeing morality only

as a matter of keeping or breaking laws, of fulfilling or failing to fulfil obligations, on which there is no neutral ground, in which one can always be said to have done *the* right thing or *the* wrong thing. We need to see morality also as a question of availing ourselves of or of missing out on invitations, calls, gifts – opportunities – which could lead to a richer, fuller life for the agent as well as for others" (Camenish 1981: 18).

17. A similar view is defended by Parens: "the shared recognition and acceptance of human neediness can be profoundly valuable" (1995: 145).

REFERENCES

Agar, N. 2004. *Liberal Eugenics*. Oxford: Blackwell.

Agar, N. 2010. *Humanity's End*. Cambridge, MA: MIT Press.

Appiah, K. A. 2008. *Experiments in Ethics*. Cambridge, MA: Harvard University Press.

Appleyard, B. 2007. *How to Live Forever or Die Trying*. London: Pocket Books.

Aristotle 1908. *Nicomachean Ethics*, W. D. Ross (trans.). Oxford: Clarendon Press.

Barak, B. 1999. "Perceived Youth". *International Journal of Aging and Human Development* **49**(3): 231–57.

Barch, D. M. 2004. "Pharmacological Manipulation of Human Working Memory". *Psychopharmacology* **174**(1): 126–35.

Baum, S. K. 1983. "Age Identification in the Elderly". *International Journal of Aging and Human Development* **18**(1): 25–30.

Berger, F. R. 1975. "Gratitude". *Ethics* **85**(4): 298–309.

Berger, T. W. & D. L. Glanzman (eds) 2005. *Toward Replacement Parts for the Brain: Implantable Biomimetic Electronics as Neural Prostheses*. Cambridge, MA: MIT Press.

Berger, T. W., A. Ahuja, S. H. Couresllis *et al.* 2005. "Restoring Lost Cognitive Function: Hippocampal–Cortical Neural Prostheses". *IEEE Engineering in Medicine and Biology Magazine* **24**(5): 30–44.

Berghmans, R., R. ter Meulen, A. Malizia & R. Vox 2011. "Scientific, Ethical, and Social Issues in Mood Enhancement". See Savulescu *et al.* (2011a), 153–65.

Bibel, W. (ed.) 2004. "Converging Technologies and the Natural, Social and Cultural World" (ftp://ftp.cordis.europa.eu/pub/foresight/docs/ntw_sig4_en.pdf).

Biddiss, E. A. & T. T. Chau 2007. "Upper Limb Prosthesis Use and Abandonment: A Survey of the Last 25 Years". *Prosthetics and Orthotics International* **31**(3): 236–57.

Block, N. 1978. "Troubles with Functionalism". *Minnesota Studies in the Philosophy of Science* **9**: 261–325.

Boas, F. 1916. "Eugenics". *Scientific Monthly* **3**(5): 471–8.

Bok, S. 2010. *Exploring Happiness*. New Haven, CT: Yale University Press.

Borges, J. L. 1962. "Funes the Memorious". In his *Ficciones*, 107–16. New York: Grove Weidenfeld.

Borges, J. L. 1964. "Pierre Menard, Author of the *Quixote*". In his *Labyrinths: Selected Stories and Other Writings*, 36–44. New York: New Directions.

Borrell, B. 2008. "What is Truth Serum?" *Scientific American* (4 December). www.scientificamerican.com/article.cfm?id=what-is-truth-serum (accessed January 2013).

Bortolotti, L. & Y. Nagasawa 2009. "Immortality without Boredom". *Ratio* **22**(3): 261–77.

Bostrom, N. 2004. "Golden". www.nickbostrom.com/fable/retriever.html (accessed January 2013).

Bostrom, N. 2005a. "In Defense of Posthuman Dignity". *Bioethics* **19**(3): 202–14.

Bostrom, N. 2005b. "The Fable of the Dragon Tyrant". *Journal of Medical Ethics* **31**: 273–7.

Bostrom, N. 2005c. "A History of Transhumanist Thought". *Journal of Evolution and Technology* **14**(1). Revised at www.nickbostrom.com/papers/history.pdf (accessed March 2013).

Bostrom, N. 2008. "Why I Want to be a Posthuman When I Grow Up". See Gordijn & Chadwick (2008), 107–36.

Bostrom, N. & T. Ord 2006. "The Reversal Test: Eliminating Status Quo Bias in Applied Ethics". *Ethics* **116**: 656–79.

Bova, B. 1998. *Immortality: How Science Is Extending your Life Span – and Changing the World*. New York: Avon.

Brave, R. 2003. "Germline Warfare". *The Nation* (7 April).

Brixey, Y. 2012. "Plastic Surgery Is Not Just for the Rich and Famous Anymore." http://uberarticles.com/recreation-and-sports/plastic-surgery-is-not-just-for-the-rich-and-famous-anymore/ (accessed February 2013).

Brueckner, A. L. & J. M. Fischer 1986. "Why Is Death Bad?" *Philosophical Studies* **50**(2): 213–21.

Brumberg, J. J. 1998. *The Body Project: An Intimate History of American Girls*. New York: Vintage.

Buchanan, A. 2008. "Enhancement and the Ethics of Development". *Kennedy Institute of Ethics Journal* **18**(1): 1–34.

Buchanan, A. 2009. "Moral Enhancement and Moral Status". *Philosophy and Public Affairs* **37**(4): 346–81.

Buchanan, A. 2011. *Beyond Humanity? The Ethics of Biomedical Enhancement*. Oxford: Oxford University Press.

Buchanan, A., D. W. Brock, N. Daniels & D. Wikler 2000. *From Chance to Choice*. Cambridge: Cambridge University Press.

Burgess, A. 1962. *A Clockwork Orange*. London: Heinemann.

Burley, M. 2006. "Anticipating Annihilation". *Inquiry* **49**(2): 170–85.

Camenish, P. F. 1981. "Gift and Gratitude in Ethics". *Journal of Religious Ethics* **9**(1): 1–34.

Caplan, A. 2006. "Is it Wrong to Try to Improve Human Nature?" In *Better*

Humans? The Politics for Human Enhancement and Life Extension, P. Miller & J. Wilsdon (eds), 31–9. London: Demos

Caplan, A. 2009. "Good, Better, or Best?" See Savulescu & Bostrom (2009), 199–209.

Carlezon, W. A., R. S. Duman & E. J. Nestler 2005. "The Many Faces of CREB". *Trends in Neuroscience* **28**(8): 436–45.

Chadwick, R. 2008. "Therapy, Enhancement and Improvement". See Gordijn & Chadwick (2008), 25–37.

Chesteron, G. K. 1908. *Orthodoxy*. New York: Dodd, Mead.

Chesterton, G. K. 1923. *St Francis of Assisi*. London: Hodder & Stoughton.

Collins, W. [1860] 2009. *The Woman in White*. London: Penguin.

Cremin, M. C. 1992. "Feeling Old Versus Being Old". *Social Science Medicine* **34**(12): 1305–15.

Crockett, M. J. 2009. "The Neurochemistry of Fairness. Clarifying the Link Between Serotonin and Prosocial Behavior". *Annals of the New York Academy of Sciences* **1167**: 76–86.

Crockett, M. J., L. Clark, M. D. Hauser & T. W. Robbins 2010. "Serotonin Selectively Influences Moral Judgment and Behavior Through Effects on Harm Aversion". *Proceedings of the National Academy of Sciences of the United States of America* **107**(40): 17433–8.

Danto, A. C. 1981. *The Transfiguration of the Commonplace*. Cambridge, MA: Harvard University Press.

Davis, K. 1998. "Facing the Dilemma". In *Sex/Machine: Readings in Culture, Gender, and Technology*, P. D. Hopkins (ed.), 286–305. Bloomington, IN: Indiana University Press.

Dawkins, R. 1976. *The Selfish Gene*. New York: Oxford University Press.

Dawkins, R. 2006. *The God Delusion*. London: Bantam.

Degrazia, D. 2000. "Prozac, Enhancement, and Self-Creation". *Hastings Center Report* **30**(2): 34–40.

De Grey, A. & M. Rae 2007. *Ending Aging: The Rejuvenation Breakthroughs that Could Reverse Human Aging in Our Lifetime*. New York: St Martin's Press.

Derrida, J. 1991. *Given Time: I. Counterfeit Money*. Chicago, IL: University of Chicago Press.

Dewey, J. 1916. *Democracy and Education*. New York: Macmillan.

Diener, E. & R. E. Lucas 1999. "Personality and Subjective Well-Being". In *Well-Being: The Foundations of Hedonic Psychology*, D. Kahneman, E. Diener & N. Schwarz (eds), 213–29. New York: Russell Sage.

Diogenes Laertius 1958. *Lives of Eminent Philosophers*, with an English translation by R. D. Hicks, vol. 2. London: Heinemann.

Dobelle, W. H. 2000. "Artificial Vision for the Blind by Connecting a Television Camera to the Visual Cortex". *ASAIO Journal* **46**: 3–9.

Douglas, T. 2008. "Moral Enhancement". *Journal of Applied Philosophy* **25**(3): 228–45.

Doyle, R. 2003. *Wetwares: Experiments in Postvital Living*. Minneapolis, MN: University of Minnesota Press.

Draper, K. 1999. "Disappointment, Sadness, and Death". *Philosophical Review* **108**(3): 387–414.

Elliott, C. 1998. "The Tyranny of Happiness: Ethics and Cosmetic Psychopharmacology". See Parens (1998), 177–88.

Elliott, C. 2003. *Better Than Well: American Medicine Meets the American Dream*. New York: W. W. Norton.

Emmons, R. A. 2008. "Gratitude, Subjective Well-Being, and the Brain". In *The Science of Well-Being*, M. Eid & R. J. Larsen (eds). New York: Guilford Press.

Fenton, E. 2010. "The Perils of Failing to Enhance: A Response to Persson and Savulescu". *Journal of Medical Ethics* **36**: 148–51.

First, M. B. 2005. "Desire for Amputation of a Limb: Paraphilia, Psychosis, or a New Type of Identity Disorder". *Psychological Medicine* **35**: 919–28.

Fox, M. J. 2002. *Lucky Man*. London: Ebury.

Freedman, C. 1998. "Aspirin for the Mind? Some Ethical Worries about Psychopharmacology". See Parens (1998), 135–50.

Fukuyama, F. 2002. *Our Posthuman Future*. New York: Farrar, Straus & Giroux.

Galton, F. 1873. "Hereditary Improvement". *Fraser's Magazine* **7**: 116–30.

Gems, D. 2003. "Is More Life Always Better? The New Biology of Aging and the Meaning of Life". *Hastings Center Report* **33**(4): 31–9.

Glannon, W. 2002. "Identity, Prudential Concern, and Extended Lives". *Bioethics* **16**(3): 266–83.

Glannon, W. 2011. "Diminishing and Enhancing Free Will". *AJOB Neuroscience* **2**(3): 15–26.

Glover, J. 2007. *Choosing Children*. Oxford: Clarendon Press.

Godbout, J. T. 1998. *The World of the Gift*. Montreal: McGill-Queen's University Press.

Goleman, D. 1996. *Emotional Intelligence: Why it Can Matter More Than IQ*. London: Bloomsbury.

Gooch, B. 2009. *Flannery: A Life of Flannery O'Connor*, London: Little, Brown.

Gordijn, B. & R. Chadwick (eds) 2008. *Medical Enhancement and Posthumanity*. New York: Springer.

Greenemeyer, L. 2011. "Robotinc Exoskeletons from Cyberdyne Could Help Workers Clean Up Fukushima Nuclear Mess". *Scientific American* (9 November).

Greenstreet, R. 2011. "Q&A: Margaret Atwood". *Guardian* (28 October). www.guardian.co.uk/lifeandstyle/2011/oct/28/margaret-atwood-q-a (accessed February 2013).

Guarente, L. & C. Kenyon 2000. "Genetic Pathways that Regulate Aging in Model Organisms". *Nature* **408**: 255–62.

Habermas, J. 2003. *The Future of Human Nature*. Cambridge: Polity.

Haiken, E. 1997. *Venus Envy: A History of Cosmetic Surgery*. Baltimore, MD: Johns Hopkins University Press.

Hamermesh, D. S. 2011. *Beauty Pays: Why Attractive People Are More Successful*. Princeton, NJ: Princeton University Press.

Hanson, R. 2009. "Enhancing Our Truth Orientation". See Savulescu & Bostrom (2009), 357–72.

Hare, R. M. 1993. "Abortion and the Golden Rule". In his *Essays on Bioethics*. Oxford: Clarendon Press.

Harrington, A. 1969. *The Immortalist: An Approach to the Engineering of Man's Divinity*. New York: Random House.

Harris, J. 1993. "Is Gene Therapy a Form of Eugenics?" *Bioethics* **7**(2–3): 178–87.
Harris, J. 2002. "A Response to Walter Glannon". *Bioethics* **16**(3): 284–91.
Harris, J. 2007. *Enhancing Evolution: The Ethical Case for Making Better People.* Princeton, NJ: Princeton University Press.
Harris, J. 2009. "Enhancements are a Moral Obligation". See Savulescu & Bostrom (2009), 131–54.
Harris, J. 2010. "Moral Enhancement and Freedom". *Bioethics* **25**(2): 102–11.
Hauskeller, M. 2007. *Biotechnology and the Integrity of Life.* Aldershot: Ashgate.
Hauskeller, M. 2009. "Making Sense of What We Are: A Mythological Approach to Human Nature". *Philosophy* **84**(1): 95–109.
Hauskeller, M. 2011. "No Philosophy for Swine: John Stuart Mill on the Quality of Pleasures". *Utilitas* **23**(4): 428–46.
Hayashi, M., M. Kato, K. Igarashi & H. Kashima 2007. "Superior Fluid Intelligence in Children with Asperger's Disorder". *Brain and Cognition* **66**(3): 306–10.
Hayflick, L. 2002. "Anarchy in Gerontological Terminology". *The Gerontologist* **42**: 416–21.
Hayles, N. K. 1996. "How Cyberspace Signifies: Taking Immortality Literally". In *Immortal Engines: Life Extension and Immortality in Science Fiction and Fantasy*, G. Westfahl, G. W. Slusser & E. S. Rabkin (eds), 111–21. Athens, GA: University of Georgia Press.
Hekimi, S. & L. Guarente 2003. "Genetics and the Specificity of the Aging Process". *Science* **299**: 1351–4.
Hochberg, L. R., M. D. Serruya, G. M. Friehs *et al.* 2006. "Neuronal Ensemble Control of Prosthetic Devices by a Human with Tetraplegia". *Nature* **442**: 164–71.
Hoehn-Saric, R., J. R. Lipsey & D. R. McLeod 1990. "Apathy and Indifference in Patients on Fluvoxamine and Fluoxetine". *Journal of Clinical Psychopharmacology* **10**(5): 344–8.
Holm, S. & M. McNamee 2011. "Physical Enhancement: What Baseline, Whose Judgment?" See Savulescu *et al.* (2011a), 291–303.
Housman, A. E. 1896. *A Shropshire Lad.* London: K. Paul, Trench, Treubner.
Jonas, H. 1992. "The Burden and Blessing of Mortality". *Hastings Center Report* **22**(1): 34–40.
Jotterand, F. 2011. "'Virtue Engineering' and Moral Agency: Will Post-Humans Still Need the Virtues?" *AJOB Neuroscience* **2**(4): 3–9.
Kadmon, A. 2003. "Mind Uploading: An Introduction". Transtopia – Transhumanism Evolved. http://www.transtopia.net/uploading.html (accessed February 2013)).
Kahane, G. 2011. "Reasons to Feel, Reasons to Take Pills". See Savulescu *et al.* (2011a), 166–78.
Kamm, F. 2009. "What Is and Is Not Wrong with Enhancement". See Savulescu & Bostrom (2009), 91–130.
Kant, I. [1786] 1974. *Grundlegung zur Metaphysik der Sitten*, 2nd ed. In *Immanuel Kant, Werkausgabe VII*, W. Weischedel (ed.). Frankfurt: Suhrkamp.
Karp, D. 1988. "A Decade of Reminders". *The Gerontologist* **28**(6): 727–38.
Kass, L. 2003. "Ageless Bodies, Happy Souls". *The New Atlantis* (Spring): 9–28.

Kass, L. 2004. "L'Chaim and Its Limits: Why not Immortality?" In *The Fountain of Youth*, S. G. Post & R. H. Binstock (eds), 304–20. Oxford: Oxford University Press.

Katz, S. & K. R. Peters 2008. "Enhancing the Mind? Memory Medicine, Dementia, and the Aging Brain". *Journal of Aging Studies* **22**: 348–55.

Klein, B. 2003. "Building a Bridge to the Brain". www.imminst.org/forum/index.php?act=ST&f=67&t=938&s (accessed January 2013).

Klein, M. 1957. *Envy and Gratitude*. London: Routledge.

Kline, A. D. 2007. "Giftedness, Humility and Genetic Enhancement". *Human Reproduction and Genetic Ethics* **13**(2): 16–21.

Koenigs, M., L. Young, R. Adolphs *et al.* 2007. "Damage to the Prefrontal Cortex Increases Utilitarian Moral Judgements". *Nature* **446**: 908–11.

Kolber, A. J. 2006. "Therapeutic Forgetting. The Legal and Ethical Implications of Memory Dampening". *Vanderbilt Law Review* **59**(5): 1561–626.

Kosfeld, M., M. Heinrichs, P. J. Zak, U. Fischbacher & E. Fehr 2005. "Oxytocin Increases Trust in Humans". *Nature* **435**: 673–6.

Kramer, P. D. 1994. *Listening to Prozac*. London: Fourth Estate.

Kurzweil, R. 1999. *The Age of Spiritual Machines*. New York: Penguin.

Kurzweil, R. & T. Grossman 2005. *Fantastic Voyage*. New York: Plume.

Labiaenhancement 2006. "Welcome to Labia Enhancement". www.labiaenhancement.com (accessed February 2013).

Landeweerd, L. 2011. "Asperger's Syndrome, Bipolar Disorder and Mood, Cognition, and Well-Being". See Savulescu *et al.* (2011a), 207–17.

Lane, R. 2000. *The Loss of Happiness in Market Democracies*. New Haven, CT: Yale University Press.

Levy, N. 2011. "Enhancing Authenticity". *Journal of Applied Philosophy* **28**(3): 308–18.

Lewis, C. S. 1955. *The Abolition of Man*. New York: Macmillan.

Liao, S. M. 2006a. "The Right of Children to Be Loved". *Journal of Political Philosophy* **14**(4): 420–40.

Liao, S. M. 2006b. "The Idea of a Duty to Love". *Journal of Value Inquiry* **40**(1): 1–22.

Liao, S. M. 2011. "Parental Love Pills: Some Ethical Consideration". *Bioethics* **25**(9): 489–94.

Liao, S. M. & R. Roache 2011. "After Prozac". See Savulescu *et al.* (2011a), 245–56.

Little, M. O. 1998. "Cosmetic Surgery, Suspect Norms, and the Ethics of Complicity". See Parens (1998), 162–76.

Locke, J. 1894. *An Essay Concerning Human Understanding*, collated and annotated by A. C. Fraser. Oxford: Clarendon Press.

Lucke, J. C. & W. Hall 2005. "Who Wants to Live Forever?" *EMBO reports* **6**(2): 98–102.

Lucke, J. C., S. Bell, B. Partridge & W. D. Hall 2011. "Deflating the Neuroenhancement Bubble". *AJOB Neuroscience* **2**(4): 38–43.

Lundquist, L. 1996. "Images of Immortality in Children's Literature". In *Immortal Engines. Life Extension and Immortality in Science Fiction and Fantasy*, G. Slusser, G. Westfahl & E. S. Rabkin (eds), 201—10. Athens, GA: University of Georgia Press.

Luria, A. R. 1969. *The Mind of a Mnemonist*. London: Jonathan Cape.

Lyons, D. 1969. "The Odd Debt of Gratitude". *Analysis* **29**: 92–7.

Maberry, J. 2010. *The Dragon Factory*. London: Gollancz.

Macintyre, A. 1981. *After Virtue. A Study in Moral Theory*. London: Duckworth.

Martel, Y. 2002. *Life of Pi*. Edinburgh: Canongate.

Mauss, M. 1990. *The Gift*. New York: W. W. Norton.

McKibben, B. 2003. *Enough*. London: Bloomsbury.

Mill, J. S. 1998. *Utilitarianism*, R. Crisp (ed.). Oxford: Oxford University Press.

Minsky, M. 1986. *The Society of Mind*. New York: Simon & Schuster.

Moore, A. W. 2006. "Williams, Nietzsche, and the Meaninglessness of Immortality". *Mind* **115**(458): 311–30.

Moorhead, J. 2012. "Removing a Child is Terrible". *Guardian* (14 January).

Moravec, H. 1989. *Mind Children: The Future of Robot and Human Intelligence*. Cambridge, MA: Harvard University Press.

More, M. 1994. "On Becoming Posthuman". /www.maxmore.com/becoming.htm (accessed February 2013).

More, M. 1996. "Transhumanism: Towards a Futurist Philosophy" www.maxmore.com/transhum.htm (accessed January 2013). Originally published in *Extropy* **6** (1990): 6–12.

Morgan, K. P. 1998. "Women and the Knife: Cosmetic Surgery and the Colonization of Women's Bodies". In *Sex/Machine: Readings in Culture, Gender, and Technology*, P. D. Hopkins (ed.), 261–85. Bloomington, IN: Indiana University Press.

Nagel, S. K. 2010. "Too Much of a Good Thing? Enhancement and the Burden of Self-Determination". *Neuroethics* **3**: 109–19.

Nagel, T. 1970. "Death". *Nous* **4**(1): 73–80.

Natural Beauty Enhancement 2012. "Welcome to Natural Beauty Enhancement: Permanent Makeup, Medical Camouflage and Tattoo Removal". www.lovenbe.com (accessed February 2013).

Nietzsche, F. 1966. *Werke in drei Bänden*. Munich: Carl Hanser.

Nilsson, M., A. Sarvimäki & S.-L. Ekman 2000. "Feeling Old: Being in a Phase of Transition in Later Life". *Nursing Inquiry* **7**(1): 41–9.

Noë, A. 2009. *Out of Our Heads*. New York: Hill & Wang.

Odling-Smee, P., K. Laland & M. Feldman 2003. *Niche Construction: The Neglected Process in Evolution*. Princeton, NJ: Princeton University Press.

Parens, E. 1995. "The Goodness of Fragility: On the Prospect of Genetic Technologies Aimed at the Enhancement of Human Capacities". *Kennedy Institute of Ethics Journal* **5**(2): 141–53.

Parens, E. (ed.) 1998. *Enhancing Human Traits*. Washington, DC: Georgetown University Press.

Parens, E. 2009. "Toward a More Fruitful Debate About Enhancement". See Savulescu & Bostrom (2009), 181–97.

Parker, E. S., L. Cahill & J. L. McGaugh 2006. "A Case of Unusual Autobiographical Remembering". *Neurocase* **12**(1): 35–49.

Paul, G. S. & E. D. Cox 1996. *Beyond Humanity: CyberEvolution and Future Minds*. Rockland, MA: Charles River Media.

Pearce, D. 1995. *The Hedonistic Imperative* 0.1. www.hedweb.com (accessed January 2013).

Persson, I. & J. Savulescu 2008. "The Perils of Cognitive Enhancement and the Urgent Imperative to Enhance the Moral Character of Humanity". *Journal of Applied Philosophy* **25**(3): 162–77.

Persson, I. & J. Savulescu 2010. "Moral Transhumanism". *Journal of Medicine and Philosophy* **35**(6): 656–69.

Persson, I. & J. Savulescu 2011a. "Getting Moral Enhancement Right: The Desirability of Moral Bioenhancement". *Bioethics* (29 July, online). http://onlinelibrary.wiley.com/doi/10.1111/j.1467-8519.2011.01907.x (accessed January 2013).

Persson, I. & J. Savulescu 2011b. "The Turn for Ultimate Harm: A Reply to Fenton". *Journal of Medical Ethics* **37**: 441–4.

Persson, I. & J. Savulescu 2011c. "Unfit for the Future? Human Nature, Scientific Progress, and the Need for Moral Enhancement". See Savulescu *et al.* (2011a), 486–500.

Pico della Mirandola [1486] 1985. *On the Dignity of Man, On Being and the One, Heptaplus*. London: Macmillan.

Plato, 1997. *Protagoras*. In Plato, *Complete Works*. Indianapolis, IN: Hackett.

Potts, St. 1996. "IBMortality: Putting the Ghost in the Machine". In *Immortal Engines: Life Extension and Immortality in Science Fiction and Fantasy*, G. Slusser, G. Westfahl & E. S. Rabkin (eds), 102–10. Athens, GA: University of Georgia Press.

President's Council on Bioethics 2003. *Beyond Therapy: Biotechnology and the Pursuit of Happiness*. New York: Dana Press.

Richard, N. 1988. "Is Humility a Virtue?" *American Philosophical Quarterly* **25**(3): 253–9.

Roco, M. C. & W. S. Bainbridge (eds) 2003. *Naontechnology, Biotechnology, Information Technology and Cognitive Science*. Dordrecht: Kluwer.

Sandberg, A. 2011. "Cognitive Enhancement: Upgrading the Brain". See Savulescu *et al.* (2011a), 71–91.

Sandberg, A. & N. Bostrom 2008. *Whole Brain Emulation: A Roadmap*. Oxford: Future of Humanity Institute.

Sandel, M. 2007. *The Case against Perfection*. Cambridge, MA: Harvard University Press.

Savulescu, J. 2001. "Procreative Beneficence: Why We Should Select the Best Children". *Bioethics* **15**(5–6): 413–26.

Savulescu, J. 2009. "The Human Prejudice and the Moral Status of Enhanced Beings: What Do We Owe the Gods?" See Savulescu & Bostrom (2009), 211–47.

Savulescu, J. & N. Bostrom (eds) 2009. *Human Enhancement*. Oxford: Oxford University Press.

Savulescu, J. & B. Foddy 2011. "Le Tour and Failure of Zero Tolerance: Time to Relax Doping Controls". See Savulescu *et al.* (2011a), 304–12.

Savulescu, J. & A. Sandberg 2008. "Neuroenhancement of Love and Marriage: The Chemicals Between Us". *Neuroethics* **1**: 31–44.

Savulescu, J., B. Foddy & M. Clayton 2004. "Why We Should Allow Performance Enhancing Drugs in Sport". *British Journal of Sports Medicine* **38**: 666–70.

Savulescu, J., R. ter Meulen & G. Kahane (eds) 2011a. *Enhancing Human Capacities*. Chichester: Wiley-Blackwell.

Savulescu, J., A. Sandberg & G. Kahane 2011b. "Well-Being and Enhancement". See Savulescu *et al.* (2011a), 3–18.

Scarre, G. 1997. "Should We Fear Death?" *European Journal of Philosophy* 5(3): 269–82.

Schacter, D. 2001. *The Seven Sins of Memory*. New York: Houghton Mifflin.

Schopenhauer, A. 2008. *The World as Will and Presentation*, vol. 1. New York: Pearson Longman.

Searle, J. 1990. "Is the Brain's Mind a Computer Programme?" *Scientific American* 262: 26–31.

Shelley, P. B. 1924. *Poems Published in 1820*. Oxford: Clarendon Press.

Simmons, R. G., S. D. Klein & R. L. Simmons 1977. *The Gift of Life: The Social and Psychological Impact of Organ Transplantation*. New York: Wiley.

Sinrex 2013. "Male Enhancement Pills for Real Male Enhancement". www.sinrex. com/ (accessed February 2013).

Solomon, R. C. 2002. *Spirituality for the Skeptic: The Thoughtful Love of Life*. New York: Oxford University Press.

Spicer, M. N. 2004. "Letter re: Quest to Forget". *New York Times Magazine* (18 April).

Stock, G. 2002. *Redesigning Humans: Choosing Our Children's Genes*. London: Profile.

Sunstein, C. 2007. *Worst-Case Scenarios*. Cambridge, MA: Harvard University Press.

Szalavitz, M. 2009. "Popping Smart Pills. The Case for Cognitive Enhancement". *Time* (6 January). www.time.com/time/health/article/0,8599,1869435,00.html (accessed January 2013).

Tamburrini, C. & T. Tännsjö 2011. "Enhanced Bodies". See Savulescu *et al.* (2011a), 274–90.

Tännsjö, T. 2009a. "Ought We to Enhance Our Cognitive Capacities?" *Bioethics* 23(7): 421–32.

Tännsjö, T. 2009b. "Medical Enhancement and the Ethos of Elite Sport". See Savulescu & Bostrom (2009), 315–26.

Taylor, J. S. 2009. *Practical Autonomy and Bioethics*. London: Routledge.

Temkin, L. S. 2008. "Is Living Longer Living Better?" *Journal of Applied Philosophy* 25(3): 193–210.

Thompson, P. R. 1992. "I Don't Feel Old: Subjective Ageing and the Search for Meaning in Later Life". *Ageing and Society* 12: 23–47.

Titmuss, R. 1970. *The Gift Relationship: From Human Blood to Social Policy*. London: Allen & Unwin.

Todd, T. 1987. "Anabolic Steroids: The Gremlins of Sport". *Journal of Sport History* 14(1): 87–107.

Turner, D. C., T. W. Robbins, L. Clark, A. R. Aron, J. Dowson & B. J. Sahakian 2002. "Cognitive Enhancing Effects of Modafinil in Healthy Volunteers". *Psychopharmacology* 165: 260–69.

Vedder, A. & L. Klaming 2010. "Human Enhancement for the Common Good: Using Neurotechnologies to Improve Eyewitness Memories". *AJOB Neuroscience* 1(3): 22–33.

Voltaire [1759] 2007. *Candide*. London: Harmondsworth.

Visser, M. 2008. *The Gift of Thanks*. New York: HarperCollins.

Vos, R. 2011. "What is Good or Bad in Mood Enhancement?" See Savulescu *et al.* (2011a), 194–206.

Wade, G. 2005. "Seeing Things in a Different Light". www.bbc.co.uk/devon/news_features/2005/eyeborg.shtml (accessed January 2013).

Wall, R. J., A. M. Powell, M. J. Paape *et al.* 2005. "Genetically Enhanced Cows Resist Intramammary *Staphylococcus aureus* Infection". *Nature Biotechnology* **23**(4): 445–51.

Wells, H. G., J. Huxley & G. P. Wells 1934. *The Science of Life*. New York: Literary Guild.

Wikler, D. 2009. "Paternalism in the Age of Cognitive Enhancement". See Savulescu & Bostrom (2009), 341–55.

Williams, B. 1973. "The Makropulos Case: Reflections on the Tedium of Immortality". In his *Problems of the Self*, 82–100, Cambridge: Cambridge University Press.

Yeoman, A. 1998. *Now or Neverland: Peter Pan and the Myth of Eternal Youth*. Toronto: Inner City Books.

Young, L. & R. Saxe 2009. "Innocent intentions: A Correlation Between Forgiveness for Accidental Harm and Neural Activity". *Neuropsychologia* **47**: 2065–72.

Zuboff, A. 1990. "One Self: The Logic of Experience". *Inquiry* **30**: 39–68.

INDEX